————— THE —————
UNITED STATES
SINGAPORE

FREE TRADE AGREEMENT
Highlights and Insights

—————— THE ——————
UNITED STATES
SINGAPORE

FREE TRADE AGREEMENT
Highlights and Insights

edited by

TOMMY KOH
CHANG LI LIN

World Scientific

iPS Institute of
Policy Studies

SINGAPORE
BUSINESS
FEDERATION

Published by

Institute of Policy Studies
29 Heng Mui Keng Terrace
Singapore 119620

and

World Scientific Publishing Co. Pte. Ltd.
5 Toh Tuck Link, Singapore 596224
USA office: Suite 202, 1060 Main Street, River Edge, NJ 07661
UK office: 57 Shelton Street, Covent Garden, London WC2H 9HE

British Library Cataloguing-in-Publication Data
A catalogue record for this book is available from the British Library.

Photo on the cover: From left to right
George Yeo, Minister for Trade and Industry, Singapore; Goh Chok Tong, Prime Minister of Singapore; S. Jayakumar, Minister for Foreign Affairs and for Law, Singapore; George W. Bush, President of the United States of America; and Colin L. Powell, U.S. Secretary of State.

Source: Reuters

ISBN 981-238-848-6

Inhouse Editor: Juliet L C Lee

Printed in Singapore by World Scientific Printers (S) Pte Ltd

Foreword

Foreword

Every free trade negotiation has its unique history. The United States-Singapore Free Trade Agreement (USSFTA) was conceived one dark stormy night in Brunei after a round of night golf between Prime Minister Goh and President Clinton. Then USTR Charlene Barshefsky played a critical role in making this happen. It was one of the final acts of the Clinton Administration. When George W. Bush became President two months later, he and USTR Bob Zoellick were fully committed to the early conclusion of the negotiations. Ambassador Zoellick reminded me that years earlier, when he was Undersecretary to Secretary of State James Baker, he had proposed an FTA with us but we were then not prepared to open up some of our services sectors.

Apart from the benefits of increased trade and investment in goods and services, both sides wanted the agreement for strategic reasons. For the U.S., a good agreement establishes a template for future free trade agreements with other countries particularly in the area of intellectual property. It also signals the U.S.'s long-term commitment to Asia.

For Singapore, the Free Trade Agreement strengthens us as a hub for manufacturing and services. We also knew that it was the first step towards a closer relationship between ASEAN and U.S., which is of strategic importance not only to Singapore but to all of Southeast Asia. The Agreement is therefore an important bridge across the Pacific built at the right place and at the right time. So many people on both sides took part in its construction. As was to be expected, there were many problems to be solved along the way. In the end, we were able to build in less than two years a structure which is solid and elegant, and already serving the purposes for which it was intended. I thank IPS and SBF for compiling this record.

George YEO
Minister for Trade and Industry, Singapore
February 2004

January 2004 is indeed a historical moment as the United States-Singapore Free Trade Agreement (USSFTA), the first ever agreement between the U.S. and an Asian-Pacific country has been implemented. It has been a long but patient wait of three years since the announcement by the leaders of the two countries to launch the USSFTA back in November 2000. We have finally reached this stage, when the agreement has finally become law where businesses will be able to benefit from it.

The past few years had been most difficult: gloomy global economic situation; terrorist attacks; Severe Acute Respiratory Syndrome (SARS); and bird flu outbreak had all affected businesses worldwide. However, there are some signs that we are heading towards a recovery. The U.S., the world's largest economy, is showing evidence of recovery: manufacturing and property markets are picking up, and the improvement in employment and consumption also point to an improving economic performance in 2004.

Thus the implementation of the U.S.-Singapore trade pact comes at the most appropriate time. Besides, enabling improved market access and tariff savings for Singapore's exports to the U.S., the agreement will help generate better-paying jobs and opportunities for businesses and people, both in Singapore and in the United States.

I must appraise the great work done by the Singapore negotiation team, led by our Ambassador-at-Large Professor Tommy Koh. Under his guidance, the team comprising senior government officials and subject experts had worked hard for the past three years with many rounds of negotiation to reach an agreement with their U.S. counterparts. On behalf of all businesses in Singapore, I would like to express our sincere appreciation to every single member of the team.

It interested me when Professor Koh told me about writing this book, with the idea of sharing the insights they faced throughout the negotiation process. I am glad to listen to some light-hearted stories from Professor Koh himself, amidst the hard work of negotiation. As his books usually are, I find this book very enjoyable, and I believe you would share my sentiments after reading it.

Stephen LEE
Chairman
Singapore Business Federation

The United States-Singapore Free Trade Agreement (USSFTA) came into force on 1 January 2004. This is a significant agreement for both countries for three reasons. First, this is America's first free trade agreement with an Asian country. Second, this agreement is a token of the U.S.'s engagement with the region. Third, the USSFTA can serve as a useful template for America's negotiations with other Asian countries and economies. It can also serve as a building block for an eventual ASEAN-U.S. FTA.

As the Institute of Policy Studies (IPS) focuses, *inter alia*, on United States-Singapore relations, and as our director is also Singapore's chief negotiator, it seems only logical for the institute to publish a book on the USSFTA.

In this book, we have tried to capture insights into the negotiating process as well as highlights of the most important chapters of the agreement. It is our hope that this book will be useful to a wide community of readers including business people, trade negotiators and students of negotiations.

Hsuan OWYANG
Chairman
IPS Board of Governors

Contents

Section II: Selected Chapters of the Agreement

Section III: Getting the FTA through Congress

List of Abbreviations

List of Abbreviations

AFL-CIO	American Federation of Labour-Congress of Industrial Organizations
AFTA	ASEAN Free Trade Area
AGC	Attorney-General's Chambers
AGO	African Growth and Opportunities Act
AmCham	American Chamber of Commerce in Singapore
ANZSCEP	Agreement Between New Zealand Singapore on a Closer Economic Partnership
APEC	Asia-Pacific Economic Cooperation
ASEAN	Association of Southeast Asian Nations
ATM	Automated Teller Machine
ATPA	Andean Trade Preference and Drug Eradication Act
CBTPA	Caribbean Basin Trade Partnership Act
CDs	Compact Discs
CODEL	Congressional Delegation
CSFTA	Canada-Singapore FTA
CSIS	Centre of Strategic and International Studies
CTC	Change in tariff classification
DIY	Do-It-Yourself
DMCA	Digital Millennium Copyright Act
DOC	Department of Commerce
DVD	Digital Video Discs
EAI	Enterprise for ASEAN Initiative
EFTA	European Free Trade Association
EPO	European Patent Office
ERC	Economic Review Committee
FCC	Federal Communications Commission
FDI	Foreign Direct Investment
FICPI	International Federation of Intellectual Property Attorneys
FTA	Free trade agreement
FTAA	Free Trade Area of the Americas
GATS	General Agreement on Trade in Services
GATT	General Agreement on Tariffs and Trade
GDP	Gross Domestic Product
GLC	Government-linked Companies
GNP	Gross National Product
GST	Goods and Services Tax
HS	Harmonised Commodity Description and Coding System
ICT	Information and Communication Technology
IDA	Infocomm Development Authority
IES	International Enterprise Singapore
IIE	Institute for International Economics
IISS	International Institute for Strategic Studies
ILO	International Labour Organisation
IM	Intersessional meetings

IMC	Inter-Ministry Committee
IPR	Intellectual Property Rights
IPS	Institute of Policy Studies
ISI	Integrated Sourcing Initiative
ISP	Internet Service Provider
IT	information technology
ITU	International Telecommunication Union
ITC	International Trade Commission
JPO	Japan Patent Office
JSEPA	Agreement between Singapore and Japan for a New Age Economic Partnership
MAS	Monetary Authority of Singapore
MFA	Multi-Fibre Arrangement
MFN	Most Favoured Nation
MNCs	Multinational Companies
MOF	Ministry of Finance
MTI	Ministry of Trade and Industry
NAFTA	North American Free Trade Agreement
NTM	Non-Tariff Measures
NWC	National Wages Council
OP	Outward Processing
PhRMA	Pharmaceutical Research and Manufacturers of America
PNTR	Permanent Normal Trading Relations
QFB	Qualifying Full Bank
ROO	Rules of Origin
RVC	Regional value content
SAFTA	Singapore-Australia FTA
SARS	Severe Acute Respiratory Syndrome
SBF	Singapore Business Federation
SIT	Substantially Impeded Transfer
SME	Small and Medium Enterprise
SME	Square Meter Equivalents
SNEF	Singapore National Employers Federation
SNTUC	Singapore National Trades Union Congress
STAFFDEL	Staffers' Delegations
TAFF	Textile and Fashion Federation
TEU	Twenty-foot Equivalent Unit
TIFA	Trade and Investment Framework Agreement
TPA	Trade Promotion Authority
TPL	Tariff Preference Level
TRIPS	Trade-Related Aspects of Intellectual Property Rights
UNCLOS	United Nations Convention on the Law of the Saw
UPOV	International Union for the Protection of New Varieties of Plants
UPS	United Parcel Service
UPU	Universal Postal Union
USABC	United States-ASEAN Business Council

USSFTA	United States-Singapore Free Trade Agreement
USTR	United States Trade Representative
UTC	United Technologies
WB	Wholesale Bank
WCT	WIPO Copyright Treaty
WDA	Workforce Development Agency
WIPO	World Intellectual Property Organization
WMD	weapons of mass destruction
WPPT	WIPO Performances and Phonograms Treaty
WTO	World Trade Organization
WTO-ATC	WTO Agreement on Textiles and Clothing

Section I
Introduction

Section 1

Introduction

1 The USSFTA: A Personal Perspective

Tommy T. B. KOH[1]

This is the story of the vision to conclude a free trade agreement between the United States and Singapore. It is the story of how that vision was eventually realised.

THE BACKGROUND

1982: Bill Brock's Proposal

The journey began in 1982. At that time, the United States Trade Representative (USTR) was Senator Bill Brock of Tennessee. Senator Brock had an able young staffer called Doral Cooper. She was an early supporter of the Association of Southeast Asian Nations (ASEAN). She persuaded Senator Brock to propose the idea of concluding a free trade agreement between ASEAN and the United States. ASEAN was, however, not ready for such a bold idea and did not take up Senator Brock's proposal.

---

[1] Chief Negotiator, Singapore. Tommy Koh is Ambassador-At-Large at the Ministry of Foreign Affairs; Director of the Institute of Policy Studies and Chairman of the National Heritage Board. He is a Director of SingTel and Chairman of the Chinese Heritage Centre. He is also a Professor of Law at the National University of Singapore. He served as Singapore's ambassador to the United States from 1984 to 1990. The views expressed in this article are those of the author and do not necessarily represent the views of the Singapore Government.

1984 to 1990: In Washington

From 1984 to 1990, I served as the Ambassador of Singapore to the United States. During my tenure in Washington, I became a good friend of Doral Cooper and tried to revive Senator Brock's proposal. At that time, neither ASEAN nor the U.S. was receptive to the idea. I tried to promote the alternative idea of a free trade agreement between the U.S. and Singapore, and of using Singapore as a stepping stone to an eventual U.S.-ASEAN agreement. I left Washington in 1990 with this dream unfulfilled. I had hoped, however, that one day my dream would come true.

1992: Zoellick and Lavin

The current USTR, Bob Zoellick, had stated that in 1992 he had proposed the idea of a free trade agreement between the U.S. and Singapore. On 6 October 1992, the current U.S. Ambassador to Singapore, Frank Lavin, who was then the Deputy Assistant Secretary of the U.S. Commerce Department, spoke to the Heritage Foundation. In his speech, entitled "After NAFTA: Free Trade and Asia", Ambassador Lavin proposed that the U.S. should consider entering into free trade agreements with several economies in Asia, such as Singapore, Taiwan, Australia and New Zealand. It is fortuitous that eight years after that speech he would be posted to Singapore as the U.S. Ambassador.

The Age of Multilateralism

In the 1990s, the intellectual climate surrounding the debate on multilaterism, regionalism and bilateralism in trade policy began to change. In the beginning, the moral consensus was clearly in favour of multilateralism. The near universal preference was to bring all trade problems and initiatives to the General Agreement on Tariffs and Trade (GATT) (and subsequently to the World Trade

Organization (WTO)) and to negotiate global solutions and agreements. Regional arrangements such as the European Common Market and North American Free Trade Agreement (NAFTA) were regarded as undesirable aberrations which threatened to divide the global trading system into rival blocs. Bilateral trade agreements were viewed in an equally poor light.

APEC's Endorsement of FTAs

The pendulum began to swing the other way as the WTO expanded its membership and as its greater number and diversity made it increasingly difficult to arrive at agreements. As the pendulum moved, the idea that bilateral and regional agreements might not be harmful but could actually help the global system, gained ground. The argument is that bilateral and regional agreements, which are consistent with the WTO and which set higher standards than the WTO norm, could help to spur the global system to embrace those higher standards. In 1999, the Asia-Pacific Economic Cooperation (APEC) Leaders, at their annual Summit in New Zealand, endorsed the legitimacy of using bilateral free trade agreements as a means to achieve multilateral trade liberalisation. Today, bilateral, plurilateral, regional and inter-regional free trade agreements are all regarded as legitimate instruments of trade liberalisation as long as they are deemed to be WTO-consistent and WTO-plus.

U.S.-Singapore Relations

The Singapore government's relationship with the Clinton Administration was not good during President Clinton's first term because of the Michael Fay incident. During President Clinton's second term, he sent a new Ambassador, Steven Green, to Singapore. Green had been a very successful businessman. Although this was his first diplomatic posting, he performed brilliantly and helped to turn U.S.-Singapore relations around.

Steve Green's Initiative

In November 2000, the then USTR, Charlene Barshefsky, stopped over in Singapore en route to the APEC Leaders' meeting in Brunei. She asked to pay a farewell call on the Senior Minister. Although the mandate of the Clinton Administration would expire in two months, Steve Green persuaded Barshefsky to broach the idea of launching the U.S.-Singapore FTA with the Senior Minister. The Senior Minister conveyed the message to Prime Minister Goh, who had already left for Brunei. Since the idea was hatched in Singapore, between Charlene Barshefsky and Steve Green, the other leaders of the Clinton Administration, such as Secretary of State Madeleine Albright and National Security Adviser Sandy Berger, were not aware of it. For the idea to prosper, it was necessary for Prime Minister Goh to pitch it directly to President Clinton. During the Summit, Prime Minister Goh invited President Clinton to play a game of golf with him. President Clinton agreed and, after reviewing his crowded schedule, proposed playing after the state dinner on 15 November 2000.

Golf Diplomacy in Brunei

During the dinner, the sky opened up and unleashed a tremendous thunderstorm. When the dinner ended, the storm continued to rage. The faint-hearted among the Prime Minister's staffers asked him whether to call the game off. The Prime Minister said "no" and so the two leaders proceeded to the golf course in a driving rain. Miraculously, when they arrived, the storm passed and the rain stopped. At 11.45 pm, the two leaders started their game. After the game, at around two in the early hours of 16 November, the two leaders went to the clubhouse for coffee. It was during this time that Prime Minister Goh made his case to President Clinton for an U.S.-Singapore FTA. President Clinton accepted the Prime Minister's proposal and reasoning. Later that day, at 6.00 pm on 16 November

2000, the two leaders issued a joint statement launching the U.S.-Singapore FTA (see Appendix I).

A Fateful Call at the West Lake

On 16 November 2000, I was in Hangzhou, China, carrying out my responsibility as a Visiting Professor to Zhejiang University. I was accompanied by my good friend from the Asia-Europe Foundation, Cai Rongsheng. I had delivered a public lecture in the morning and was hosted to an enormous lunch by the President of the University. After lunch, I asked to be taken to the West Lake to admire the scenery and to clear my head before addressing a faculty seminar in the afternoon. While standing on the bank of the West Lake, I received a call on my cell phone from Neo Gim Huay of the Ministry of Trade and Industry. She said Minister George Yeo wanted to speak to me. The Minister told me that earlier that morning the Prime Minister and President Clinton had agreed to launch the U.S.-Singapore FTA. He said the Prime Minister had asked him to check with me whether I would be willing to be Singapore's chief negotiator. I told the Minister that I would be delighted to do so. I was so happy that fate was giving me a second chance to fulfill one of my dreams.

THE RATIONALE FOR THE FTA

Why does Singapore want an FTA with the U.S.? Why does the U.S. want an FTA with Singapore?

Singapore's Reasons

Singapore wants an FTA with the U.S. for a combination of economic and strategic reasons. The U.S. is Singapore's largest foreign investor and second largest trading partner. The U.S. is also Singapore's most important source of technology and management know-how. Singapore's interest in the U.S., however, transcends business and economics. Singapore wishes to entrench the presence of the U.S. in the region because it underpins the security of the whole Asia-Pacific region. Singapore regards the U.S.-Singapore FTA as a symbol of continued U.S. commitment to the region. Therefore, for Singapore, the USSFTA is not just about securing tariff-free entry for Singapore's exports to the U.S. market. It is not just about attracting more Foreign Direct Investment (FDI) to Singapore. It is also about enhancing the prospects of peace and stability in the region.

The U.S.'s Reasons

I am, of course, only speculating when I suggest that the U.S. may want an FTA with Singapore for the following reasons. Singapore is U.S.'s 11th largest trading partner in the world and the largest in Southeast Asia. The U.S. exports more to Singapore than it does to Indonesia, India, Brazil or Egypt. The U.S. has a cumulative FDI of US$30 billion in Singapore. There are over 1,500 U.S. companies operating in Singapore and 17,000 American residents in Singapore. Singapore is the 2nd largest Asian investor in the U.S., after Japan. Therefore one reason for the FTA would be that the U.S. has a substantial economic stake in Singapore. Also, an FTA with Singapore could serve as a template for the U.S. in its negotiations with other Asian countries and economies. The U.S. might also have wished to use the USSFTA to signal to ASEAN and East Asia that it is committed to the region.

It has been said that U.S. international trade policy is driven, in part, by commercial interests and, in part, by strategic interests. Sometimes, as in the cases of Canada and Mexico, there is a congruence of U.S. economic and strategic interests. In other cases, such as Israel and Jordan, the interests are more strategic than economic. In the case of Singapore, the U.S. has a congruence of economic and strategic interests. How does Singapore contribute to U.S. strategic interests in the region and the world?

Singapore is not a treaty ally but a close partner of the United States. The two countries share a common worldview and threat perception. The U.S. does not have bases in Singapore, but it has access to Singapore's naval and air facilities. Singapore was the first Asian country to join the U.S. Container Security Initiative. Singapore was a member of the 1991 Gulf War coalition. Singapore supported the U.S. war against the Taliban in Afghanistan. Since 11 September 2001, Singapore has supported the U.S.-led war against terrorism. In 2003, Singapore joined the coalition for the immediate disarmament of Iraq. Singapore has sent police officers to train the new Iraqi police force. Singapore has also sent ships, aircraft and armed personnel to undertake logistical and peace-keeping duties in the Gulf. Singapore is an important stop-over for U.S. armed forces, moving from their bases in Northeast Asia, to Diego Garcia in the Indian Ocean and westward to the Middle East.

IMPLICATIONS FOR ASEAN

I have often been asked whether Singapore's bilateral free trade agreements, especially the one with the U.S., are harmful to ASEAN. My answer is that they not only do no harm but actually help ASEAN. One criticism is that the USSFTA may serve as a back door for the U.S. to gain entry to the ASEAN market through Singapore. This is without merit because a product must satisfy the requirements of the rules of origin before it can be regarded as a product of Singapore origin. A product made in the U.S. will not qualify as a product of Singapore origin.

Singapore does not seek an exclusive relationship with any of its FTA partners. On the contrary, Singapore would like its FTAs to serve as building blocks for FTAs between ASEAN and the different FTA partners. Thus, Singapore is gratified that its FTA with Japan will lead to a comprehensive economic partnership agreement between ASEAN and Japan. In the same way, Singapore would like its FTA with the U.S. to lead eventually to an FTA between the U.S. and ASEAN. Singapore was therefore very pleased when President Bush announced, at his meeting with ASEAN leaders, in Los Cabos, Mexico, in 2002, the Enterprise for ASEAN Initiative or EAI. Under the EAI, the U.S. would negotiate either a trade and investment framework agreement (TIFA) or a free trade agreement with like-minded ASEAN countries. The U.S. and Thailand have agreed to launch negotiations for an FTA. Singapore and India are currently negotiating an FTA which will probably be concluded this year. Singapore hopes that its FTA with India will pave the way to an eventual FTA between India and ASEAN. Singapore is therefore not a lone ranger, as some of its critics have alleged, but a path finder for ASEAN. Singapore's FTA policy is intended to benefit and not harm ASEAN.

THE UNIQUE EXPERIENCE OF NEGOTIATING WITH AMERICA

Another question which I have been asked is whether the experience of negotiating with the U.S. is different from my experiences of negotiating with other countries. My answer is "yes". The following are some lessons I have learnt about America and the way in which she negotiates.

Uniqueness of U.S. Democracy

First, the U.S. democracy is unique. Normally, when you negotiate with another country, your negotiating partner is the executive branch of that government. However, when you negotiate with the U.S., you have no choice but to negotiate not only with the administration but also with the United States Congress, U.S. business and industry and the civil society. This is necessary because the U.S.

political system is a system of checks and balances. It is a system in which power is dispersed and there are many stakeholders in the decision-making process. Therefore, a top-down approach can work in Singapore but it cannot work in the U.S. Prime Minister Goh had the power to conclude an FTA with the U.S. without having to consult Parliament, business and industry and the civil society. President Clinton did not have such power. The situation in Singapore is, however, evolving with the private sector and civil society taking advantage of the consultation processes to articulate their views and interests.

U.S.'s Need for Time to Forge Consensus

Second, evolving a consensus between the executive and legislative branches of the U.S. government and among the different departments and agencies of the executive branch takes time. Unlike Singapore, the different departments and agencies of the U.S. government very often have their own institutional interests, agendas, demands, sub-cultures, historic memories, preferences and prejudices. The USTR's role is that of coordinator, convenor, facilitator and negotiator. Although the USTR is the lead agency, it cannot speak for or deliver other powerful departments, such as State, Treasury, Commerce, Defence or the Customs Service. The USTR is, in fact, a very small agency. With a very small team, it nevertheless performs its tasks admirably.

Intensive and often protracted inter-agency meetings must take place first before the USTR is in a position to negotiate with a foreign country. In the case of the USSFTA, we had to wait for 18 months before the U.S. was in a position to table its proposal for the chapter on investment. A foreign country can help to move the process along by lobbying the relevant department or agency and by helping to alleviate their concerns or to find solutions to their problems. To its credit, the USTR never asked Singapore to speak to any of the departments or agencies during the negotiation.

Consulting the Congress

Third, the Congress cannot be ignored. Because of the unique circumstances surrounding President Clinton's and Prime Minister Goh's decision to launch the USSFTA, President Clinton had not consulted the relevant Congressional leaders in advance. Consequently, they were upset. Minister George Yeo and our Ambassador in Washington, Chan Heng Chee, worked very hard to persuade the Congressional leaders to support President Clinton's decision. During the two years when the negotiations were taking place, Minister Yeo and Ambassador Chan regularly updated the Congressional leaders, both Republicans and Democrats, on the status of the negotiations, answered their questions and responded to the concerns of their constituents. We were careful to make sure that our supporters in the Congress came from both parties. In the end, we succeeded in creating a bi-partisan Singapore Congressional Caucus with Congressman Solomon Ortiz, a Democrat, and Congressman Curt Weldon, a Republican, as co-chairs. The caucus has 59 members in the House of Representatives (see Appendix II).

Necessity to Work with U.S. Business

Fourth, I know of no other country in the world in which business enjoys such a pervasive influence as in the United States. There is truth in the dictum that the business of America is business. An important objective of U.S. trade policy is to advance the interests of U.S. business and industry. We therefore decided, from the beginning of the negotiation, to be pro-active and to reach out to every important business organisation. These included the U.S. Chamber of Commerce, the National Association of Manufacturers, the U.S.-ASEAN Business Council and others. We also reached out to associations which represent specific industries, such as the pharmaceutical industry, the software industry, the services industry, the financial services industry, the music industry, the movie industry, the logistics industry, etc. We even reached out to individual companies, such as Amway and Wrigley. As a result of our hard work, we managed to build a powerful U.S.-Singapore FTA Business Coalition, comprising 75 members and co-chaired by Boeing, Exxon Mobil and UPS, to support the FTA (see Appendix III).

Power of U.S. Civil Society

In his classic book, *Democracy in America*, Alexis de Tocqueville observed that the U.S. had a vibrant civil society. This has remained a constant feature of life in America. The civil society probably enjoys more power and influence in America than in any other democracy. In the U.S., an initiative driven by people power or civil society can sometimes either defeat a government policy or compel a government to adopt a new policy. It was therefore wise to think of a strategy to engage the U.S. civil society in order to build support for the FTA and to prevent the emergence of any pressure group or interest group to oppose it. My nightmare scenario would have been an anti-USSFTA coalition consisting of organised labour, the human rights lobby and the green movement. We encouraged our trade union movement, NTUC, to engage the AFL-CIO, in a dialogue which culminated in a joint statement welcoming the USSFTA (see Appendix IV). I had hoped that the AFL-CIO would therefore support the USSFTA. I was disappointed that it did not do so. However, it agreed not to campaign against it and not to punish the members of Congress who voted in its favour.

THE NEGOTIATING PROCESS

Every negotiation is unique. No two negotiations are alike because each negotiation has its own agenda, its challenges and complexities, its cast of negotiators, its tone and momentum. Every negotiation between two or more countries is also a cross-cultural experience. The USSFTA's negotiating process is therefore different from other negotiating processes. Let me describe some of its special features.

First, the USSFTA was started by the Clinton Administration and concluded by the Bush Administration. Conscious that the negotiation would straddle two administrations, Ambassador Chan Heng Chee and I contacted our close friends in the incoming Republican Administration in order to ensure that they would support the negotiation when they joined the new administration. Thus, during the first and second rounds of the negotiations in Washington, in December 2000 and January 2001 respectively, we met with USTR Bob Zoellick, Deputy Secretary of State Richard Armitage and Deputy Secretary of Defence Paul Wolfowitz, to brief them. They assured us that the Bush Administration would support the USSFTA. There was, however, a four-month interval, between the second round in January 2001 and the third round in May 2001 because the new administration needed time to organise itself and to formulate its policy. We were grateful that in this case, the new administration did not repudiate an initiative started by the previous administration.

Second, in the joint statement issued by President Clinton and Prime Minister Goh, the two leaders stated that they had "directed Ambassador Charlene Barshefsky and Minister George Yeo to endeavour to conclude negotiations before the end of the year". This was mission impossible. Under U.S. law, the Clinton Adminis-tration had to inform the public of its intention to negotiate with Singapore. The public was given six weeks to give its inputs and comments. The administration had to analyse and consider the public's responses in formulating its negotiating strategy and demands. At the same time, the administration had to consult Congress and obtain its blessings. The USTR had to begin the elaborate process of consulting the various relevant departments and agencies and to forge an internal consensus. All these activities would take time, much more time than the two months remaining in the life of the Clinton Administration. Therefore, when my government instructed the delegation to proceed to Washington in December 2000, and to stay for as long as was necessary in order to conclude the negotiation, I knew in my heart that the job could not be done in such a short time. At our first meeting in Washington, on 4 December 2000, the U.S. Chief Negotiator, Ralph Ives, and I agreed that the negotiation could not be concluded in one or two months. It took us 24 months to conclude the main negotiation. We needed an extra two months to wrap up the balance of payments issue.

Third, January 2001 was the month in which power was transferred from the Clinton to the Bush Administration. At the insistence of the Clinton Administration, we held our second round from 10 to 17 January during which a difficult issue arose. The Clinton Administration proposed that the two governments should adopt a joint declaration to lock in the progress which had been achieved during the first two rounds. Since not much progress had been made, there was not much substance to lock in. I felt that the real agenda of the Clinton Administration was to lock in the U.S.-Jordan FTA's templates on labour and environment (see Appendix V) and to prevent the incoming Bush Administration from watering down those templates. In announcing the launch of the FTA, President Clinton and Prime Minister Goh had referred to the U.S.-Jordan FTA as the model. However, we were not sure whether some of the templates in that FTA were acceptable to the incoming administration and did not want to tie our hands. We succeeded in persuading our U.S. counterparts to use the joint statement (see Appendix XX) as a through train between the Clinton and Bush administrations.

Fourth, negotiations succeed best when the rapport between the negotiators is good and when they share a bond of mutual trust and confidence. Therefore, from the commencement of the negotiation, I urged all my colleagues to build rapport with their American counterparts and to conduct themselves in such a way as to earn their respect and trust. I told my colleagues that we should use the negotiating experience to expand our personal networks in America and to build goodwill between our two governments and countries. I also urged my colleagues to indulge in "makan diplomacy" or "dining diplomacy". Eating together is a bonding exercise. I am very pleased to say that the good rapport and friendships between the U.S. and Singapore negotiators created a happy ambience for our work and contributed to the success of our negotiations.

Fifth, the USSFTA has 21 chapters. Ralph Ives and I agreed to create 21 negotiating groups,[2] one for each chapter. In each negotiating group, we appointed a lead negotiator. Several of the more experienced negotiators were asked to be the lead negotiator in more than one group. My deputy chief negotiator, Ong Ye Kung, and I supervised the work of all the negotiating groups. During the negotiating sessions, we would ask each lead negotiator to report on the work in his or her negotiating work at our daily delegation meeting. Ye Kung and I would, whenever necessary, suggest solutions to problems encountered. In-between sessions, we would meet with our colleagues in the different negotiating groups in order to take stock of their progress and to assist them in preparing for the next round.

Sixth, what role did personalities play in the success of the negotiations? As a general rule, the success or failure of a negotiation is, in part, dependent upon the ability and character of the negotiators. In the case of the USSFTA, much of the credit must go to the two Ministers, George Yeo and Bob Zoellick. The two Ministers are intellectually brilliant, very focused on both the big as well as the small pictures, and enjoy a high regard for each other. During the two years of negotiation, the two Ministers met several times, often on the sidelines of other meetings. Each time, they would take stock of progress, discuss the problems encountered, suggest possible ways of moving forward and energise their two delegations. On the final day of the final round in Singapore, the

---

[2] Refer to Appendix VI.

negotiation was held at the ministerial level. I would like to pay a tribute to my U.S. counterpart, Ralph Ives, and to my deputy chief negotiator, Ong Ye Kung. Ralph Ives is an outstanding trade negotiator and a gentleman. I would describe Ye Kung as the most valuable player in the Singapore team. He contributed to the solution of more problems than any other member of the Singapore delegation. I would also like to put on record my gratitude to the entire Singapore delegation. I had a great team and we enjoyed the experience of working together.

Seventh, the work of the negotiations was done both during the 11 formal rounds and in many inter-sessional meetings. Inter-sessional meetings can play an important part in the life of a negotiation. This was true in the case of the USSFTA. I remember that between the first and second rounds, Martin Walsh led a fact-finding mission to visit Singapore in order to see the Singapore port, to visit Batam and to understand the labour conditions in Singapore. On another occasion, the new U.S. lead negotiator on textile, David Spooner, led a delegation to visit Singapore in order to get a better sense of Singapore's textile and garment industry. I recall that other inter-sessional meetings were held in Washington, with our negotiating groups on goods, services, textile, telecommunications and financial services.

Eighth, extensive use was made of email, audio-conference and video-conference, as modalities of negotiation, in between negotiating rounds. Sometimes, we would start with email. At a certain point, we would decide to have a audio-conference in order to clarify certain issues or to have a more spontaneous exchange. At other times, we would hold a video-conference, which is the next best thing to meeting face-to-face. Information and communication technology is a wonderful thing. There is, however, still no substitute for face-to-face interaction.

Ninth, what was the nature of the internal decision-making process in Singapore? At the apex was the Cabinet. During the course of the negotiation, the delegation submitted several papers to the Cabinet to ask for new instructions. Under the Cabinet was a committee consisting of Deputy Prime Minister Lee Hsien Loong, as Chairman, and the Ministers of Trade and Industry, Foreign Affairs and Finance. The delegation met this Cabinet committee on several occasions. The deputy chief negotiator and I held a number of consultations with representatives of different ministries and agencies. These meetings were always helpful as we needed some of the ministries, such as Finance, to modify certain long-standing policies of the government. We had also convened meetings involving a large number of stakeholders from various statutory boards and government-linked companies in order to brief them on certain developments in the negotiations and to seek their help. We had also held meetings to brief the private sector on the negotiations and to solicit their feedback and cooperation.

BENEFITS OF THE USSFTA FOR SINGAPORE

First, the FTA will result in improved market access and tariff savings for Singapore's exports to the United States. The U.S. will abolish import duties on all goods originating from Singapore. We calculate that we will achieve tariff savings of S$178 million in the chemical industry (HS[3] 28-38); S$54 million in the minerals industry (HS 25-27); S$4 million in the instrumentation equipment industry (HS 90); and S$16 million in several other sectors. The biggest beneficiaries will be the U.S. companies based in Singapore. They account for 60 percent of Singapore's exports to the United States.[4]

---

[3] The Harmonised System (HS) codes is an international method of classifying products for trading purposes. This classification is used by customs officials around the world to determine the duties, taxes and regulations that apply to the product.

[4] These figures were based on the year 2000 Singapore trade statistics.

Second, the merchandise processing fee of 0.21 percent ad valorem, imposed on all imports entering the U.S. will be waived for goods originating from Singapore. We calculate the waiver to be worth S$51 million annually.

Third, Singapore-based companies will be able to take advantage of the value-added rule of origin and the integrated sourcing initiative for a wide range of products, including components in the Information and Communication Technology (ICT) industry and the medical equipment industry. The USSFTA, like Singapore's other FTAs, recognises the realities of distributed manufacturing in the region and allows the accumulation of value-add in Singapore, as the product and its components shuttle to and fro between Singapore and the neighbouring countries.

Fourth, the textile and garment industry will enjoy a competitive price advantage of 5–15 percent for such goods originating from Singapore provided they use Singapore-made or U.S.-made yarn or fabric. The industry will have to restructure in order to take advantage of this development. Singapore's manufacturers should explore the possibility of sourcing yarn from the U.S. or diversify into using synthetic fabrics which can be produced by our chemical industry.

Fifth, the vessel repair duty will be waived for Singapore. This duty is assessed on the basis of 50 percent of the value of repair work done on U.S. ships outside the United States. We estimate this waiver to be worth S$7.7 million per annum.

Sixth, Singapore's service suppliers are guaranteed access to the U.S. market. This includes such important sectors as information and communication technology and financial services. Singapore's service suppliers will be accorded the same treatment as that accorded to an U.S. service supplier by any of the 50 states of America.

Seventh, professional bodies from the U.S. and Singapore, especially those in architecture and engineering, will consult in order to develop mutually acceptable standards and criteria for licensing and certification of professional service providers.

Eighth, both U.S. and Singapore-based companies will enjoy increased protection for intellectual property rights. Singapore will amend its IP laws in line with technological changes and international developments. It will accede to World Intellectual Property Organization (WIPO) treaties on copyright and implement anti-circumvention measures, amongst others. Singapore will have the best Intellectual Property Rights (IPR) regime in Asia. This is likely to attract more FDI to Singapore, especially in the knowledge-intensive industries.

Ninth, Singapore's investors in the U.S. will enjoy strong protection under the FTA. An aggrieved Singaporean investor can take the U.S. government to an international arbitration tribunal if it feels that the U.S. has acted in breach of its obligations under the FTA.

Tenth, the U.S. will make two changes to its visa system for Singapore. The U.S. will extend the E1 and E2 visas to Singapore. E1 visa is available to traders with enterprises engaged in trade with the U.S. The E2 visa is available to investors who have invested or are actively in the process of investing a substantial amount of capital in the United States. The E1 and E2 visa holders and their spouses can extend their stay in the U.S. indefinitely. In addition, the U.S. will grant Singapore a special quota of 5,400 visas (H1B1) a year. This category applies to professionals such as IT personnel. Unlike the H1B visa, employers of such visa holders need not satisfy the market test, i.e., they do not have to show that there is no American who can do the job. The visa is renewable on an annual basis with no limit.

SIGNATURE AND RATIFICATION

On 30 January 2003, President Bush notified Congress of his intention to enter into the FTA with Singapore. Under the Trade Promotion Authority Act, the President had to give Congress 90 days notice before he could sign the agreement. On 7 March 2003, the USTR released the draft of the 800-page text of the agreement. Of the Administration's 31 trade advisory committees, all except the Labour Advisory Committee, endorsed the agreement.

In the meantime, the Singapore Embassy and the U.S. Chamber of Commerce in Washington, the U.S.-ASEAN Business Council, the U.S. Embassy and the American Chamber of Commerce in Singapore, waged a campaign to build support for the FTA, in the Congress and in the U.S. business community. I must express my deep gratitude to Tom Donohue, Myron Brilliant and Erin Pham of the U.S. Chamber of Commerce in Washington D.C., to Ernie Bower of the U.S.-ASEAN Business Council, and to Landis Hicks, Kristin Paulson and Nick de Boursac of the American Chamber of Commerce in Singapore for their wise counsel and sterling support. I must also express my admiration for the brilliant manner in which Ambassador Chan Heng Chee and her team garnered support for the FTA and orchestrated its passage through the U.S. Congress. Thanks are also due to the U.S. Ambassador to Singapore, Frank Lavin, and his team at the U.S. Embassy in Singapore (see Appendix VII).

The USSFTA was signed by President Bush and Prime Minister Goh at the White House on 6 May 2003. The statements of the two leaders are attached in Appendix VIII.

The agreement was approved by the House of Representatives, on 24 July 2003 by a vote of 272 in favour and 155 against. The Senate approved the agreement on 31 July 2003 by a vote of 66 in favour and 32 against. The agreement came into force on 1 January 2004. The chapter on intellectual property rights will come into force on 1 July 2004.

CONCLUSION

I am very pleased that my dream of the United States-Singapore Free Trade Agreement has come true. I hope that this will lead, step by step, to an eventual U.S.-ASEAN FTA. I am confident that the USSFTA will increase the flows of trade and investment between the U.S. and Singapore; increase Singapore's attractiveness as a destination for U.S. FDI; and create jobs for Singaporeans. The USSFTA is also a shining symbol of the close partnership which exists between our two countries. The joint ministerial committee to be established under the USSFTA will constitute an important institutional link between the two countries.

2 The USSFTA: Personal Perspectives on the Process and Results

Ralph F. IVES[1]

INTRODUCTION

I plan to explain the process leading to the successful conclusion of the United States-Singapore Free Trade Agreement (USSFTA) and the significance of the results. I believe there are important lessons in the relationship between process and outcome, particularly for the long-term.

First, let me put this FTA in the context of broad U.S. trade policy. The USSFTA was initiated by the Clinton Administration and concluded under the Bush Administration. This Agreement was the first FTA the United States had concluded with a major trading partner since the North American Free Trade Agreement (NAFTA) a decade ago. Singapore is the United States' 12th largest trading partner, with annual two-way trade in goods and services exceeding US$40 billion. This FTA is the first United States has with an Asian nation.

---

[1] U.S. Chief Negotiator for the USSFTA, Ralph F. Ives was appointed to the position of Assistant U.S. Trade Representative for Asia-Pacific and APEC Affairs on 12 June 2000. Mr. Ives is responsible for developing and implementing U.S. bilateral and multilateral trade policy toward countries in the Asia-Pacific region (except China and Japan, for which there are separate offices in USTR). Mr. Ives is the chief trade negotiator for countries in the region. In addition, he serves as one of two U.S. senior officials to the Asia-Pacific Economic Cooperation (APEC) process and is responsible for developing and implementing trade and investment initiatives in APEC. The views expressed in this article are those of the author and do not necessarily represent the views of the U.S. Government.

PROCESS

The United States enters FTAs for economic and foreign policy reasons. The Bush Administration's policy is to seek trade liberalisation on a global, regional and bilateral basis and to pursue FTAs with countries in nearly every region — Latin America, Africa, the Middle East and Asia.

The ultimate objective of expanding trade and economic growth is to contribute to world prosperity, peace and security. FTAs, or even global free trade, could not achieve this goal on its own — a point often ignored by anti-trade forces. Trade between people is another form of freedom and communication that promotes understanding and rapport. To quote Alexis de Tocqueville:

> "Trade is the natural enemy of all violent passions. Trade loves moderation, delights in compromise, and is most careful to avoid anger."

How did the FTA negotiating process promote this objective?

FTA negotiations are tough. The issues involved are concrete. At stake are real people, real investments, real jobs, real products, real property and real ideas. Differences cannot usually be papered over with flowery language or vague intentions. Each nation's commitments in an FTA can be subjected to formal dispute settlement arbitration, which can require a nation either to come into compliance with the FTA's provisions or face the prospect of trade retaliation. This reality can lead to contentious debates during the negotiations, possibly creating lasting ill will and mistrust.

With Singapore, I believe interpersonal relations between the U.S. and Singapore delegations were enhanced by the negotiating experience, and this improved the results of the FTA. Let me start on my relationship with my counterpart, Ambassador Tommy Koh.

My first meeting with Ambassador Koh was at lunch in November 2000. We immediately established a candid and positive interaction. We both agreed that it would be impossible to complete an FTA in the six-week deadline set by the Clinton Administration. We both pledged to do our best to do the impossible. In the two years that followed, I gained immense respect for Ambassador Koh, who set a constructive and optimistic tone for the overall negotiations.

Other members of the U.S. delegation had similar experiences with their counterparts. The 60-plus members of the U.S. delegation were always impressed with their Singaporean counterparts. I cannot count how many times my delegation praised the Singapore team who worked relentlessly, intelligently and with good humour to help us solve many problems during the negotiations.

Among the problems with which Singapore had to contend with was the change of U.S. administrations. As negotiation began on the basis of an understanding between former President Clinton and Prime Minister Goh before the November 2000 U.S. election, it had to await policy guidance under President Bush. Similarly, former USTR Charlene Barshefsky and Trade Minister George Yeo had adopted an approach to the FTA that had to be revisited and revised by USTR Ambassador Robert B. Zoellick. Fortunately, Ambassador Zoellick and Minister Yeo had developed a long and close relationship which served the negotiations particularly well in the final months.

One of the major differences between the Clinton Administration and the Bush Administration was their respective view about the comprehensiveness of the FTA. Charlene Barshefsky envisaged an FTA modelled on the U.S.-Jordan FTA, which was purposefully modest in scope — reflecting the small size of the trading relationship. This approach was designed to enable negotiations to conclude within the short time remaining for the Clinton Administration.

Ambassador Zoellick reviewed this approach, heard the strong views expressed by a wide range of business interests about the need for a comprehensive FTA that built on NAFTA and the World Trade Organization (WTO) agreements, and decided to seek a comprehensive world-class agreement. This revised policy meant that Singapore often had to wait — sometimes for months — for the U.S. side to develop a position on a particular issue.

Three specific examples illustrate this point. The previous administration adopted a "positive list" approach for services — i.e., only those services sectors explicitly listed in the FTA were bound by the terms of the agreement. The Bush Administration decided to use a "negative list" approach, which is more liberalising but required a more detailed and careful analysis by both the United States and Singapore to cnsure all sectors not listed could, in fact, be bound by the FTA.

Another example is the investment provisions of the FTA. The Clinton Administration could not adopt a policy on key features of a new investment chapter — such as the terms under which a private company could seek arbitration against a government. Resolving the investment issues took about 18 months in the Bush Administration.

A third example is intellectual property rights (IPR). Copyright protection, in particular, has become even more complicated than before in the new digital environment. The various interested sectors in the United States had reached a difficult domestic compromise under the Digital Millennium Copyright Act (DMCA). The U.S. side wanted to embed the basic provisions of the DMCA in the new FTA — a complicated and time-consuming exercise.

Of course, once the U.S. position was established on these, and other, sensitive issues it was difficult to revise them in the course of the negotiations. Singapore's patience and persistence were tested. Instead of becoming aggravated and annoyed, the Singapore team helped resolve issues in a way that met both countries' political needs.

This problem-solving attitude prevailed throughout the negotiations. Both sides approached issues with an attitude of producing the best possible FTA within their respective political constraints. It is this approach that helped maintain a positive spirit at the negotiating table and a successful outcome in the form of an FTA both sides can be proud of — a world-class FTA that will serve as a model for future U.S. free trade agreements with other nations.

SUBSTANCE

So, what was achieved in the FTA?

The final USSFTA consists of about 250 pages of text and roughly 1,200 pages of annexes. There are 21 chapters,[2] covering **trade in goods, textiles and apparel, rules of origin, services — including general services, financial services and telecommunication — investment, competition policy, intellectual property, e-commerce, customs cooperation, government procurement, labour/environment protections, and dispute settlement provisions**. Let me describe some of the key provisions.

Services are a major segment of the U.S. economy and a growing share of Singapore's economy. Under the FTA, both sides committed to provide substantial access for all types of services — subject to a few exceptions — and treat each other's services suppliers as well as it treats its own suppliers. The FTA will also ensure that both nations receive the best treatment that other foreign suppliers receive. Some of the services sectors covered by the FTA include: financial services, such as banking and insurance; construction and engineering; computer and related services; telecommunications services; tourism; professional services, such as architects, accountants and lawyers; express delivery; and energy services.

The USSFTA also provides important protection for U.S. investors. U.S. foreign direct investment in Singapore as of 2001 was over USD$27 billion. The Agreement ensures a secure and predictable legal framework for such investment. U.S. investors will be treated as well as Singaporean investors or any other foreign investor, and vice versa. The investment provisions draw from U.S. legal principles and practices, including due process and transparency. These investor rights are backed by effective and impartial procedures for dispute settlement.

---

[2] Refer to Appendix VI for a list of the 21 chapters. The full text of the USSFTA can be found on the web at http://app.fta.gov.sg/asp/fta/us_text.asp.

The FTA is innovative and state-of-the-art in a number of other ways, including its IPR protection. The FTA builds upon the WTO's Agreement on Trade-related Intellectual Property Rights, provides strong protection for new and emerging technologies and reflects standards of protection similar to those in U.S. laws. **The FTA's provisions also contain IPR enforcement provisions that are significantly stronger than those contained in the TRIPS[3] Agreement, thereby enhancing the ability of IPR owners to protect their rights.**

Enhanced transparency is another important feature of this FTA. An entire chapter is devoted to notice and comment procedures that are modelled on the U.S. Administrative Procedures Act. In addition, many of the other chapters contain specific provisions to ensure regulatory transparency — e.g., in the chapters on services, financial services, competition, government procurement, customs administration, investment, telecom, and dispute settlement.

Improved transparency can be an effective deterrent to combat corrupt business practices, creating an important precedent for future U.S. free trade agreements. In addition, the United States and Singapore expressly affirm in the FTA their strong commitments to effective measures against bribery and corruption in international business transactions.

The chapter on electronic commerce also breaks new ground. The FTA establishes for the first time explicit guarantees that the principle of non-discrimination applies to digital products delivered electronically (e.g., software, music, and videos). This chapter also creates the first binding prohibition on customs duties being levied on digital products delivered electronically, and where these products are stored on physical media (e.g., on a CD or DVD) duties are assessed on the value of media as opposed to the content. In addition, the chapter memorialises the principle of avoiding barriers that impede the use of electronic commerce.

---

[3] Trade-Related Aspects of Intellectual Property Rights.

Similarly, the telecommunications chapter achieves significant advances over the work undertaken in the WTO. The full range of telecommunication issues, i.e., reasonable and non-discriminatory access to networks, transparent rule making by an independent regulator, and adherence to the principles of deregulation and operator choice of technology.

The competition chapter[4] of the FTA is worth noting because there is a somewhat unique situation in Singapore — the presence of Government investment in the private sector through so-called government-linked companies (GLCs). While Singapore has welcomed foreign investment and treated it fairly, the United States wanted the FTA to contain certain protections for U.S. firms relating to sales to, and purchases from, these companies. In particular, the U.S. side wanted to make sure that GLCs in which the Government of Singapore could have effective influence acted in accordance with commercial considerations; did not discriminate against U.S. goods, services and investments; and did not engage in anti-competitive practices.[5]

The USSFTA addresses the sensitive areas of trade and labour and environment. The FTA has provisions for both sides to consult their laws in these areas and conduct cooperative activities. The FTA also commits both countries to enforce their respective labour and environment laws and recognises that it is inappropriate to weaken or reduce such laws to encourage trade or investment.

The FTA contains a number of provisions to ensure that the United States and Singapore are the actual beneficiaries of the Agreement. First, the FTA uses strong but simple rules of origin designed to ensure that it is U.S. and Singaporean goods that benefit from the FTA.

---

[4] Refers to the Anticompetitive Business Conduct, Designated Monopolies, and Government Enterpries chapter in the USSFTA.

[5] To better understand the role and rationale of the Singapore Government in GLCs, please refer to Appendix IX.

Second, the chapter on customs administration improves the exchange of information between the United States and Singapore, which is critical to modern risk management practices. The FTA also contains specific, concrete obligations on how customs procedures are to be conducted. Such procedures will help enable U.S. customs to combat illegal transhipments of goods, including on products violating the intellectual property rights provisions — such as pirated CDs.

Third, the textile and apparel chapter contains specific rules on monitoring Singapore's production and extensive anti-circumvention commitments — such as reporting, licensing, and announced factory checks. These provisions are designed to ensure that only Singaporean textiles and apparel receive tariff preferences.

Finally, the dispute settlement provisions of the FTA encourage resolution of disputes in a cooperative manner and provide an effective mechanism should such an approach prove to be unsuccessful. If a Party is found to be in breach of the FTA, it will be asked to bring its offending measure into compliance. Failing that, the preferred remedy is trade enhancing compensation. If compensation is not possible, the system allows the aggrieved Party to take other action without formal approval of a dispute settlement body.

In summary, the result is a world-class agreement providing positive economic gains to both nations. Various economic studies have attempted to assess in quantitative terms the value of these benefits. However, the models on which such estimates are based severely underestimate the FTA's potential economic value. Most models highlight the gains from tariff elimination and cannot accurately predict the value of strengthening commitments related to services, investment and IPR. Yet, in the case of the USSFTA, tariff elimination is a relatively modest feature, since Singapore had very few applied tariffs and U.S. tariffs were fairly low. A quantitative estimate that accurately accounted for the full range of the FTA's provisions would certainly be much higher than what the existing models suggest.

PROCESS PRODUCES RESULTS

Why does the right process improve the results of the FTA?

The complexity of a comprehensive FTA implies at least two points. The people negotiating the provisions must be able to understand them to negotiate them. Both Singapore and the United States had such people.

Second, understanding breeds trust, both of which are important for a successful negotiation — in terms of the actual FTA text and in terms of the ability and willingness to implement the provisions. Both sides need to feel that the other side is making a good faith effort to understand and work through a particular issue. Negotiations can focus for a long time around particular phrases or words. There needs to be a mutual recognition that the time spent on such discussions is truly leading to a resolution of an important substantive issue and not a tactic to delay negotiations and dilute the provisions.

Understanding must be achieved during the negotiations for implementation to be successful. The Parties to the agreement must clearly appreciate the implication of the provisions being negotiated for the FTA to have a good chance of being successfully implemented.

The goodwill and constructive engagement occurring in the U.S.-Singapore negotiations will, therefore, serve both sides for years to come. The FTA itself is a better agreement for this attitude. The FTA is more likely to stand the test of time.

The process and results also have a strategic value. The USSFTA is one part of a policy in both nations to keep the United States actively engaged in Southeast Asia. Successful conclusion of the FTA was a necessary step in the vision embodied in President

Bush's Enterprise for ASEAN Initiative (EAI). The President sees using the USSFTA as the foundation for future FTAs in the ASEAN region.

It is also this goodwill that will help improve U.S.-Singapore relations as countries — both in terms of interpersonal bonds formed and deeper understanding of each nation's respective sensitivities. This deeper understanding and respect carries on into other areas of work and is likely to prevail and spread through the delegation members' careers in and out of government service.

CONCLUSION

The United States has strong political and economic interests in Southeast Asia. Singapore is viewed as a leader in that region and recognises the need to maintain U.S. engagement there. The leadership of both nations shares the same strategic vision for the region. We expect the FTA with Singapore will serve as an important contribution to further enhancing the U.S. relationship with Singapore and the rest of Southeast Asia and assist its economic development. The process of negotiating and successfully concluding the FTA, as well as the strength of the FTA itself, should encourage this goal.

3 Lessons from the USSFTA Negotiations

ONG Ye Kung[1]

I got involved in the United States-Singapore Free Trade Agreement (USSFTA) negotiations when I was the Director of Trade at the Ministry of Trade and Industry (MTI), staffing Minister George Yeo at the November 2001 APEC meeting in Brunei. When we returned to Singapore, we conveyed to our colleagues the good news that the USSFTA was finally launched. We also told them the not-so-good news that many of us had to venture into the cold winter in Washington D.C. and work through Christmas if necessary to conclude the negotiations by the end of the year. The then Permanent Secretary of the Ministry of Trade and Industry, Mr. Khaw Boon Wan, asked me to be stationed in Washington to co-ordinate the first and supposedly only round of negotiations. As it turned out, it was not a fruitful round of negotiations. But on hindsight, I am grateful to him for giving me this assignment. The negotiations stretched much longer than originally intended, but the experience of seeing the negotiations from start to end has helped

---

[1] Former Deputy Chief Negotiator and Director (Trade) at the Ministry of Trade and Industry. Since July 2002, Ong Ye Kung has been appointed the Principal Private Secretary to Deputy Prime Minister Lee Hsien Loong. His only negotiating experience before USSFTA was the two Collective Agreements he was involved in while serving at the Public Service Division, Prime Minister's Office, from April 1997 to December 1998. The views expressed in this article are those of the author and do not necessarily represent the views of the Singapore Government.

me to grow and mature as a public service professional. I got to work very closely with United States Trade Representative (USTR) officials, collaborated with my colleagues in other ministries, and engaged the private sector. It was an opportunity that I was fortunate to have. So when Professor Tommy Koh asked me to contribute an article to this book, I decided to share the lessons I have learnt. There are three. First, stay true to our conviction. Second, negotiate, not bargain. Third, internal negotiations are harder.

STAY TRUE TO OUR CONVICTION

Singapore is committed to advancing freer trade at multilateral, regional and bilateral levels. It is a simple, honest policy that reflects our smallness and our need for the global market in order to survive. We do not draw philosophical lines between different initiatives. Neither do we eschew bilateral deals in order to hide behind the complexity of multilateral deals to avoid opening up our markets. It is therefore with conviction that we went about our FTAs.

The U.S., being the largest market in the world, is particularly important to Singapore. In 2001, Prime Minister Goh in his keynote address to the U.S.-ASEAN Business Council in Washington, D.C. explained:

> "The sheer weight of the U.S. economy and its pre-eminent strategic position, among other factors, ensure that the U.S. will have a primary influence on the overall environment in which East Asia evolves."[2]

---

[2] Keynote Address by Singapore Prime Minister Goh Chok Tong at the U.S.-ASEAN Business Council 9th Annual U.S. Ambassadors' Tour Dinner on Tuesday, 12 June 2001 at Willard Intercontinental Hotel, Washington D.C., USA.

"The key issue is how to 'embed', to borrow a popular term, the U.S. in this process of East Asian regionalism, and ensure that the two sides of the Pacific remain in happy embrace. This is a strategic as well as economic imperative. Without the U.S., East Asian regionalism will, over time, be dominated by one player. This will give less breathing room for others in the region."[3]

This captured the essence of our strategic view that the United States played an important role in contributing to the growth and stability of the region.

When we first started our FTA initiatives, various concerns were raised. Some thought FTAs are messy and resembled an unpleasant "spaghetti bowl". Others feared that FTAs could be used as a backdoor into the ASEAN Free Trade Area (AFTA) and work against the ASEAN spirit of solidarity. Some of the arguments were seductively popular. But we persisted, explained our position and stayed on the course that we have chosen.

Years later, I believe that our approach has borne fruit. Several of our neighbours are now engaged in FTA negotiations themselves. The U.S., upon concluding the USSFTA negotiations, is now working with other ASEAN countries, and has launched bilateral FTA negotiations with Thailand. Our most recent bilateral partners, such as India and South Korea, saw their negotiations with Singapore as first steps towards deeper and broader engagement with ASEAN. The lesson is that Singapore as a small country has to act in its own interest and be convicted of its cause.

---

[3] Keynote Address by Singapore Prime Minister Goh Chok Tong at the Asia Society Gala Dinner, The Fairmont Hotel, Washington D.C., 7 May 2003.

NEGOTIATE, NOT BARGAIN

I have also learnt to differentiate between bargaining and negotiating. Bargaining is what we do at the flea market. The seller quotes an opening price, I ask for a 50 percent discount, and we settle somewhere in-between.

Negotiations are different in a few aspects. They do not involve just the two persons engaging face to face, but the layers of interests and influence behind them. For Singapore, MTI was negotiating on the positions provided by various stakeholders and ministries. The U.S. has an even more complex system of decision-making and checks and balances. So while the negotiators were at one battle front, our Mission in Washington was at another, working tirelessly to meet with government and business representatives that influence the U.S.'s negotiating positions. So although the negotiators met formally once every two months, real progress was made outside of the formal meetings.

Negotiations must also be interest-based. Each side must understand the interests at stake and work together to reach a position that both sides can uphold. Let me cite an issue which I thought both sides negotiated particularly well. The issue relates to the Government-Linked Companies (GLCs) of Singapore. We started off badly, with wide ideological differences. The U.S.'s position was that governments should not be in the business of owning and running commercial enterprises. This is the domain of the private sector and should be left to market forces. It is a key principle that made the U.S. private sector the most innovative and vibrant in the world. Singapore's starting point was that GLCs were part of our historical legacy. At the point of independence, we hardly had a private sector, but the Government set up these companies to offer essential services, create employment and generate wealth. Many started off as government departments, which we later corporatised and privatised. Further, GLCs operate commercially and had to compete in the market place. There is nothing wrong with government ownership.

If we had persisted with negotiations along the two different ideologies, never the twain would have met. Fortunately, both sides were able to set aside the ideological differences and focus on our interests. The U.S.'s real interest is not to advance their ideology, but to ensure that GLCs do not become anti-competitive or monopolistic companies and hurt their business interests. The U.S. was also concerned that GLCs may become vehicles for the Singapore Government to implement discriminatory policies. Having learnt that, the Singapore side concluded that it was in fact in our interest to address the U.S.'s concerns. Having our GLCs that operate commercially and on a level playing field with other market players is a key differentiating factor between them and other state-owned enterprises around the world, and explains why GLCs are viable companies which are not a drain on national resources. Hence in the USSFTA, we have committed to maintain Singapore's current regime on GLCs but have given the U.S. the assurance that GLCs: act in accordance with commercial considerations; do not discriminate against U.S. goods, services and investments; and do not engage in anti-competitive practices.

At the first round we were literally debating Adam Smith's theory, but by the time we reached the last round, we were quibbling over drafting format and choice of words.

Negotiation is therefore far more complex than bargaining. It is the constructive process of navigating through competing interests and complex spheres of influences to reach a mutually acceptable solution. It is not a dirty word.

It is to the great credit of the U.S. team for always taking a constructive and non-ideological approach to our negotiations. Of course, the bargaining powers are different — Singapore is a small market with practically no tariffs, while the U.S. is the world's largest economy and a superpower. But that did not stop both sides from negotiating with mutual respect and as equal, sovereign entities. Each issue was debated based on the merit of the reasoning. If Singapore felt arm-twisted into positions we cannot accept, we would probably have walked away, to the detriment of both sides.

INTERNAL NEGOTIATIONS ARE HARDER

The final lesson is that the bigger challenge of the negotiations came from within. There is a perception that the notion of the "Singapore Inc." implies that all ministries think alike and obey the same orders. This is untrue. In reality, the Government is a complex organisation. Various ministries have to take into account economic, social and security considerations of every Government action. On a daily basis, the agencies have to work closely together to harmonise these often competing objectives and arrive at a common position that has buy-in from all stakeholders and will take the nation forward.

The USSFTA brought to light many issues that different agencies have to collaborate on and resolve. A good illustration is the protection of intellectual property rights (IPR). The U.S. requested that we raise the standard of protection of IPR in Singapore. Although we recognise that better protection for knowledge means the potential to attract more foreign investments, we are also mindful that consumers' interests must be addressed and that they should not be exploited by the IP owners. In the end, we managed to strike a new balance in our regime, where we updated and improved our IP in view of advances in information technology. That way, in the knowledge-based economy, Singapore will stand out as a country that protects IP rights vigorously and is attractive to investors.

It is also not easy to co-ordinate the effort of 21 negotiating groups with team members drawn from different ministries and agencies. We had to create new frameworks and tools to foster closer inter-agency teamwork. One small idea which helped a great deal was the FTA Fund. It is a S$5m one-off fund granted by the Ministry of Finance and administered by MTI. Through this fund, MTI paid for all the travelling and hotel expenses of all members of the negotiating team, and reimbursed various agencies the salaries of their officers involved in the negotiations (since it was almost a full time assignment for many members). This helped lubricate friction inherent in inter-agency work. The Chief and Deputy Chief Negotiators also wrote staff appraisals for some of the members, so that their excellent performances during the negotiations are recognised by their parent organisations. Moving forward, as the civil service engages in more projects that straddle across ministries, we should perhaps come up with more tools that facilitate a networked Government.

CONCLUSION

There were of course many other lessons learnt — some professional, some personal. I realised how important it is to have a strong team. Not everyone is involved in high profile or glamorous work that received attention. The best example is our Rules of Origin Team, which had to scrutinise over 6000 lines of rules, buried deep in the Annexes of the Agreement, but absolutely essential in making sure that Singapore businesses can benefit from the FTAs. They are known to be the people with the gentlest temperament in any negotiating team. Part of the extended team are the families, who had to manage with a missing spouses, parents, or children for the two years that the negotiations took. They deserve recognition too.

On a lighter note, I learnt that one can live on adrenalin. During the last round of negotiations, a few of us were so highly strung that we found ourselves losing our appetite totally and needing very little sleep. Someone told me that it was because we were surviving on our adrenalin. Now that the USSFTA is in force, the anxiety continues. We hope that we have delivered a good and fair deal. We hope there would be no disputes. We hope that the good relations developed with our U.S. counterparts will be enduring and will last beyond this Administration. We hope that with the help of MTI, our businesses could better access the U.S. market. We hope that the USSFTA will help Singapore grow and remain connected to the key markets of the world.

4 The USSFTA: The Socio-Political Context

Franklin L. LAVIN[1]

A quote variously ascribed to Dorothy Parker and other writers reveals the ambiguity the craftsman feels toward the craft: "I don't like writing. I like having written". I suppose this is how most people feel about trade negotiations. There might be little that is inherently enjoyable in the process, but it is pleasant in retrospect to see that the hard work, travel, and occasional heartburn of negotiations can result in a world-class agreement. With the United States-Singapore Free Trade Agreement (USSFTA), both countries have taken an important step forward in commercial terms as well as politically. Indeed, it might be the political dimension that is more consequential over time.

A LITTLE HISTORY

In 1992 I was running the U.S. Department of Commerce's Asia operations in the "other" Bush Administration, serving as Deputy Assistant Secretary, and I gave a speech at a Washington think-tank

---

[1] Frank Lavin is currently the United States Ambassador to Singapore. He was sworn into to this post on 13 August 2001, culminating over two decades of work in Asian affairs in both government and the private sector. From 1996 until his present position, Lavin worked as a banker and venture capitalist in Hong Kong and Singapore. In the George H. W. Bush Administration, he served in the U.S. Department of Commerce, and in the Reagan Administration he served on the National Security Council and White House Staff. The views expressed in this article are those of the author and do not necessarily represent the views of the U.S. Government.

in which I suggested that several economies in Asia might be good partners for Free Trade Agreements with the United States.[2] Singapore, Taiwan, New Zealand, and Australia all came to mind as economies that were both relatively advanced as well as relatively open, at least when compared to the rest of Asia.

Although to my mind, no one in the U.S. Government had explicitly mentioned these possibilities, it was not an extraordinary speech. However, the fact that I specifically mentioned some economies by name netted a bit of publicity, most of it favourable. In fact, the single unfavourable comment came, unfortunately, from the office of the Secretary of Commerce. The Secretary's Chief of Staff told me that the Secretary was unhappy my speech had received more publicity than a speech she had given the same day. I was a bit mystified by all this and never heard any word directly from the Secretary so I was at a loss as to how to interpret the comments. Still, it was a reminder that trade issues can be sensitive, that all negotiations take place in a context of bureaucracy and politics, and sometimes the greatest problems can come from within one's own institution.

Let us flash forward eight years to the end of the Clinton Administration.

All parties owe President Clinton a debt for agreeing to free trade negotiations. This had the helpful political impact of giving the negotiations a Democratic Party parentage, a useful pedigree to militate against partisan opposition. Party loyalty and White House management would ensure that the FTA received majority support from President Bush's party, the Republicans, but the Democratic Party was more of an open question, due in part to the role of industrial unions in its make-up.

We can see why this initiative would appeal to President Clinton. Liberalisation with Singapore allowed him to occupy the high

---

[2] "After NAFTA: Free Trade and Asia", The Heritage Foundation, 6 October 1992.

ground on trade, with minimal dislocation in the U.S. In a sense, Singapore represented a low risk: It was prosperous, with few industries that the U.S. would consider import sensitive, making job migration from the U.S. on the basis of labour costs unlikely. There would be no "giant sucking sound", to invoke arch-protectionist Ross Perot's prediction of North American Free Trade Area job loss. The Singapore economy would be unlikely to be seen as a threat to the U.S. Finally, according to U.S. trade data, the U.S. had been running a trade surplus with Singapore, which would put the minds of the deficit hawks at ease that we were somehow giving away too much.

The Clinton Administration's decision to launch negotiations also deserves praise for improving the bilateral relationship, especially given the Michael Fay incident which occurred in the first half of Clinton's Presidency and had put bilateral ties under a bit of a cloud.

THE BUSH ADMINISTRATION AND THE START OF NEGOTIATIONS

The Bush Administration came to office positively disposed to both Singapore and to trade liberalisation. It was clear that this was an Administration priority from the start. In fact, the FTA was so central to the view of Singapore that it figured prominently in my discussions whether I should serve as Ambassador. The White House specifically raised the importance of the FTA negotiations when I was asked to take this position in February 2001.

The Bush Administration also saw FTAs as an important political statement, helping to provide leadership in the region. The FTA helps the U.S. think more seriously about Southeast Asia and helps the region think more seriously about the United States. Strengthening the bonds of peaceful, voluntary, and mutually beneficial commercial interchange reminds the political leadership on both sides of the Pacific that the societies have much in common and much to gain by working together.

A second goal was to instigate a virtuous cycle of liberalisation. The Singapore FTA was important not only in itself but for what it might promote in the region. President Bush formalised this approach in 2002 when the United States launched the Enterprise for ASEAN Initiative (EAI) at the Asia-Pacific Economic Cooperation (APEC) summit in Mexico. This was an invitation to other ASEAN nations to enjoy the benefits of free trade with the U.S. The USSFTA stands as the model for these additional agreements.

This approach is already bearing fruit. In October 2003, President Bush announced our intention to launch FTA negotiations with Thailand. Trade and Investment Framework Agreements (TIFAs) are in place or are being negotiated with a number of other ASEAN members. Beyond Southeast Asia, the U.S. has negotiated an FTA with Australia. It is not surprising that, in the wake of the launch of negotiations for the USSFTA, China has also offered the ASEAN countries a preferential trade arrangement, and Japan has followed suit, albeit more tentatively.

The USSFTA and these other initiatives reinforce the shift in Southeast Asia toward further liberalisation. Once a country makes a decision to liberalise with one trading partner, it becomes easier to extend that liberalisation to others. The expanding number of FTAs being negotiated by ASEAN or by ASEAN members is a clear example of this phenomenon, which in turn feeds global trade liberalisation.

TIMETABLES AND STOVEPIPES: WHAT KIND OF FTA?

As Bush Administration negotiations began in Singapore, we had an early question of definition — how broad and deep would the FTA be? Would it be a symbolic FTA or a real one? The U.S. side had a concern on this point because Singapore had just concluded an FTA with New Zealand that we regarded as largely symbolic with close to no new market openings. In addition, the Clinton Administration seemed to have envisaged a quick negotiation that would have made it near impossible to achieve a substantive agreement. We were determined that our FTA negotiations would not be an empty exercise. It was unclear if everyone on the Singapore side felt the same way. In fact, there were some troubling initial indicators that Singapore might not have the desire to pursue the type of ambitious accord we were seeking.

In the course of trade negotiations, some countries occasionally give the impression of having two distinct goals: to garner the political or symbolic benefit of an FTA and to garner the economic benefits of an FTA. The political benefit could be achieved simply through declaration, without any of the difficult steps needed to liberalise. Both sides would state they have an agreement. The spotlight would switch on; smiles and applause all around. On the other hand, to attain the economic benefits of an FTA would require painstaking negotiations, the ability to work across the government systems to build a consensus, and a series of technical discussions on the minutia of international commerce.

Governments want progress, but they also want the perception of progress. This can be a seductive approach to policy, in which the hard decisions are pushed aside for the empty declaration. The peril in the approach of setting a deadline is that as that deadline for completion approaches, the parties have a strong incentive to stall — or settle for a least-common denominator approach — rather than to address the issues. Why should we struggle to solve problems when the deadline would soon be upon us, and we can simply declare victory?

In this regard, it was worrying when we heard preferences to establish a timetable to complete the negotiations. The first attempt was when President Clinton and Prime Minister Goh launched the negotiations at the end of 2000 and stated that they wanted the agreement finished by the end of Clinton's term — only a few months away. This was so unrealistic that it was hard to take it seriously, and the implication was that Singapore and the U.S. might not genuinely be interested in a Free Trade Agreement — only in a declaration of a Free Trade Agreement.

The Bush Administration wanted as ambitious an FTA as possible. As I stated at the time, you only get one shot at an FTA so we might as well take the time to get it right. There is a paradox in negotiations, in that if you insist on one hundred percent, you will likely end up with zero percent, so we were prepared from the start to accept less than 100 percent market openings. At the same time, we felt there had to be concrete openings in specific sectors. We wanted to avoid the type of agreements Singapore reached with New Zealand, Japan and the European Free Trade Association, which resulted in little new market access in Singapore. We thought a largely symbolic exercise would be merely a waste of time and intellectually a bit thin. If we were going to put in the effort to open something up, we needed to end up with measurable improvements. And as a practical political matter, we needed "champions" — U.S. companies that would be sufficiently pleased with the results that they would advocate ratification of the FTA. So one clear challenge opened up early on in the negotiations: the need to avoid deadlines while at the same time aiming for an ambitious FTA. We had to work constantly to keep set on these goals.

This process did not always lend itself to the sort of quiet harmony that some would have preferred. Singapore's political culture is more subdued and consensus-oriented. The United States has a more contentious style in which issues and criticisms are openly discussed. Indeed, when a member of the U.S. delegation, at my direction, stated at a negotiating round that we rejected the idea of a deadline and saw little point in negotiating an agreement that would simply codify the status quo, some of our Singapore friends complained about his "behaviour" to the State Department.

A second structural challenge became clear early on as well, somewhat related to the first. Each particular sectoral negotiation would be led by an expert from that sector, usually from a government ministry or a regulatory body. But these government agencies (on both sides) tended to be status quo oriented. Having designed and operated the current system, they had enormous psychological attachment to it and did not necessarily have much of an incentive to liberalise it. This was what we called the stovepipe issue, because government management tends to take place through particular silos or stovepipes of expertise and mandates. Civil servants guard their particular sectoral responsibilities jealously and can be quite unenthusiastic about openings in their sector. Only when decision-making rises to the national level or the political level are people more inclined to look at the national benefits of liberalisation.

Thus part of the embassy's role was to escalate the issues — on both sides, when necessary — from the stovepipe specialist to the national leadership. We knew that any liberalisation might cause some minor dislocation, but that overall it would improve the aggregate economic benefits to each side. We had to continue to focus on these macro benefits. I developed this theme in a speech to the American Chamber of Commerce in March 2002:[3]

> Trade negotiation is an area that is fraught with unrealised promise and contradictory impulses. Indeed, with the possible exception of high school dating, there is perhaps no area of human activity more burdened with misplaced hopes. The reasons are simple. In the abstract, we all know that open trading systems provide the best path for economic growth, but there can be dislocation. Even though market openings will result in net job creation, this is small solace to those who might be displaced. The combination of dispersed benefits of trade and the more acute, though more modest costs, makes for powerful

---

[3] "U.S.-Singapore FTA: Taking Singapore Higher", Speech to the American Chamber of Commerce, 22 March 2002: http://singapore.usembassy.gov/speeches/2002/mar22.shtml.

constituencies against market openings. We all favour trade liberalisation in the abstract, but when the time comes to open up, we sometimes fall short of the mark. So it is not uncommon to hear perfectly rational people agreeing to trade liberalisation … only just not right now. It calls to mind St. Augustine's prayer as he was attempting to turn away from his earlier sinful life, "O Lord, make me chaste, but not yet".

This makes Singapore and America's commitment to a world-class FTA all the more impressive. It would be easy enough to establish an agreement that would bring us 80 percent success — and then we could declare victory. Indeed, on the day that negotiations commenced both countries probably enjoyed something close to 80 percent free trade. But why not aim higher? Why not work for an A+ instead of a C? Why not do what we can to get as much benefit as possible from this agreement?

I went on to delineate six areas where I felt Singapore was not being as responsive as we hoped to market openings. This led to an unhappy response from Singapore including critical press coverage in the pro government newspaper as well as an informal chiding for "negotiating in public".

Perhaps some in Singapore would view it as impolitic to concede that my points were either valid or that the way that I made them was constructive, although some did acknowledge as much. A cynical interpretation is that there are two great sins in public life: not telling the truth, and (potentially the greater sin) telling the truth. In the end, virtually every point I raised was eventually addressed in the FTA.

MOVING TOWARD PASSAGE

As the agreement moved to completion, several issues remained unresolved. We made sure we undertook regular consultations with the U.S. business community to help manage these issues. On a practical level, the businesses were the ones who would have to operate under the FTA and we wanted to make sure we were taking their concerns into account. On a political level, we wanted to make sure we had responded to every concern we could. Working primarily through the American Chamber of Commerce in Singapore, we held a number of round-tables to explore concerns and to make sure our proposals were responsive.

One such issue was Singapore's proposal to broaden the FTA to accord privileges to third countries under an "Integrated Sourcing Initiative" (ISI). The ISI as originally proposed would have allowed components of Singapore items that had been manufactured offshore (in Indonesia, for example) to count as Singapore goods. Initially, this privilege would only exist in the medical equipment and information technology sectors and apply only to products that already enter duty-free. In other words, a hard drive manufactured in Indonesia could be assembled into a computer manufactured in Singapore, and the computer would be considered a Singapore product. This would be a boon to Singapore as a manufacturing hub and would be an inducement to companies in the region to find some way to link to Singapore to get the benefit of ISI.

However the proposal ran into criticism in the United States from those who believed it might create a backdoor through which imports from low-wage countries, like Indonesia, could enter the United States. This criticism ignored the fact that ISI covered products that had long faced a zero duty rate in the U.S. and were made on sophisticated production lines, not sweatshops. There was also concern that the ISI sectoral list could be expanded beyond information technology and medical equipment without Congressional approval. As a result of this concern, the benefits originally proposed in the ISI were substantially reduced.

Visas were another issue. Both sides wanted improved visa treatment for their professionals. Singapore sought treatment similar to that granted to Canada and Mexico under NAFTA. In response, we agreed to provide a special enhanced visa category for a limited quota of professionals. We thought that was the end of the story, but some Members of Congress were displeased that a trade agreement dealt directly with immigration. The concerns were magnified because of the unemployment situation in the U.S. and because of post-9/11 sensitivities over control of our borders. In the end, the visa provisions stayed in, with a Congressional warning to USTR not to negotiate immigration issues again.

A third issue was professional services in Singapore. It is difficult for U.S. professionals such as architects, engineers, and lawyers, to practice freely in Singapore. We put this on the table for the FTA negotiations, but made very little progress, with Singapore preferring to protect these industries than to open them to competition, to the detriment of both countries' economies.

THE UPSHOT

The economic benefits of the FTA for Singapore and the United States are delineated elsewhere in this book. But the enduring commercial benefit of the FTA might not be in any particular sectoral opening, but primarily as a signal. The FTA, in essence, is a seal of approval, a statement to businesses in the U.S. that Singapore is one of a select group of trading partners. Singapore is now the only country in Asia with which we have an FTA. The message to companies is that Singapore is now the easiest market in Asia for U.S. firms. The message I give companies in the U.S. is: If you can do business in Canada, you can do business in Singapore.

The USSFTA was the biggest U.S. trade agreement since NAFTA. It was also the first since the lapse of Fast Track and its replacement with Trade Promotion Authority. So the success of the FTA was helpful in U.S. policy evolution, helping re-establish a consensus in the U.S. in favour of liberalisation.

I would like to thank Assistant U.S. Trade Representative Ralph Ives, who served as lead negotiator on the U.S. side, First Secretary of our Economics Section Paul Brown who coordinated the embassy role, Ambassador Robert Zoellick whose interventions were constructive and elegant, and who used his considerable energy level and policy antennae to help keep the Administration focused. I also want to thank the American Chamber of Commerce in Singapore and the U.S.-ASEAN Business Council for coordinating business suggestions in the negotiations.

Most of all, the people who deserve credit are our Singapore counterparts. Ambassador Tommy Koh was diligent, fair-minded, and ever patient, but with a keen mind and a sense of Singapore's core goals. He oversaw a formidable inter-agency team that prepared well and worked hard. I would also like to pay respects to my counterpart, Singapore Ambassador to the U.S. Chan Heng Chee, who ensured the broader Washington policy community, especially the legislative branch, was kept apace of the negotiations.

As for me, my role was part strategist, part publicist, part team-builder, part business contact, part congressional liaison — all the while working to make sure the FTA improved our bilateral relations. Tommy Koh set a high tone for the negotiations when he told both sides of the negotiators that he wanted an agreement of which we could all be proud. I am happy to say that, indeed, we have exactly such an agreement. Both countries are the better for it. And Dorothy Parker's aphorism to the contrary, I enjoyed the negotiations as well.

5 The *A* to *Z* of the USSFTA[1]

William CHOONG[2]

A for Authority

U.S. President George W. Bush was given beefed-up trade negotiation powers by Congress in 2002 to get trade deals done more quickly with foreign countries like Singapore.

B for Beer

Beer is cheaper now, thanks to the scrapping of tariffs on some alcoholic beverages. Let's drink to that!

C for Chewing Gum

Chew on this — the FTA will lift the ten-year ban on some types of gum sold for therapeutic purposes.

---

[1] This is an adaptation of an article first published in *The Straits Times* on 8 May 2003 by William Choong.

[2] William Choong is a Correspondent with *The Straits Times* newspaper in Singapore, covering foreign news such as the war in Iraq, U.S. foreign policy and global trade issues. In 2000, he graduated from the University of Queensland with an MA in International Relations, focusing on American grand strategies in East Asia as well as strategic missile defence.

D for Doha

Singapore and the U.S. argue that such bilateral deals can even help grease the wheels of World Trade Organization processes such as the Doha round of global trade talks.

E for Enterprise for ASEAN Initiative (EAI)

Singapore and Washington agree that their FTA will have a positive impact on the EAI proposal by U.S. President George W. Bush to have trade agreements with ASEAN members, depending on their level of development.

F for Fish Head Curry

At times, Singaporean negotiators turned to their "secret weapon" — good Singapore food — to help keep talks moving. Besides fish head curry, they plied their American counterparts with some hot local favourites: chilli and pepper crab, fish otah, garlic prawns and roti prata.

G for Golf

Prime Minister Goh Chok Tong and former U.S. President Bill Clinton first talked of a possible FTA over a midnight golf game in Brunei in November 2000.

H for "How Can?"

One of the many Singlish terms that Americans learnt during the negotiations. Others included: kiasu, garang, and balik kampung.

I for Indonesia

The FTA makes the Indonesian Riau islands more attractive, as some components made there will be counted as being of Singapore origin.

J for Jobs

The deal is expected to generate work for thousands of Singaporeans. Companies which locate some part of their operations in Singapore can benefit from its tariff exemptions.

K for Koh

Professor Tommy Koh, Singapore's Chief Negotiator, was likened to soccer star David Beckham for his playmaker skills which helped wrap up the FTA talks.

L for Law Degrees

Under the deal, Singapore will recognise degrees from four U.S. law schools for admission to the Singapore Bar.

M for Manufacturing

Singapore's key economic engine will benefit. The pact eliminates 92 percent of current tariffs levied on its U.S.-bound exports.

N for Non-Tariff Barriers

Both countries are committed to simplifying customs procedures.

O for Opportunities

American banks get better access to Singapore's retail banking sector — if they meet local banking standards.

P for Pizza

Comfort food was offered to the American team in the hours of intensified talks leading up to their culmination in November 2002.

Q for Quit

Something some of Singapore's 50 or so negotiators felt like doing at some points during the talks. Thankfully they never did.

R for Regional Effects

The U.S.-Singapore deal has spawned similar initiatives across Asia. For example, Japan — which had for some time shunned FTAs — is now starting talks with Malaysia, Thailand and the Philippines. Japan already has an FTA with Singapore.

S for Smellmarks and Soundmarks

Trademarks governing the sounds and smells of various products. They are immensely critical for the protection of intellectual property rights, which were — for the first time — included in a bilateral or multilateral deal.

T for Tariffs

The reduction or elimination of import taxes will save Singapore more than S$200 million annually in tariffs.

U for U.S.-Singapore Business Coalition, U.S.-ASEAN Business Council, and the U.S. Chamber of Commerce

The three groups fought hard for the FTA.

V for Virtuous Promiscuity

Prof. Koh used this somewhat provocative term to describe Singapore's policy of making so many trade deals. For some time, some countries have criticised Singapore's FTA policy, saying it would derail trade liberalisation within the World Trade Organization.

W for White House

The historic FTA was signed at the White House on 6 May 2003.

X for Xerox

Someone's photocopier must have been working overtime. The final FTA agreement between Singapore and the U.S. runs into thousands of pages.

Y for Yeo

Singapore's Trade and Industry Minister George Yeo personally oversaw the FTA talks.

Z for Zoellick

The steely-eyed, hard-talking American trade czar Robert Zoellick spared no effort in wrapping up the FTA.

Section II

Selected Chapters
of the Agreement

6 The Goods Package

ROSSMAN Ithnain[1]

SINGAPORE-U.S. TRADE RELATIONS

The U.S. is Singapore's second largest trading partner and second top export destination. Exports to the U.S. made up almost 15 percent of Singapore's exports. The two-way trade with the U.S. is highly significant for Singapore — in 2002, 62.4 billion Singapore dollars worth of goods were traded between the U.S. and Singapore.

The Trade in Goods chapter of the USSFTA could be divided into three important sections:

a. Tariffs
b. Rules of Origin
c. Non-Tariff Measures or NTMs for short.

Sections a. and c. can be found in the chapter on "National Treatment and Market Access Goods" of the United States-

---

[1] Rossman Ithnain has been Deputy Director, Trade Division — Directorate B, Ministry of Trade and Industry, Singapore, since 1 April 2002. He was the lead negotiator for Goods (Market Access for Goods and Rules of Origin) for the USSFTA and Singapore-Australia FTA. He was also the lead negotiator for Rules of Origin for the Agreement between Singapore and Japan for a New Age Economic Partnership (JSEPA). Rossman was also involved in exploratory talks and initial stages of negotiations for the Singapore-Canada Free Trade Agreement and is currently involved in the FTA negotiations with India (as Goods Lead) and Sri Lanka (as Chief Negotiator) respectively. Rossman is trained as a lawyer and has an LL.B, National University of Singapore and LL.M, Fitzwilliam College, Cambridge University, United Kingdom. The views expressed in this article are those of the author and do not necessarily represent the views of the Singapore Government.

Singapore Free Trade Agreement (USSFTA), whilst section b. is in the "Rules of Origin" chapter. The key annexes of the Goods package are Annexes 2A, 2B, 3A, 3B and 3C.

GENERAL PRINCIPLES

Some general principles should be borne in mind before a discussion of the three sections. It should be noted that the USSFTA directly benefits only the U.S. and Singapore, i.e., the parties to the Agreement. Although the Indonesian islands of Batam and Bintan could benefit from their close economic ties with and proximity to Singapore, they are formally not parties to the USSFTA.

Second, the coverage of the Trade in Goods chapter does not extend to internal taxes such as Goods and Services Tax (GST) and excise duties.

In addition, the rules of origin determining that Singapore is the origin of an export must be practical and reflect local production realities. Otherwise, it would be difficult for Singapore-made goods to qualify for the tariff-free treatment. Non-tariff measures, such as cumbersome customs procedures have the potential to impede trade as well. We have therefore tried to conclude customs procedures in the USSFTA which facilitate and not impede trade.

TARIFF SAVINGS

This is one of the most direct and tangible benefits of an FTA. 100 percent of Singapore's domestic exports to the U.S. will get to enjoy preferential duty-free treatment under the USSFTA, subject to the goods satisfying the rules of origin under the Agreement. This means that no single product has been excluded from tariff concessions. However, the concessions are staged, i.e., some tariffs are eliminated immediately on 1 January 2004, while others are reduced over a period of time until it becomes zero. We have estimated that the tariff savings Singapore could enjoy from the USSFTA would be around S$200–S$300 million.

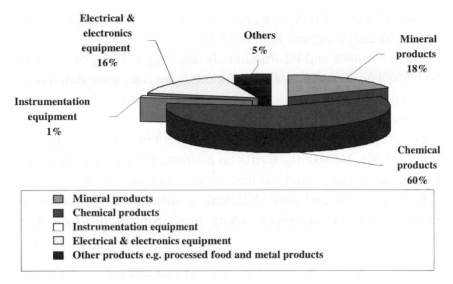

Fig. 1. Tariff savings for non-textile products.

The chart in Fig. 1 shows a breakdown of potential tariff savings in different sectors.

Of the tariff savings for non-textile products, the largest proportion comes from the chemical sector, followed by the mineral products sector, the electronics and electrical sector and the instrumentation equipment sector. Tariff savings in other sectors such as processed food and metal products, etc. constitute about 5 percent of total tariff savings for non-textile products.

Let me illustrate the above by selecting four sectors and show how the staging works.

TARIFF: STAGING CATEGORIES

The explanation of the staging categories *A* to *E* is in the agreement, but basically *A* means that tariffs on the goods will be eliminated immediately on the date the USSFTA comes into force. *B* means that tariffs will be phased out over four years and so on. *E* or Most

Favoured Nation (MFN-zero) means that all goods, Singapore and foreign, already enter the U.S. tariff-free.

For electronics and Information Technology (IT) exports, before the USSFTA, 44 percent of the exports to the U.S. were dutiable — i.e., subject to tariffs. Now, 100 percent will be tariff free on entry into force of the FTA.

For instrumentation equipment, 52 percent of exports to the U.S. were dutiable. Most of the tariffs on instrumentation equipment will be eliminated immediately as this sector is in Category A.

For chemicals and petrochemical, a substantial 74 percent of chemical and petrochemical exports from Singapore to the U.S.

Table 1. Tariff elimination — selected examples.

Sectors	Electronics and IT	Precision Instruments	Chemicals and Petrochemicals	Processed Food
Pre-USSFTA	56% of products free 44% of products dutiable	48% of equipment free 52% of equipment dutiable	26% of products free 74% of products dutiable	15% of products free 85% of products dutiable
Post-USSFTA	100% of products free	100% of equipment free	100% of products free	100% of products free
Staging A (immediate)	39%	44.7%	28.9%	45.1%
Staging B (4 years)	4.9%	5.1%	30.3%	15%
Staging C (8 years)	0.5%	1.9%	14.6%	9.3%
Staging D (10 years)	–	–	0.1%	1.6%
Staging E (MFN-zero)	55.6%	48%	26%	15%

used to be dutiable. After the USSFTA comes into force, all tariffs on chemicals and petrochemicals will be eliminated, but not immediately for all. For the products in categories B and C, the tariffs will be eliminated over a period of time.

Processed food also constitutes a sector that stands to gain substantially. Previously, 85 percent of processed food exports to the U.S. was subject to tariffs. More than half of those exports will now have tariffs eliminated when the agreement comes into force.

The details of the tariff concessions for the products are set out in the Annexes 2A and 2B of Chapter 2 of the USSFTA.

MORE SAVINGS

Singapore's businesses will also enjoy savings from the removal of other fees and duties. Take, for instance, the merchandise processing fee that is currently imposed on all goods imported into the U.S. It is a customs-user fee collected by the U.S. customs for the processing of merchandise imported into the U.S. With the USSFTA, this fee will be waived for Singapore goods. This will save businesses a projected S$51m per year.

The U.S. currently also imposes a 50 percent *ad valorem* duty on the cost of equipment and repairs obtained by U.S.-flagged vessels outside the U.S. This duty will be removed under the USSFTA. The potential savings are estimated at S$7–S$9m. Singapore will also remove its tariffs on U.S. exports of beer, stout, samsoo and medicated samsoo. So, not only will U.S. beer exporters benefit, but Singapore's consumers will also enjoy cheaper U.S. beer.

However, tariff elimination cannot be seen in isolation. In order to qualify for the tariff elimination, there are rules which must be adhered to. The benefits under the USSFTA only accrue to goods "made in" either the United States or Singapore. There are rules that ensure that only exports of goods of Singapore origin will enjoy the benefits of the USSFTA.

RULES OF ORIGIN (ROO)

Rules of origin determine where a good is "made in". Just as there are laws to determine a person's nationality, these ROO determine the country of origin of a product. This is a difficult and complex area. I will only attempt to explain generally the features of the ROO regime of the USSFTA.

Only a product that is deemed "Singaporean" or "originating" will benefit from the tariff concessions. Products manufactured in Singapore are not automatically considered originating. Whether a good is "made in Singapore" depends on the degree of transformation which the inputs undergo within Singapore.

The USSFTA adopts a product-specific approach — which means that there is a separate and distinct ROO for each product. The ROO could be a single rule, they could be alternative rules, or they could be a combination of criteria. To see what ROO a product of interest has to meet, refer to Annex 3A of Chapter 3 in the USSFTA. In general, there are three types of ROO: change in tariff classification (CTC), local content (which is technically referred to as Regional Value Content (RVC) in the USSFTA), and process rules.

Change in Tariff Classification (CTC)

The rule is fulfilled if the imported inputs used in the manufacture of the final good within Singapore are classified under a different tariff classification from the final good. See Fig. 2 as an example.

Value Add Rule (Local Content)

The rule is fulfilled if the Singapore content of the final good is above the specified threshold. See Fig. 3 as an example.

ROO Criteria for Beer (HS 2203) is "CHANGE TO HS2203 FROM ANY OTHER CHAPTER"

Water (HS 11) + Imported Malt (HS 25) + Other imported Inputs (HS32) → Beer (HS 2203)

→ Beer is considered as a Singapore originating good as the imported input (Malt) undergoes a Change in Tariff Classification. Hence, beer will enjoy preferential tariffs under the USSFTA

(Note: 11, 25, 32, 2203 represent tariff classification under the Harmonised System Nomenclature)

Fig. 2. Example of CTC.

ROO Criteria for Sparkling Beverages is "A REGIONAL VALUE CONTENT OF 40%"

Sugar ($1) + Beer ($2) + Imported Juice (S$3) + Labour (S$3) + Profit (S$1) → Sparkling Beverage (S$10)

→ As the local content of the Sparkling Beverage is 70%, it is above the requisite threshold of 40%. Hence, sparkling beverage will enjoy preferential tariffs under the USSFTA.

Fig. 3. Example of value add rule.

ROO Criteria for Polyethylene is a Chemical Reaction Rule

Chemical Reaction involves a biochemical process, which results in a molecule with a new structure. Mere dilution with water and another substance, which do not change the characteristics of the input, will not be considered to be a chemical reaction

- Ethylene → Polyethylene

The process of deriving polyethylene from ethylene is considered a chemical reaction.

Fig. 4. Example of process rule.

Process Rule

This rule is fulfilled if the specified process occurs in Singapore. In the USSFTA, this rule is confined to chemical products. See Fig. 4 as an example.

Besides the three fundamental types of ROO I have mentioned, the USSFTA actually incorporates some further innovations of traditional ROO concepts. These innovations were created so that Singapore's unique manufacturing situation can be taken into account. I refer to "Outward Processing" and the Integrated Sourcing Initiative.

OUTWARD PROCESSING

I am using the term "Outward Processing" (OP) loosely. It describes the manufacturing situation in which there is shuttling of parts and components of products between Singapore and the region.

Singapore is a small country. Therefore, in many of our products, some parts of the manufacturing process are done in the region. To illustrate, an electric iron is assembled in Batam from parts and components made in Singapore. The iron is tested in Singapore before its export to the United States. Usually, ROO only count the last stage of the process, i.e., the value of testing as the Singapore content of the iron. But ROO that recognise OP will count all Singapore value of the parts and components as well. The Singapore content of the product is thus enhanced. If the applicable rule is a local content rule, the recognition of OP helps to accumulate all Singaporean content in the manufacturing process. OP allows the accumulation of all the Singaporean value even though there is a break in the production chain. Ultimately, the good must return to Singapore prior its export to the United States.

For our businesses, this means that they can make use of the comparative advantages of the region, by retaining the higher-value activities in Singapore while out-sourcing labour-intensive processes to regional manufacturing base in, for example, Batam or Bintan.

INTEGRATED SOURCING INITIATIVE (ISI)

This novel concept in the ROO chapter became one of the most controversial provisions of the Goods negotiation. The core principle of the ISI is this: that certain goods, although not made in Singapore, will be deemed as originating from Singapore, and hence enjoy the preferential benefits accorded to a Singapore good. Under the ISI, a product listed in Annex 3B of the USSFTA (otherwise known as the ISI Annex) that is imported into U.S. from Singapore will be deemed as originating in Singapore.

The ISI is hence both a novel and a unique concept for an FTA because finished products that are not made in Singapore but exported through Singapore, can also enjoy the savings from the waiver of the Merchandise Processing Fee. The ISI only covers 266 products which are mainly products negotiated under the First World Trade Organization (WTO) Information Technology Agreement, and some medical/precision equipment. These products already enter Singapore and the U.S. duty-free. It is necessary to note that the list of ISI products is not closed. There is a provision in the USSFTA which allows the product coverage of the ISI to be expanded.

For companies that use the ISI scheme, they will be able to enjoy the following benefits. First, there will be a waiver of the Merchandise Processing Fee for ISI products shipped from Singapore to the U.S., even if these products are not manufactured in Singapore. Second, there will be savings in time-to-market costs because paperwork is reduced as it becomes unnecessary to prove origin of an ISI product.

CALCULATION OF THE LOCAL CONTENT

FTAs traditionally only permitted one formula to be used to calculate the local content rule. Under the USSFTA, two formulae — the build up or build down methods — can be used. This provides our manufacturers and exporters with flexibility in the manner in which they conduct their operations and their accounting systems.

NON-TARIFF MEASURES

The Trade in Goods chapter also deals with Non-Tariff Measures (NTM). NTMs cover any measure, other than tariff, that impacts trade. Things like customs clearance forms and administrative requirements on import/export are NTMs. The U.S. importer declaration will be the only document necessary at point of entry, to prove origin. This means faster customs clearance. This permits greater flexibility for traders to make commercial arrangements regarding the necessary documentary trail.

NEGOTIATING PROCESS: A PERSONAL REFLECTION

The Trade in Goods team[3] was responsible for three chapters: Trade in Goods, Rules of Origin and Safeguards. The U.S. had different leaders for each of these chapters: Elena Bryan (Goods), Matt Rohde (ROO) and Will Martyn (Safeguards). All of them are from the Office of the United States Trade Representative (USTR). Depending on the chapters, the U.S. team also included officials from U.S. Customs, Labour, State Department, Finance and Commerce. I led the Singapore team comprising officials from International Enterprise (IE) Singapore (Trade Policy and Trade Facilitation Divisions) and the Attorney-General's Chambers. The

---

[3] Refer to Appendix XI.

divisions that were formerly from IE Singapore have since been transferred to the Ministry of Trade and Industry and Singapore Customs respectively. Compared to the Americans, we had a relatively young team.

It was also providence that my counterpart for ROO, Matt Rohde, turned out to be a friend from my previous posting in Geneva. Having worked together before, we knew each other well. This mutual trust between us helped us navigate through the complexity of drafting and updating preferential ROO that we could accept. We also had excellent rapport with Elena and Will. Right from the start, we recognised that we had a massive task ahead of us. We had to agree on the main chapters and the annexes containing the tariff commitments of the two countries and the rules of origin. The discussion on the safeguard chapter took place only towards the end of the USSFTA negotiations.

Compared to some of the other negotiating groups, the negotiations on the Goods chapter went on smoothly from day one. There were of course difficult issues but these were overcome with doses of humour and goodwill. We made progress with each formal round or intersessional meeting. By the final round in Singapore, in November 2002, few outstanding issues were left on the table except chewing gum, Vessels Repair Duty, the goods coverage and ROO. The Americans could not ask us to lower our tariffs because our tariffs were virtually zero. However, they did press us on difficult areas such as chewing gum and harmonisation of excise duties on liquor, amongst others. The Goods package was negotiated through a protracted process of request and offer and counter request. The package was reviewed many times to ensure that we had the best possible package. The lobby of U.S. companies was another force we had to contend with. They were often effective in blocking requests made by Singapore. Singapore's companies, in comparison, were not as organised.

Over the two years of negotiations, we had 11 formal rounds and as many as eight intersessional meetings, mainly in Washington.

We met our counterparts practically every month in the final stages of the negotiations, whether during formal sessions or the inter-sessionals. The discussions were held in small groups. Each morning, during the formal round of negotiations, we reported to the Chief Negotiator and updated the entire delegation. It was important that each negotiating group was kept informed of the progress in the other negotiating groups for co-ordination and to ensure that there were sufficient chips left on the negotiating table for trade-offs. Where Singapore was concerned, the Goods and ROO chapters were key demands. The intensity of the negotiations and the consultation process contributed to the close camaraderie among the various Singapore ministries and agencies.

We had many intersessionals in Washington in-between the formal rounds of negotiations in London or Singapore, especially towards the closing stages of the negotiations. We needed face-to-face meetings particularly for the Goods chapter as the work involved going through thousands of tariff lines and the corresponding rules of origin. Many pairs of eyes were needed to ensure that there were no errors. The ROO and Goods Annexes ran into hundreds of pages. The length was necessary because the annexes form the substantive commitments of the parties.

The tariff concession package was settled in November 2002 at the end of the final formal round of negotiations. The ROO chapter was, in fact, finalised about a month later in December 2002 as my U.S. counterpart was unable to travel to Singapore in November 2002. My team flew up to Washington in early December and tied up various loose ends. With the negotiations completed, the Goods team was involved in the legal scrubbing process and the passage of the USSFTA in the U.S. Congress over the next four months. That was when the ISI provision in the ROO chapter attracted much attention and the concept had to be tweaked to ensure a smooth passage through the U.S. Congress.

We found that we were able to make progress as we had by then established excellent rapport and took a problem-solving approach to our work. We never had angry words or confrontation. It seems quite unreal on hindsight. We pushed hard at the negotiating table. But outside the negotiations, "makan diplomacy"[4] took centre stage. Over roast duck in London, fish head curry in Singapore and sandwiches in Washington, our friendship blossomed. At the end of the negotiations, we became good friends. Another Singaporean trait also helped — our love for shopping! We ensured that our U.S. friends brought back to the States good bargains from Singapore.

The negotiations took two years. During that time, our families grew, with the addition of four children born in the course of the negotiations. We could not have done our job without our families' support.

The goods negotiation did not take place in a vacuum. It was difficult initially to get information or feedback from Singapore companies. Often, the attitude was one of the "Government knows best". Things have changed with the signing of the USSFTA and the media profile it has attracted. Singapore's companies are increasingly savvy about the usefulness of the FTAs and how they can leverage on them.[5]

---

[4] Makan is Malay for "eat".

[5] The Ministry of Trade and Industry has put in place a comprehensive outreach programme. We have also launched a website — **www.fta.gov.sg** — which we hope, will evolve into the platform for companies to provide us with feedback.

7 Customs Administration

LIM Teck Leong[1]

INTRODUCTION

Customs is one of the oldest professions in history and has its beginnings as the role of a revenue collector. As trade became more complex and countries enacted more and increasingly complex trade rules, customs took on the role of import and export controls. In the wake of security concerns, the role of customs expanded to controlling the movement of strategic goods and weapons of mass destruction (WMD) from entering the borders.

The notion of "free trade" appears to imply the undisrupted flow of trade and therefore a less important role for customs. On the contrary, customs is expected to ensure legitimate and compliant trade under the Free Trade Agreement (FTA). The challenge for the customs authorities is to balance effective controls with facilitation of trade to ensure that goods could move freely between the parties without unnecessary delays.

---

[1] Lim Teck Leong is Head of Intelligence in the Singapore Customs. He was a member of the USSFTA negotiating team for the Customs chapter. He was then working in the Customs Research & International branch, dealing with various FTAs and customs international matters. Apart from the USSFTA, he was also involved in the ANZSCEP (Agreement between New Zealand and Singapore on a Closer Economic Partnership) and the JSEPA (Agreement between Japan and Singapore for a new-age Economic Partnership). The views expressed in this article are those of the author and do not necessarily represent the views of the Singapore Government.

The Singapore team for the negotiations on the Customs chapter of the United States-Singapore Free Trade Agreement (USSFTA) was from the Singapore Customs Department.[2] Singapore's goal for the chapter was clear. We wanted to facilitate the movement of goods traded between the countries and, at the same time, ensure that there is no circumvention of the rules of trade. Being a member of World Trade Organization (WTO), we also sought to reaffirm the customs-related obligations of the WTO agreements.

DIFFERENT SYSTEMS ...

Both the U.S. and Singapore are major trading nations. The trade value of the U.S. is about USD1900 billion (about one-fifth of GDP[3]) while that for Singapore is about USD240 billion (almost three times of GDP). For Singapore, trade is our life-blood.

The U.S. is a vast continental state. The U.S. customs looks over more than 300 ports of entry scattered across the country. Singapore, on the other hand, is an island trading hub. We have few major ports of call for cargo, but the traffic volume at these ports is tremendous. As a case in point, our sea port is the second busiest in the world, handling 17 million TEUs[4] a year. Over the years, Singapore evolved a regulatory framework that emphasised electronic submission and speedy clearance.

Given our geographical differences, the two customs authorities adopt different approaches to manage the flow of goods. They therefore have different customs procedures and practices. There are just as many procedures unique to the U.S. as there are procedures unique to Singapore.

---

[2] Refer to Appendix XII.

[3] Gross Domestic Product.

[4] A twenty-foot equivalent unit (TEU), or 20-foot dry-cargo container.

... BUT SIMILAR PHILOSOPHY

Despite the differences in operating environments and customs practices, both Customs authorities share the same regulatory philosophy. Both are pro-trade. We believe that rules should be simple and just enough to protect national revenue and society. There should not be excessive rules that will inhibit trade. Rules and processes should be transparent. Traders should be consulted on the rules. There should be channels for appeal.

The fact that the U.S. and Singapore Customs have a common philosophy did much to bridge the difference in actual customs procedures. It was also helped by the fact that the two sides had well-meaning negotiators.

The U.S. negotiators were seasoned negotiators with vast experience in the negotiations of the North American Free Trade Agreement (NAFTA) and Free Trade Area of the Americas (FTAA). They were well prepared in every meeting and presented cogent arguments with relevant facts. At the same time, the U.S. negotiators responded to logic and common sense. If we could find some logical explanation on why a particular proposal was not relevant to or suitable in our context, they would accept the explanation and drop the demand. On the other hand, if the U.S. proposals made sense, we were ready to adopt them.

A solid foundation based on common regulatory philosophy and supported by well-meaning negotiators made possible the successful conclusion of a Customs chapter worthy of a world class FTA.

CONVERGENCE ON COMMON ISSUES

Half the battle was won at the onset of the negotiations because there was agreement on many issues. Specifically, there was agreement on the Articles on Transparency and Application of Risk Management.

TRANSPARENCY

The principle of transparency is embodied in Article X of the General Agreement on Tariffs and Trade (GATT) and is an important trade facilitation measure. Traders need timely and pertinent information to aid them in their business. Knowing the customs procedures allows traders from both countries to benefit from the business opportunities offered by the FTA.

Singapore and the U.S. already ensure the transparency of their customs procedures, either through the use of the Internet or other media. The USSFTA obligation is thus a re-affirmation by both parties that they would continue to explore and adopt new ways of enhancing transparency of customs information to traders.

RISK MANAGEMENT

Risk management, from the customs' perspective, is a systematic framework to assess the risk on goods imported, allowing the customs authorities to focus their limited resources on target high-risk goods or high-risk traders. For the trade, it means that the majority of honest, legitimate traders are given an easier time. This saves cost for the traders. Essentially, risk management allows customs authorities to facilitate trade without compromising its revenue protection mission.

Singapore customs had fully implemented a risk management regime by 1997. Singapore customs uses a computerised Pre-Clearance System to first pre-clear cargo consignments, using permit information submitted to customs prior to the physical arrival of the consignments. Based on risk profiling, customs selects cargo for physical inspection at the checkpoints and relies on risk profiling techniques and a good intelligence system to effectively target high-risk cargo consignments for checks.

Singapore customs also has in place a post-importation clearance audit system to eliminate the need for detailed scrutiny of clearance documents at the checkpoints. This system allows cargo consignments to be cleared speedily at the checkpoints. Post-importation audit officers rely on risk assessment and intelligence to target and select firms for back-end checks to minimise inconvenience to the trade.

The U.S. customs practises risk management as well, though the actual procedures are different. Therefore, in the FTA Customs chapter, both parties pledged to adopt risk management in their daily work to target high-risk goods while allowing the majority of legitimate cargoes to be cleared expeditiously through the checkpoints.

KEY ISSUES

Notwithstanding the agreement on most issues, there were several areas that required intense clarification, in order for the U.S. and Singapore customs to understand how they performed their work. Three issues are highlighted in this chapter.

DEFERRED PAYMENT

The Customs chapter included an article on "Release and Security" which relates to the deferred payment system practised by the United States. The objective of the article is to ensure the expedited clearance of goods without the need for assessment and payment of duty at the checkpoints. Such a system is relevant in the U.S. context because of the complexity and difficulty of revenue accounting on a per-shipment basis at the entry points.

In Singapore, the TradeNet System provides the means for the trading community to submit permit applications electronically to government bodies (Singapore customs and the various controlling authorities) for processing. The assessment of duties and taxes is automatically done and payment is deducted electronically from the traders' bank accounts. It takes less than ten minutes in 99 percent of the time to have the permits approved along with the assessment and deduction of duties and taxes. Today, more than half a million applications are processed through TradeNet every month.

In essence, there are no substantial differences between the U.S. and Singapore systems with regard to the objective of the FTA article. It was just a matter of seeking consensus on the text to cater to the two systems.

ADVANCE RULINGS

Advance Rulings is another trade facilitating measure that offers the importer the assurance that goods are eligible for preferential duty. Traders can use this ruling to place orders for goods and enjoy the preferential rate.

In Singapore's context, there are only a few products subject to customs duties. Furthermore, the assessment of value for the purpose of Goods and Services Tax (GST) is also done electronically via TradeNet and traders already enjoy the certainty and efficiency provided under the current system.

While Singapore importers have less need for advance rulings, Singapore customs recognised the importance of advance rulings in international trade and we have agreed on a robust set of advance ruling provisions covering all aspects of customs matters, including valuation, origin, tariff classification and eligibility for preferential tariff.

TRADE ENFORCEMENT

Trade enforcement is a multi-faceted issue. But, at its heart, is a simple question: Since the U.S. and Singapore are going to facilitate goods from each other, how do we build a secure link given that both countries also handle goods from other countries?

Singapore is a transhipment hub. Our ports host 400 shipping lines and are linked up with 600 ports around the world. On average, the containers on a third generation vessel will be unloaded in Singapore to be transported to 40 other ports. Containers from another 50 ports will be loaded onto the same vessel before it sails to its next destination. The port therefore provides 90 connection services per vessel. This is a unique characteristic of the Singapore ports.

The U.S. customs was therefore concerned about illegal mixing of goods. From a trade perspective, this would mean that errant traders can try to free-ride on the trade concessions offered under the FTA.

This concern was addressed after the Singapore team conducted detailed briefings on our port and trade systems and hosted the U.S. team to tour the ports and observe their operations. Illegal mixing of goods cannot be carried out in our ports, which are highly secured facilities. Our ports are fenced and covered by guards and cameras. All containers are individually identified; their locations are known at all times and tracked electronically. Basically, our ports can handle such high traffic volumes and so many connections because we have developed sophisticated systems and procedures supported by the latest information technology (IT). The operational mastery of our port operators ensure that cargoes handled in Singapore are at all times tracked and tamper-proof.

Trade enforcement was also strengthened with a Customs Cooperation Article. This allowed both customs authorities to work together against smugglers and errant traders. Such cooperation is important for risk management — by working together against a small number of errant traders, we allow legitimate trade to flow smoothly. In this way, the Customs Cooperation Article is an important pillar for trade facilitation and enforcement. One aspect of customs cooperation is the sharing of trade information to safeguard legitimate trade, while recognising and respecting the commercial confidentiality of trade documents.

CONCLUSION

The trade benefits arising from the Customs chapter has to be seen in a larger context as an overall package within the USSFTA. Nevertheless, Singapore exporters should benefit from the fact that goods professed to be of Singapore origin would be trusted and granted easier access to the U.S. market. Our importers would be able to import goods more easily from our FTA partner and be granted preferential tariff rate for selected goods.

All in all, the negotiations for the USSFTA Customs chapter had been a fulfilling experience for the customs team. The experience gained in the negotiations would be useful in our negotiations of other FTAs.

8 Textiles and Apparel

NG Kim Neo[1]

INTRODUCTION

The chapter on textiles and apparel is an interesting chapter in the USSFTA. This is because not only did we have to negotiate bilaterally, we also had to take into consideration the existing multilateral agreements. Take the issue of textile and clothing import quota for instance. Both U.S. and Singapore are parties to the World Trade Organization Agreement on Textiles and Clothing (WTO-ATC).[2] Under the ATC, an importing country is allowed to specify how much it will accept from each country individually.[3] This specified amount is known as the import quota. Under the framework of the ATC, U.S. has a bilateral arrangement with Singapore that imposes an import quota on exports from Singapore. This means that Singapore can only export a pre-agreed quantity of

---

[1] Ng Kim Neo is the lead negotiator for the chapters on Textiles and Apparel as well as Technical Barriers to Trade. She is a Consultant in Trade Division A in the Ministry of Trade and Industry (MTI). She joined MTI in April 2001 following her retirement as Senior Director in charge of Trade Policy in the Trade Development Board, now known as IE Singapore. She has a BA (Hons) degree in Economics from the University of Singapore and an MA (Economics) from the University of Pittsburgh, USA, done under a Ford Foundation Fellowship. The views expressed in this article are those of the author and do not necessarily represent the views of the Singapore Government.

[2] Previously known as the GATT (General Agreement on Tariffs and Trade) Arrangement Regarding International Trade in Textiles (commonly referred to as the Multi-Fibre Arrangement or MFA).

[3] This is an exception to the GATT principle of treating all trading partners equally.

textiles and apparel products (e.g., 30,000 dozens of shirts made from cotton fibre, cut and sewn in Singapore) to the U.S.

During our negotiations, we became aware that some ATC quotas would have already been phased out but others would still be in place until December 2004. Knowing that the USSFTA would come into force before December 2004, one important item in the negotiation was to ensure that there was adequate enforcement to prevent the ATC quotas from being circumvented under the USSFTA. For these reasons, although textiles and apparel are goods and could have been included under the Goods chapter, they were negotiated separately.

NEGOTIATING TEAMS

Unlike other teams, our U.S. counterparts did not have a Chief Textile Negotiator at the onset. For the first half of the two-year negotiations, I was negotiating with the Deputy Chief Textile Negotiator, Caroyl Miller. Halfway through, the United States Trade Representative (USTR) appointed David Spooner as their Chief Textile Negotiator. The U.S. team comprised representatives from the Office of Textiles and Apparel, Department of Commerce; Textiles Enforcement and Operations Division of the U.S. Customs and Border Protection which is now under the Department of Homeland Security; State Department; and the Department of Labour. My team included officers from the Trade Facilitation Division and Lifestyle Division of International Enterprise (IE) Singapore and Singapore Customs.[4]

TEXTILES AND APPAREL COVERAGE

Our negotiations were divided into three parts which are: market access; enforcement and cooperation; and safeguard actions. The

---

[4] Refer to Appendix XIII.

results of the negotiations have been incorporated into the relevant chapters of the USSFTA.

For market access, the results were included in Chapter 2: National Treatment and Market Access for Goods and Chapter 3: Rules of Origin, as textiles and apparel trade is also accorded the same privileges as well as being subject to the general rules that are applicable to trade in goods, e.g., exemption from merchandise processing fees.

Enforcement and cooperation results have been incorporated mainly in Chapter 5: Textiles and Apparel, Articles 5.1–5.8, 5.10–5.11. Safeguard actions have also been incorporated in the same chapter on Textiles and Apparel, Article 5.9. A specific provision for textiles and apparel has been negotiated under safeguard actions. The requirements are largely similar to the provision that is applicable to the rest of the goods sector. Like the goods sector, the provision provides for the importing country to impose controls, subject to specific conditions on imports of textiles and apparel if the importing country's domestic industry is seriously injured or under threat of serious injury linked directly to the tariff preferences given to the import of textiles and apparel.

THE TEXTILES AND APPAREL COMMITMENTS AND OBLIGATIONS

Made in Singapore

The Market Access package requires that the textiles and apparel be fully processed and assembled in Singapore in order to enjoy the tariff preference including the exceptions to the originating rules outlined below. Tariff preference will come into effect when the Textiles and Apparel chapter comes into force.

To qualify for immediate duty-free entry into the U.S., the textiles and apparel from Singapore must be made from yarn sourced from Singapore or the U.S., technically referred to as the "yarn forward" rule of origin and considered as "originating goods".

An exception provides for "non-originating goods" for which the materials and inputs can be sourced from outside Singapore and the U.S. This exception to the originating rule covers all cotton and man-made fibre apparel under Harmonised Commodity Description and Coding System (HS), Chapters 61 and 62. The tariff phase-out to zero is over five years in equal annual reduction. This exception or "Tariff Preference Level" (TPL) is applicable for exports from Singapore up to an initial quantity of 25 million square meter equivalent (SME), roughly equivalent to 50 million shirts. The TPL will be reduced to zero over eight years in equal annual increments. A table setting out the conversion to SME for each type of apparel is incorporated. See Appendix X.

We were fortunate in that the subsequent investigation by the U.S. Trade Advisory Committee — the Committee on Textiles and Apparel — did not object to the elimination of duties and quotas on imports in this sector from Singapore. It recognised that some of the quotas were due to be eliminated under the WTO-ATC and they did not foresee Singapore becoming a major trading partner in the textile and apparel sector.[5]

A second exception to the origin rule is the "short supply" provision. This provision allows for the tariff-free entry of textiles and apparel made from yarn and fabric from outside Singapore and the U.S. in the event that Singapore and U.S. yarn and fabric become unavailable, in commercial quantities and in a timely manner. The U.S. will determine the existence of a "short supply" situation based on request from any of the U.S. FTA partners for any specific yarn, textile or fabric. There is already an approved list of "short supply" yarn for U.S. FTA partner countries.[6] For Singapore, our approved

---

[5] For a discussion on the role of the trade advisory committees, please see the USSFTA Chronology in Appendix XVI.

[6] The list of U.S. FTAs are NAFTA (North American Free Trade Agreement), AGO (African Growth and Opportunities Act), CBTPA (Caribbean Basin Trade Partnership Act) and ATPA (Andean Trade Preference and Drug Eradication Act).

list of "short supply" yarn or fabric contains approvals given by 15 November 2002, the date when our negotiation concluded. For any approvals after 15 November 2002, Singapore will need to make separate requests. Even for "short supply" yarn that has been approved for another U.S. FTA partner, Singapore will also need to request for it.

A third exception is the "percentage de-minimis rule". This rule allows for up to seven percent by weight of that component for the textiles and apparel product to be sourced from outside Singapore and the U.S., except for elastomeric yarn.[7] For elastomeric yarn, it has to be sourced from Singapore and the U.S. even if the weight is less than seven percent.

Enhanced Customs Control

While the WTO-ATC will still be in force until the end of 2004, circumvention of bilateral export quota is one of the major problems encountered in international trade in textiles and apparel. Circumvention broadly means false declaration or provision of information to violate or evade quota, country of origin labelling, trade laws, tariff or other preferences, concessions or other controls given or imposed by the importing country on the exporter. Some examples of circumvention are illegal transhipment, re-routing, fraud, false declaration concerning country of origin, fibre content, quantities, description or classification, falsification of documents and smuggling.

Even with post-WTO-ATC, there are some countries which are still subjected to quota for a few more years. Circumvention is therefore a continuing problem encountered in international trade in textiles and apparel.

---

[7] A rubber-like synthetic polymer that will stretch when pulled and will return quickly to its original shape when released.

With the USSFTA and the tariff and other preferences which are extended to textiles and apparel exports from Singapore to the U.S., circumvention issues are a great concern for the U.S. Singapore shares the view that circumvention should not be condoned. As a U.S. FTA partner, it is also incumbent on Singapore to put in place the needed systems and safeguards to ensure that Singapore meets its commitments and obligations as an FTA partner to ensure that only legitimate trade in textiles and apparel enjoyed the preferences. However, Singapore, as one of the world's major transhipment ports, also has its commitments to ensure that trade transhipping through Singapore is not disrupted. At the same time, Singapore, in meeting its obligations as a U.S. FTA partner does not have the power to interfere in third country trade. The enforcement and cooperation provisions on the textiles and apparel exports to the U.S. are therefore negotiated against the background of these considerations.

The enforcement and cooperation to prevent the circumvention of textiles and apparel benefits involve the Singapore government as well as the exporters or the trading community. On the part of the Singapore government, the Singapore Customs, as the implementing agency, is required to do three things.

First, it has to establish and maintain a programme to register all enterprises engaged in the production and export of Singapore textiles and apparel to the U.S. These enterprises cover all textiles and apparel manufacturers, sub-contractors, traders and exporters and freight forwarders. This means that it will be mandatory for textile and apparel companies to be registered with IE Singapore.

Second, it has to establish a system to monitor, inspect and verify import, export and production of Singapore textiles and apparel destined for the U.S. market. This includes any process or manipulation in Singapore's free trade zone.

Third, Singapore needs to have the necessary laws and regulations to allow for the sharing of information and cooperating with the U.S. in investigating circumvention and on-site visits to enterprises engaged in textiles and apparel manufacturing and trade with the U.S. To that end, the Singapore Government has amended the Regulation of Imports and Exports Act. This includes moves to criminalise country of origin falsification, such as affixing Singapore-made labels on non-Singapore origin textiles and apparel goods.

The exporters or trading establishments manufacturing or exporting textiles and apparel to the U.S. are also required to maintain records and documents for five years from the time when the records are created. This is a change from the current policy of keeping the records for two years. These records and documents include those relating to material supplies, production information, sub-contractors' records and any outward processing arrangement records. Other documents include bills of lading, transaction records, cutting and assembling records including workers' time cards, payment slips, export records, sub-contractors' work records, etc. Penalties for violations can range from being black-listed to public announcement of companies' names, revocation of benefits or export suspension of varying periods.

Safeguard Actions

The article on safeguard actions was separately negotiated, but eventually incorporated into the main text. This article allows the importing country to suspend or reverse the tariff reduction (in cases of phased tariff elimination) or tariff elimination obligations by the importing country. The tariff rate following the suspension/reversal cannot be above the Most-Favoured-Nation (MFN) applied rate that is applicable to all non-FTA members.

The suspension/reversal is normally operational for two years, with extension by another two years if the importing country determines that the action continues to be necessary. This action can only be taken once on a particular textiles and apparel product.

When a safeguard action is taken, the exporting country is allowed to seek compensation from the importing party. This compensation has to be equivalent to the loss of the concession which is given by the importing country elsewhere in the USSFTA. If no agreement is reached between the two countries on the compensation package, the exporting country can take retaliatory action which again must be equivalent to the concession lost arising from the safeguard action by the importing country. Retaliatory action is however not permitted in the first two years that the safeguard action is in effect.

Safeguard action is also temporary in the sense that it is applicable in the first ten years after entry into force of the USSFTA. After the ten years, this provision cannot be invoked.

NEGOTIATING PROCESS

Market Access Package

The textiles and apparel sector is extremely sensitive. In the U.S., the industry is concentrated in a few states which are politically influential. As such, the U.S. negotiators had to settle on a market access package which they could sell to the U.S. Congress.

The market access package tabled by the U.S. at the second round was merely a listing of the 1,539 tariff lines for which Singapore is a source country. The tariff offers were minimal with almost all tariff phase-outs being over ten years and covering all the tariff lines of export interest to Singapore. There was no serious discussion on the market access package until the tenth round with the U.S. maintaining the position that the rules of origin should be the "yarn forward" rule. Throughout the negotiations, the Singapore negotiators continued to maintain that the "yarn forward" rule was not acceptable and unrealistic as U.S. yarn is not competitive in terms of price and quality with yarn and fabric sourced from the region. Studies were commissioned and presented and the case argued at each session.

It was not until 12 November 2002, the second last day of the last formal negotiating round, that there was serious engagement by the U.S. team to talk about market access. Four-eyed meetings between the two chief negotiators where frank exchanges were made finally resulted in an offer of "immediate tariff elimination" with the "yarn forward" rule for all tariff lines coupled with "tariff preference level" offer to be negotiated as an exception but with tariff staging phased out. When the offer was made formally, it was already the end of the day and the meeting had adjourned for the day.

We had to quickly consult the Singapore textiles and apparel manufacturers about the offer. That same evening, the Singapore side brought in representatives of the Textile and Fashion Federation (TAFF) (Singapore) and discussed the new offer with them. The TAFF response was positive. The TPL would provide the industry with a window for the industry to adjust to the yarn forward rule. As textiles and apparel of export interest to the industry were facing tariffs from about 10 percent to a high of 33 percent, TAFF reckoned that the zero tariff would absorb part of the increased cost of sourcing the yarn from the U.S. compared to the current tariffs ranging from 10–33 percent.

Given that the WTO-ATC will lapse in January 2005, the zero tariff will provide the Singapore textiles and apparel industry with a competitive edge vis-à-vis other suppliers. The tariff preferences will therefore help the industry to continue to be an employment-generating sector in Singapore. The industry will probably need some restructuring but remain viable after the end of the WTO-ATC. Total tariff savings can be as high as S$140 million based on the current level of trade. The price advantage can range from 5–15 percent depending on the current MFN tariffs.

The TPL, which covered primarily apparel products, should give the Singapore textile and apparel industry a period of eight years with tariff preferences to adjust and restructure to the new material sourcing requirements. The overall net outcome will be that the Singapore textile and apparel industry, which has an export value of over S$500 million a year will be given a new lease of life. The current 10,000 jobs in the industry can be retained with prospects of new jobs being created.

From the U.S. perspective, the deal that has been struck means that the U.S. yarn and fabric industry has a potential market in Singapore. U.S. consumers will also gain in terms of lower prices of the end products as the tariffs will be brought down if sourced from Singapore.

The following day, when the formal negotiation session re-convened we gave our response. Through a process of bargaining, we negotiated and agreed on the quantum and tariff staging for the TPL and its phasing out. The agreed terms were finally written as points of agreement on the last day of the negotiations on 15 November 2002. Several rounds of teleconferences were conducted between the Singapore team, which now had expanded to include the legal experts from the Attorney-General's Chambers (AGC), and the U.S. team and its lawyers, to finalise the legal text. This continued till the end of April 2003. It was among the last legal texts to be completed.

Enforcement and Cooperation

With circumvention issues being a priority with the U.S. nego-tiators, at least nine of the 12 formal sessions were spent discussing the enforcement and cooperation requirements. This did not include the intersessional visits to Singapore's port for briefings on the operations of the port and transhipment activities in the port.

The negotiating process for this chapter was laborious. The Singapore team spent each session reviewing new texts from the U.S. team as the texts would have only been circulated at the meeting. It would often take a day for the Singapore team to study the new texts before the negotiation could begin.

There were three extremely contentious issues relating to the U.S. demand for Singapore to change certain laws to allow for: free information exchange; enforcement in port activities relating to any textiles and apparel transit and transhipment trade; and widening of penalties to successor companies. As a result of the difficulties encountered, this particular chapter has a provision on prior consultations by both sides on the legislative changes which would be made by Singapore to implement the commitments.

Subsequently, the U.S. legal experts found that the text agreed by the negotiating groups was not sufficiently precise. To set it right, several teleconferences were held between the two teams and the legal experts between November 2002 and April 2003, when the legally "scrubbed" text was finally approved.

IMPLEMENTATION

The Singapore negotiating team's work did not end with the agreed legal text. Between April 2003 and 31 December 2003, the team met with the textiles and apparel industry in Singapore to discuss how best to share out the limited TPL and the process of meeting the "yarn forward" rules. The team also worked on the changes to the required legislation to ensure that the commitments were met. In addition, we worked on the documentation requirements to demonstrate what aspects of the market access package the consignment landing in the U.S. were applying for, i.e., the current bilateral quota items, the TPL preference or "yarn forward" preference. We also sought the U.S. Customs' agreement to accept the Singapore proposals on the documentary evidence to seek entry for the consignments.

Several additional teleconferences were conducted with the USTR legal team, U.S. Customs and the Singapore negotiating team on the changes to the Singapore legislation as well as the documentary procedures and documents. Circulars issued to advise the textiles and apparel industry were also sent to the U.S. side for their information. Agreement on all the documentation and procedures were finally reached only on 30 December 2003. The effective date for entry into force would be based on goods landing at U.S. ports from 1 January 2004.

CONCLUSION

Sometimes, benefits from an FTA may not be immediately tangible, but we are already seeing some signs in the textile sector in Singapore. With the USSFTA, it is anticipated that new areas of businesses may develop — businesses such as expansion or development of man-made fibre manufacturing or trading and warehousing activities in U.S. yarn and fabrics. From the job creation side, there are signs that the FTA will contribute to new jobs. In Singapore there are about 156 companies in the textile industries. Since November 2003, Singapore's Workforce Development Agency (WDA) has started a Textile and Fashion Re-skilling for Employment programme. This is a place-and-train scheme where workers are placed with firms and provided with training. The programme has trained 33 apparel specialists to date and another 20 are undergoing training. With the tariff savings from the USSFTA and the lifting of the MFA, it is anticipated that the Singapore textile industry will head towards a revival.[8] This augurs well for Singapore.

---

[8] "Textile firms asked to cooperate on jobs", *Business Times*, 14 January 2004, p. 11.

9 Telecommunications and Electronic Commerce

Valerie D'COSTA[1]

INTRODUCTION

When I was first asked to take on the role of lead negotiator for the Information Communications Technology (ICT) sector in December 2000, there was little time to reflect on what lay ahead. We were told to pack our bags and prepare to spend a month in Washington D.C., during which time an agreement would have to be sealed. That ambitious timeframe did not transpire and as the negotiations stretched over the next two years, my colleagues from the Infocomm Development Authority (IDA) and I found ourselves on a fascinating journey. There were roadblocks, hairpin curves and U-turns along the way, but what a ride it turned out to be.

---

[1] Valerie D'Costa presently serves as Director of the International Division at the Info-Communication Development Authority of Singapore (IDA Singapore). Formed by the merger of the Telecommunication Authority of Singapore and the National Computer Board, IDA Singapore undertakes the development, promotion and regulation of Singapore's Information and Communication Technology (ICT) industry. D'Costa is responsible for the formulation of the Singapore Government's policies on international ICT issues and the representation of Singapore's ICT interests at a number of international organisations and fora. She also oversees Singapore's bilateral relations with other countries in ICT issues. Currently, she oversees ICT negotiations under a number of bilateral Free Trade Agreements (FTAs) which Singapore is negotiating. Prior to joining the government in 1991, D'Costa worked in private legal practice. She holds a LL.B from the National University of Singapore and a LL.M from University College, University of London. The views expressed in this article are those of the author and do not necessarily represent the views of the Singapore Government.

THE ROLE OF IDA

IDA was responsible for negotiating those aspects of the Agreement that related to ICT. This meant that IDA took on the task of negotiating not just the commitments on telecommunications but also those on electronic commerce (e-commerce) and postal services.

In addition, because of the nature of ICT as a service enabler and an important service sector in its own right, IDA also took an interest in the ICT-related aspects of other chapters of the Agreement such as Government Procurement and Intellectual Property Rights (IPR). This made scheduling quite a daunting task, especially since the IDA negotiating team comprised only four individuals.

I cannot sing the praises of my IDA team[2] enough. I was very ably assisted by Muhammad Hanafiah and Gerald Wee, who not only delved into the intricacies of U.S. telecommunications law and policy but helped me formulate strategy upon counter-strategy, often into the wee hours of the night. I was also very lucky to have David Alfred from our Legal Division represent IDA's interests at the IPR negotiations. I am indebted to Hanafiah, Gerald and David for their ideas, energy, humour and tenacity.[3]

OUR AMERICAN COUNTERPARTS

Fortunately, IDA was blessed with very good negotiating counterparts. The U.S. team comprised representatives of the Office of the U.S. Trade Representative (USTR), the Federal Communications Commission (FCC) and the Department of Commerce (DOC). The team was led by Jonathan McHale from the USTR, who was capably supported by his colleagues, Demetrios Marantis (USTR), Jacqueline Ruff (FCC) and Arrow Augerot (DOC).

---

[2] Refer to Appendix XIV.

[3] Two former staff — Mark Fong and Eric Lie — were involved in earlier stages of the USSFTA negotiations, whose important contributions I also want to acknowledge.

Over the months we worked together, the U.S. team not only showed its mettle and a deep understanding of telecommunications and e-commerce trade issues, but also a level of creativity, intellectual honesty and patience that I came to admire. We became friends. Since negotiations concluded, we have all kept in touch with one another. While the negotiations were far from straightforward, the good rapport helped us nip several problems in the bud and tide us through the storms that inevitably brewed over the more thorny issues.

The one thing that contributed immeasurably to the success of the negotiations was the sincere desire on the part of the both teams to craft an agreement that was ambitious yet fair to both Singapore and the United States. Both countries' ICT markets are open but the U.S. has had a much longer experience of liberalisation and competition than Singapore and it has a far larger market in scope and scale. There was give and take on both sides as we worked hard to ensure that the agreement was reflective of both countries' realities.

TRADE RULES AND TODAY'S ICT LANDSCAPE

The term "Information Communication Technology" does not really show up in today's lexicon of international trade. While attempts to update the situation are being made at the World Trade Organization (WTO), the current language in the General Agreement of Tariffs and Trade (GATT) and the General Agreement on Trade in Services (GATS) still reflects a worldview that pre-dates the Internet and the phenomenon of technological convergence. The product classification list used by the GATT does not recognise "ICT" products as a separate category in its own right. Commitments on telecommunications services are made separately from those of audio visual services or computer and related services.

Another area where trade rules are still being developed is how international trade disciplines should treat products and services that are purchased, traded and consumed entirely in electronic form over the Internet.

However, the technological realities of this sector are quite different. Today, an Internet-enabled computer can function like a telephone or fax machine. Software, videos and music can be sold and consumed in purely electronic form over the Internet. It is becoming harder and harder to tell the difference between information technology (IT) and telecommunications products and services.

The symbiosis between telecommunications and IT is also growing. The deployment of high speed fibre optic cables now allows an IT company here to outsource software development to countries thousands of kilometres away and have the product delivered to it electronically just days later. Practical and easy access to telecommunication lines at reasonable rates is crucial to the survival of high tech IT firms and to their ability to market their products.

Yet, commitments made at the WTO still reflect a situation that assumes telecommunications and IT services are distinct sectors. Many countries have made limited commitments at the WTO on voice telephony, telex and facsimile services because these services are often offered by monopoly incumbents. At the same time, most of these countries made quite liberal IT commitments.

THE ICT NEGOTIATIONS: BENEFITS AND CHALLENGES

Benefits

The USSFTA provided Singapore and the U.S. with a chance to develop cutting edge trade disciplines that could reflect more vividly today's ICT landscape. We were aided by the fact that both the U.S. and Singapore have relatively liberal ICT regulatory regimes. The U.S. IT regime is already open and it started liberalising its telecommunications market some twenty years ago. Likewise, Singapore places no restrictions on IT services and it fully liberalised its telecommunications market in 2000.

Therefore, right from the start, both sides wanted to build upon existing WTO disciplines to reflect today's realities more fully. Few reservations were taken with respect to ICT services.

The telecommunications industry is still characterised by high capital barriers to entry. Even with unfettered access to the market, dominant incumbents can affect the ability of foreign operators to offer their services viably. This could be done by refusing to enter into interconnection arrangements with the new operator or by pricing essential services like co-location of equipment or access to poles and conduits owned by the dominant incumbent in a manner that effectively prevents the new operator from offering viable services.

The Singapore team therefore sought to put in place strong disciplines that addressed this dominance factor, so as to provide Singapore telecom companies meaningful access to the U.S. telecom market. Indeed, the USSFTA does contain strong commitments addressing the conduct of dominant telecom companies.

We were also able to develop an inventive and original chapter on e-commerce, the first of its kind in any bilateral trade agreement. This chapter put in place trade commitments covering digital products — contents such as e-books, software and e-music that exist in digitally encoded form. The chapter recognises that the value of these digital products lies in the content itself, not in the medium on which the content is stored or in the mode of its transmission. Singapore and the U.S. not only undertook a permanent moratorium on the application of customs duties to electronic transmissions; they agreed that in future, any customs duty imposed would be applied only to the physical medium, not the content. For example, for software CDs, the U.S. and Singapore will impose a duty based on the value of the plastic CD itself, not the value of the software encoded on the CD. This represents important savings for exporters and importers.

There were other successes. Firstly, the USSFTA will see the removal of all remaining tariffs on ICT equipment between Singapore and the United States. Currently, while most ICT goods already enjoy tariff-free access in both markets, there are a handful of products on which tariffs still apply, for example, certain types of remote control and radio broadcast equipment. These tariffs will be phased out over eight years. Based on figures from the Ministry of Trade and Industry, Singapore expects the removal of these tariffs to benefit the country to the tune of approximately S$25 million per annum based on current trade flows.

Singapore companies will also now enjoy better access to U.S. government tenders for telecom equipment. Before the USSFTA came into effect, there was nothing to stop the U.S. government from discriminating in favour of American companies when reviewing tender proposals for telecommunication equipment. Singapore companies will now be guaranteed non-discriminatory treatment for such contracts. Considering the size of the United States. Government procurement market for telecom equipment (about US$4.8 billion in 2001), the potential benefit to Singapore companies can be quite substantial.

Last but not least, the USSFTA will make it easier for Singapore companies to test and certify telecom equipment for sale in the U.S. market. This will be done via a mutual recognition arrangement which will allow both countries to recognise each other's conformity assessment procedures for telecom equipment. Once the arrangement is finalised, Singapore companies exporting telecom equipment to the U.S. will not need to submit their equipment for duplicative, additional testing or certification in the U.S. once it has been tested in Singapore. This will give real and tangible benefits to Singaporean companies as they would face lower testing costs and enjoy a faster time to market their products.

Challenges

Despite these many successes, it would be misleading to characterise the ICT negotiations as easy or uncomplicated. There were several provisions where a win-win solution took time to find.

While both countries' regimes are open, the laws and regulations governing telecommunications services differ quite markedly, in terms of substance, terminology and philosophical approach. For example, while Singapore does not impose any foreign equity restrictions on ownership of telecommunications companies, the U.S. imposes a 20 percent direct ownership limit on radio-communication licensees. On the other hand, the U.S. does not license or regulate the Internet or Internet Service Providers (ISPs) and views services delivered over the Internet as "information" services rather than telecommunications services. Singapore requires these services to be licensed as telecommunications services. Singapore's licensing regime differentiates licensees on the basis of whether they own or operate telecommunications facilities. The U.S. licensing regime functions on the basis of the type of service being provided over those facilities.

These difficulties led us to many a late night, poring over legal, regulatory and linguistic minutiae. Because both countries had different approaches, negotiators had to come up with creative ways of ensuring the agreement was consistent with their regimes. Because Singapore did not recognise "information services" as being separate and distinct from telecommunications services, a U.S. negotiator, glancing at the negotiating table and spying a piece of fruit, suggested we just call it a "plum" for the time being, until we were able to find a mutually satisfactory term. That word stuck, and long after the agreement was sealed, we still fondly refer to one article of the Telecommunications Chapter as the "plums issue"!

Another aspect of the negotiations which we had to come to grips with was the way the U.S. team negotiated. The U.S. negotiates on the basis of dearly-held principles which it views as important to enshrine — for example, the transparency of the regulatory process and forbearance from regulating services that are being competitively provided in the market. Their insistence on including these provisions reflected the U.S.'s traditional beliefs in the value of openness and market forces, rather than a belief that IDA was un-transparent or over-zealous in its regulation of the Singapore market.

The way American political and business interests affected the negotiations was another issue our team had to come to terms with. ICT industry representatives and congressional staffers coordinated positions with the U.S. negotiating team before and after every round. Companies and industry associations even proposed a specific language for the Agreement for USTR to consider tabling as formal U.S. proposals.

Because of this panoply of interests, the U.S. team did on occasion agree to something, only to find it untenable to some political or industry quarters back home and then have to reverse its position at the next round. This was an eye-opener to the IDA team and at times a point of frustration for us. We quite quickly had to read up on various Congressmen's positions on domestic telecom issues as well as the specific and often quite parochial needs of powerful telecom companies who wanted some language in or out of the agreement.

I marvelled at how effective a well-organised political and business lobby can be in getting a government to respond to its needs. By contrast, the Singapore's ICT industry took far less interest in pushing for their demands during the negotiations.

During the last two months of the negotiations, circumstances conspired to make the U.S. Congress pay close attention to the telecom negotiations. Some Congressmen were at that time trying to effect changes to the U.S. Telecommunications Act of 1996, which they felt were hurting the interests of U.S. telecommunications companies which they represented. These Congressmen did not want to see the very provisions they were seeking to remove from domestic legislation replicated in the USSFTA and evangelized to America's other trade partners. The U.S. negotiating team faced strong scrutiny and pressure from Congress over those last few weeks. Some substantive points of agreement had to be unravelled in the Telecoms Chapter because of this scrutiny. These developments dismayed us after having worked so hard to forge a consensus on those issues. However, it was a good reality check for us on the many, often competing interests that affect and shape U.S. foreign and trade policy.

A BOLD JOURNEY, A HAPPY DESTINATION

The provisions of the USSFTA Telecoms Chapter have not only enriched Singapore's international position as a good place for U.S. firms to do business, they also benefited IDA tremendously in terms of the negotiating experience we gained and the contacts we established with our U.S. counterparts.

The collective grappling over issues, the constant exchange of information and views and the forging of friendships over countless meals gave rise to a great agreement, of which I am very proud. It testifies to the truism that there is never just one way to approach an issue, if only negotiators think beyond existing mindsets, models and disciplines and work to find common ground. In today's ICT environment, with its high emphasis on innovation and derring-do, these lessons are particularly relevant for us all.

10 Financial Services and Capital Controls

Ravi MENON[1]

THE STRATEGIC BACKDROP

When word reached the Monetary Authority of Singapore (MAS) in November 2000 on the launch of the United States-Singapore Free Trade Agreement (USSFTA), we knew that financial services was going to be one of the focal points of the negotiations. Singapore had a more open regime than the U.S. in merchandise trade, while our services sector, including financial services, was not as open. The larger strategic bargain was thus quite obvious: the U.S. would lower its tariffs and other restrictions on merchandise trade in exchange for Singapore's liberalising of access to its services sector. And we knew that the financial services sector in particular was one of the top priorities of the U.S.

MAS had been progressively liberalising the financial services sector since 1998. The insurance and securities industries were fully open to foreign competition. In wholesale and offshore banking, foreign banks could do virtually everything that local banks were allowed to do. The principal remaining restrictions on foreign access were in domestic retail banking. The rationale for this was

[1] Ravi Menon is currently Deputy Secretary at the Ministry of Finance. Prior to this, during the USSFTA negotiations, he was Assistant Managing Director at the Monetary Authority of Singapore, responsible for the supervision of Singapore's systemically important financial groups across their banking, securities, and insurance activities. The views expressed in this article are those of the author and do not represent the views of the Singapore Government.

fundamentally one of safeguarding financial stability. It was important to have strong local banks, whose interests were aligned with those of the Singapore economy because, in a time of crisis, it is these banks that are more likely to support the stability of the system.

At the same time, we believed that the best way to strengthen the local banks was to progressively expose them to greater foreign competition. We therefore took a calibrated and phased approach to liberalisation, to give the local banks time to adjust to and meet the competition. The challenge posed by the USSFTA was how much more and how much faster we could liberalise without jeopardising our financial stability objectives.

The negotiations on financial services lasted the full two years of the USSFTA, with virtually all the critical items of contention resolved only in the final round held in Singapore in November 2002. It was a package deal where both sides had to make some careful calculations and creative compromises. Neither side got all that it wanted but it was a good deal for both sides. Singapore safeguarded its vital interests. The U.S. secured access to our financial services sector that went well beyond our current regime.

SINGAPORE: VITAL INTERESTS SAFEGUARDED

First, we retained the right to prohibit foreign control of local banks. The right of U.S. institutions to acquire local banks was a key demand of the United States. It was not an unreasonable demand. For the U.S., not having this right would have set a bad precedent for its other FTAs. But this was also an issue of practical importance for the United States. It was well-known that at least one of the major U.S. banks operating in Singapore was keen on expanding its domestic franchise through acquisition. But agreeing to the U.S. request would have run counter to our policy of fostering strong local banks to underpin the stability of the financial system in the event of a crisis. Singapore's banking industry already had one of the world's highest foreign penetration rates. Further erosion of the local banks' share in the market would have made the system more vulnerable to the vagaries of international finance and foreign banks' strategic realignments. We made it very clear that it was of vital national importance that the USSFTA recognised Singapore's right to prohibit a foreign takeover of local banks or finance companies. The U.S. agreed to drop its demand provided that Singapore agreed to discuss the issue again with the U.S. no later than January 2007 and every three years thereafter. We agreed.

Second, we retained our right of local incorporation of foreign banks. Singapore was one of few jurisdictions in the world, which allowed foreign banks to operate in their retail banking markets as branches of their head offices instead of locally incorporating as subsidiaries. In contrast, the U.S., Canada, Australia, and many other countries require foreign banks which want to take retail deposits from their citizens to locally incorporate. There are good prudential reasons for this. Local incorporation creates a separate legal entity with its own assets and capital that serve as backing for the foreign bank's domestic deposits. It also makes it easier for the regulator to ringfence the foreign bank subsidiary and minimise contagion arising from problems that may emanate from its home market or global operations. But international financial centres like Singapore, London and Hong Kong have no local incorporation requirements for foreign banks. And while we had no plans to impose such a requirement, we wanted to safeguard in the USSFTA our *right* to require systemically important foreign banks to incorporate in Singapore. As foreign banks became systemically important, it was critical that MAS had the flexibility to require them to locally incorporate if this was judged necessary to accord better protection to Singapore depositors. The U.S. was resistant to enshrining a right in the USSFTA that if exercised would seem to be regressive from the trade liberalisation perspective. Finally, the U.S. agreed to allow Singapore to retain the right of local incorporation provided that it was exercised in a reasonable, objective, and impartial manner, and the bank concerned was given six months' notice.

Third, we safeguarded our right to modify our schedule of restrictions under specified circumstances. Under the USSFTA, commitments in financial services by both the U.S. and Singapore were scheduled using a negative list approach. This means that all restrictive measures would have to be specifically listed in the schedule; no new restrictions could be put in place in future if they were discriminatory. While we agreed with this in principle, we wanted a clause that would allow us to *modify* our schedule of restrictions in future. As MAS further liberalised the banking industry, it was important to have the flexibility to put in place new safeguards (some of which could be discriminatory) to address potential risks that liberalisation might entail. Although such a right was common in WTO and other international trade agreements, the U.S. viewed such flexibility as inconsistent in a bilateral trade agreement that is based on a more ambitious liberalisation agenda. Eventually, the U.S. agreed to allow Singapore the right to modify its schedules provided that such modification was made in the context of an overall banking liberalisation programme, did not derogate from the timeframes for removal of quotas on licenses, and allowed affected banks to opt out of the liberalisation measures if they did not wish to be subject to any new restrictions that came with these measures.

UNITED STATES: ENHANCED ACCESS TO THE SINGAPORE MARKET

First, U.S. Qualifying Full Banks (QFBs) secured the right to negotiate access to the local banks' ATM networks. As a matter of policy, MAS restricted foreign banks from having access to the local banks' ATM networks. Local banks had much larger ATM networks than foreign banks and this was an important source of competitive advantage for them in the domestic retail deposit market. The policy position was consistent with our objective of safeguarding systemic stability through fostering strong local banks. We knew we had to open up the local banks' ATM networks eventually — this was the biggest and last item on the liberalisation agenda — but there was no scheduled timeline for it. We wanted to wait to see how the banking industry adapted to the two rounds of liberalisation we had undertaken since 1998. The U.S. wanted immediate access to the local banks' ATM networks. We made a careful evaluation and proposed a five-year timeframe. The U.S. felt this was far too long. Eventually, we agreed that locally-incorporated U.S. QFBs would be permitted to negotiate access to the ATM network after two-and-a-half years and QFBs operating as branches after four years.

Second, restrictions on the number of customer service locations (branches and offsite ATMs) for U.S. QFBs would be phased out. MAS restricted QFBs to no more than 15 service locations. We agreed this quota would be doubled to 30 service locations for U.S. QFBs upon entry into force of the USSFTA, and removed altogether two years after that.

Third, our existing quotas on the number of QFB licenses and Wholesale Bank (WB) licenses would be phased out for U.S. banks. MAS had a quota of six QFB licenses and twenty new WB licenses. We agreed to lift the quota on QFB licenses one-and-a-half years after entry into force of the USSFTA and the quota on WB licenses three years after entry into force of the agreement.

These commitments to liberalise represented substantive benefits to U.S. financial institutions operating in Singapore.

IMPASSE OVER CAPITAL CONTROLS

On the morning of 19 November 2002, when the respective ministers of the two countries were scheduled to hold a joint press conference to announce the successful conclusion of negotiations for the USSFTA, one important issue remained unresolved — the free transfer of capital. This had been an unresolved issue throughout the two years of negotiations but never attracted much attention. Each side assumed that the other would agree when the rest of the FTA fell into place. But it was not to be. Despite two telephone conversations between Chairman MAS Deputy Prime Minister Lee Hsien Loong and U.S. Treasury Under-Secretary John Taylor in the last couple of days of the negotiations, there was no agreement. The gap in positions was not tactical but fundamental.

The U.S. wanted clauses in the FTA requiring both countries to freely allow payments and transfers of capital into and out of their territories. The "free transfer" clause was a feature of all bilateral trade and investment agreements that the U.S. had concluded to-date. Making an exception for Singapore would set a bad precedent for all of the U.S.'s future agreements. The free flow of capital was a central tenet of U.S. international economic policy and strongly subscribed to by the U.S. Treasury in particular. It was not just an ideological position but reflected the genuine commercial interests of U.S. corporations, financial institutions and individuals who had large stocks of overseas investments. It was only natural that the U.S. would want to protect the ability of its investors to freely move their assets out of the jurisdictions in which they are held.

Singapore shared the U.S.'s strong commitment to the free and unfettered flow of capital An open capital account regime had been and remained a critical factor underpinning Singapore's economic growth. We had consistently eschewed capital controls of any kind — even at the height of the Asian financial crisis. However, in an exchange rate crisis that threatened to severely destabilise the economy, Singapore needed the flexibility to take all appropriate measures, including, as a last resort, restrictions on capital flows when conventional monetary policy tools might be inadequate. We were not opposed to a "free transfer" clause but wanted to include an exception similar to that in multilateral trade agreements, such as the GATS, which provided flexibility to impose restrictions on capital flows in the event of serious balance of payments difficulties.

BREAKING THE DEADLOCK

The two months of negotiations that followed were quite unique. There were no face-to-face meetings. The negotiations were conducted entirely through a series of telephone conversations and video-conference, punctuated by exchanges of letters formalising the evolution of our respective positions. Our embassy in Washington played a key role in building support for our position.

The breakthrough came when both sides agreed to set aside the contentious issue of whether capital controls were a legitimate macroeconomic policy tool and focus on the extent to which Singapore should be subject to claims for damages by affected investors in the event that Singapore imposed capital controls. This meant that there would be a "free transfers" clause without exception (reflecting the U.S. position) but the scope of Singapore's liability in the event we imposed capital controls was significantly reduced (largely meeting Singapore's need for flexibility of action in a crisis).

First, Singapore agreed that we would not impose restrictions on current payments and transfers such as debt servicing, profit repatriation, dividend payments, and proceeds from the sale of foreign direct investments. The critical flow that we sought to restrict in the event of a crisis was "hot money" or short-term capital flows, which were driven by speculation and could be very large. Second, the U.S. agreed that for restrictions that lasted for less than one year and did not *substantially impede transfers*, Singapore would not be liable for any claims for damages by affected investors.

The focus of the issue thus shifted to the definition of the term *substantially impede transfers*. After much discussion, both sides agreed that a measure was presumed not to *substantially impede transfers* if it was non-confiscatory, non discriminatory, price-based, did not interfere with an investor's ability to earn a market rate of return in Singapore, and did not prevent a reasonable investor from taking his money out of Singapore. In substance, it meant that

Singapore would have sufficient flexibility to implement without liability capital restrictions in the form of a tax or levy during a crisis, but not an outright ban.

It was also agreed that even if the measures were to *substantially impede transfers*, the liability that Singapore was exposed to would be limited. In effect, investors could only claim for losses in the value of investments in Singapore dollars as a result of the capital restrictions after taking account of the returns they could earn in Singapore. No liability could be claimed for opportunity costs from foregoing alternative investments outside of Singapore.

On 16 January 2003, the U.S. and Singapore released press statements[2] announcing the conclusion of negotiations on the "free transfers" issue and in effect the USSFTA itself. The way was finally clear for signing the USSFTA.

REFLECTIONS

I look back on the USSFTA negotiations with much satisfaction and fondness. It was a gradual, two-year process that culminated in an intense final week of negotiations on financial services only to be followed by another exhilarating two months resolving the "free transfers" issue. While much of the attention has focused on the final outcome of the negotiations, for many of us the real value lay in the process itself. It was a deeply fulfilling experience — to patiently and painstakingly search for creative solutions to bridge seemingly irreconcilable positions and coming up with an agreement that both sides could be happy about.

Ultimately, successful negotiations are all about how people work together and build trust. In this, I was fortunate in both the Americans I negotiated with and the team I had working with me. Mary Beasley and Marylyn Muench from the U.S. Treasury and

---

[2] Refer to Appendix XV.

Ann Main from the U.S. Trade Representative's Office were the main members on the U.S. side negotiating the financial services chapter of the USSFTA during the two years. The rapport and trust that we shared helped us get around many thorny issues. The key member of the U.S. team, however, was Treasury Assistant Secretary Randy Quarles, who was my principal counterpart during the critical week of negotiations on financial services in November 2002. He was firm yet reasonable. Randy was also my principal counterpart in the negotiations on the difficult "free transfers" issue. Right from the start, we took a problem-solving approach aimed at finding middle ground rather than trying to convert each other on ideological arguments.

I was also fortunate in the group of people who worked with me. MAS did not have a dedicated trade negotiation team nor professional expertise in trade issues. But we were able to put together a very competent team drawing from many departments and sources of expertise. Everyone had the right instincts: to see how best we could secure an agreement while safeguarding our essential interests. Throughout the negotiations, I was most ably assisted by Adrian Chua[3] who played a vital role in carefully analyzing the various clauses, evaluating policy options, and framing our negotiating positions. Two other colleagues who provided much help were Loo Siew Yee,[4] our legal counsel, and Linda Foo. Ong Ye Kung and Daren Tang offered invaluable counsel at various stages of the negotiations. I could not have asked for a better team.

---

[3] Refer to Appendix XVI.

[4] Lead Policy Analyst, Monetary Authority of Singapore. Currently leading a team of analysts formulating prudential policies for Singapore's financial sector, she previously served as Assistant General Counsel to MAS. In that capacity, she provided legal advice to the USSFTA financial services negotiation team, and assisted in drafting the financial services chapter.

11 Competition Policy[1]

MINN Naing Oo[2]

"Nothing mattered except states of mind, chiefly our own."

John Maynard Keynes

The purpose of a Competition Policy Chapter in an FTA is not immediately obvious. Unlike the Trade in Goods or the Trade in Services chapters, the Competition Policy chapter does not remove tariffs, restrictions on foreign service suppliers, or any other type of trade barriers. In fact, it is not concerned with the removal of trade barriers at all. What it does is to provide the assurance that having obtained access to each other's market through the commitments in the other chapters of the FTA, that hard-won access is not somehow impeded or nullified by an unfair business environment or unfair business practices of an incumbent in the local market. The Competition Policy chapter is thus an "enabling" chapter. It provides some of the necessary supporting structure for optimum exploitation of FTA concessions.

---

[1] Refers to the Anticompetitive Business Conduct, Designated Monopolies, and Government Enterprises chapter in the USSFTA.

[2] Deputy Director/Legal Advisor at the Ministry of Trade and Industry (MTI). Minn has practised in M/s Rajah & Tann since 1998, and was seconded to MTI in January 2002. He was a member of the U.S.-Singapore FTA (USSFTA) and Singapore-Australia FTA (SAFTA) negotiating teams. He is currently involved in the Canada-Singapore FTA (CSFTA) negotiations as well as the exploratory talks for a Sri-Lanka Singapore FTA. Minn also works on WTO matters, including Competition, Investment and Dispute Settlement issues. He obtained his LL.B from the National University of Singapore and has an LL.M from Columbia Law School. The views expressed in this article are those of the author and do not necessarily represent the views of the Singapore Government.

Typically therefore, the competition chapter in an FTA would contain several important obligations. These would include the commitment to ensure that anti-competitive business practices are proscribed, monopolies do not abuse their powers, and there are avenues for complaints of unfair practices to be initiated. There would also be commitments for cooperation and consultations between the relevant authorities to facilitate enforcement and share best practices.

The USSFTA competition chapter includes all of the above obligations. It also contains a few additional obligations, which will be elaborated on below.

LEGACIES AND PERCEPTIONS

The United States is, in many ways, the pioneer of competition regulation. Indeed, the term "antitrust" was born in America. It came about when the American public began to lash out fervently at the "trusts" (combinations of firms) that were forming in earnest in late 19th century and abusing their dominant positions at the expense of consumers. As Senator Sherman[3] put it,

> "The popular mind is agitated with problems that may disturb social order, and among them all, none is more threatening than the inequality of condition, of wealth, and opportunity that has grown within a single generation out of the concentration of capital into vast combinations to control production and trade and to break down competition." [4]

In an attempt to tame these behemoths, the U.S. Congress enacted in 1890 one of the oldest and most well-known competition

---

[3] The sponsor of the antitrust legislation which came to be known as the Sherman Act.

[4] 21 March 1890, Debate on Antitrust Bill.

legislation in the world, the Sherman Act (or the Antitrust Act). A piece of legislation consisting essentially only two substantive sections, the Act has played a significant role in the development of the modern American economy and has, remarkably, survived virtually unchanged to this day.

While believing that the government had an important role to play in refereeing the market place to ensure that every player played fairly, the United States also adhered to the view that the government should not enter the fray and be a player itself on the field.

On the other hand, owing to Singapore's unique historical circumstances and development pattern, the Singapore government has played a role in the commercial arena since the early days of the nation. Coming from a tradition of non-involvement and active regulation of competition, the U.S. negotiators were thus interested in how Singapore's government-owned companies competed and interacted with other companies, and how they were regulated.

Adding to this was the perception the U.S. negotiators had obtained from their own sources that the Singapore government-owned companies played a significant part in the country's economy and enjoyed an advantage over other companies by virtue of their ownership. This was partly due to the traditional conception of state-owned enterprises that the negotiators were familiar with, and which continue to exist in many countries, where such entities did not necessarily fulfil commercial functions but served governmental or public ones.

The U.S. therefore wished to use the Competition Policy chapter as a means to ensure that government-owned enterprises were subject to the same rules of fair competition as other companies and that U.S. companies in Singapore would be guaranteed a level playing field. While this was understandable, in the case of Singapore, its government-owned corporations were already in that position. The challenge lay in convincing the U.S. that this was in fact the case.

For a start, the Singapore side showed that government-owned companies in Singapore were no differently regulated than other companies. They were registered under the Companies Act (Cap.50) and subject to all of its laws and regulations. They were also subject to the same accounting and reporting requirements as other companies. Indeed, the only difference between a government-owned corporation and one wholly-owned by private interests was the identity of the shareholders. In all other respects, the government-owned corporation was no different and regulated no differently than the privately owned one.

Further, government-owned corporations in Singapore have received no special advantages by virtue of their ownership. So there are no special subsidies or assistance for government-owned corporations. Their boards are expected to run them as they would any other for-profit corporate entity, and be accountable to shareholders.

Most importantly perhaps, the Singapore government is not involved in the day-to-day operations or commercial decision-making of these companies. From the beginning, the Singapore government had decided on this wise course and had acted like any other prudent shareholder would — leaving the running of the company to the board and executives. This was crucial from the perspective of the U.S., which, as pointed out above, believed that the business of running businesses should be left to commercial players and the government should concentrate on the business of government.

THE OBLIGATIONS

While acknowledging Singapore's position with respect to its government enterprises, the U.S. maintained the wish to have this position articulated in the Competition Policy chapter. The chapter thus fulfilled two broad functions. The first was to act as an enabler for furthering the aims of trade liberalisation and investment flows resulting from the USSFTA. The second was to provide the assurance that all businesses would compete on an equal footing, and allied to that, the assurance that the Singapore government would continue its policy of not getting involved in the commercial operations of companies.

Critical to those aims was the commitment by Singapore to enact a general competition legislation by 2005. This put a date to the intention already expressed on previous occasions by the Singapore government that Singapore will be enacting a general competition law.[5] Both Parties also undertook specific obligations relating to monopolies and government enterprises, as set out below.

Monopolies[6]

The Parties have committed to ensuring that designated monopolies:

a) exercise any delegated governmental authority consistent with other obligations in the FTA ("the Agreement");
b) act solely in accordance with commercial considerations in their operations;
c) provide non-discriminatory treatment to goods, services and investments of the other Party; and
d) do not take advantage of their monopoly position in one market to engage in anti-competitive practices in another market.

---

[5] See for example, comments by BG (NS) George Yeo, Minister for Trade and Industry, in Parliament on 16 May 2002. Hansard, Vol 74, Column 1285: "Mr. Inderjit Singh asked whether and when we are going to introduce a Competition Law .... We have more or less settled on a few key ideas. Our aim is to have such a law within two to three years, but because of its sweep, extensive consultations with industry will have to be carried out."

[6] USSFTA, Chapter 12, Art. 12.3.

Government Enterprises[7]

Similarly, the U.S. and Singapore agreed to ensure that their government enterprises, if they exercise any delegated governmental authority, do not act inconsistently with the obligations of the FTA. Further, both Parties committed to ensuring that their government enterprises do not practice discriminatory treatment.

As alluded to above, Singapore agreed to continue its policy of ensuring that government enterprises act in accordance with commercial considerations and of not interfering in the operations of these enterprises. Singapore also agreed that it will continue with its policy of reducing the government's overall stake in government enterprises over time, subject to the state of the relevant capital markets and the interests of other shareholders.

In addition to the substantive obligations, Singapore agreed to make an annual report on government enterprises with at least S$50 million annual revenue or which have at least S$50 million worth of assets, that state the government's shareholding in the enterprise description of special share, if any, the name and government title of any official serving on the board of directors, and the annual revenue or total assets, or both, depending on the basis on which the enterprise is covered in the report.

Transparency and Information Requests[8]

In the spirit of cooperation and promoting transparency, Singapore and the U.S. committed to making information relating to competition issues, such as enforcement measures and exemptions from competition law, available to each other upon request.

---

[7] *Ibid.*

[8] USSFTA, Chapter 12, Art 12.4 and Art 12.5.

Consultations [9]

The chapter also institutes a consultation mechanism to address specific issues that might arise relating to the obligations contained in the chapter. This is to ensure that dispute settlement is a measure of last resort.

CONCLUSION

The negotiations for the competition chapter were an exercise in learning about one another's economy and historical development. While similar in several respects, differences existed that shaped the perceptions and states of mind of the negotiators. The final positions reached reflect these states of mind, and not only go some way towards addressing them without fundamentally altering each country's approach towards the issues, but also demonstrate a deeper understanding of each country's unique developmental circumstances. This can only be to the benefit of companies wishing to use the USSFTA to access the U.S. and Singapore markets, and who will enjoy the assurance of a fair and competitive business environment when they do so.

---

[9] USSFTA, Chapter 12, Art 12.6.

12 Intellectual Property Rights

LIEW Woon Yin[1]

SINGAPORE IN TRANSITION

Much has been said about the potential benefits to developing countries of implementing a strong intellectual property (IP) regime. The benefits include the stimulation and effective exploitation of local innovation, greater incentives encouraging foreign investment, and sharing of knowledge. The effects of these benefits, however, can vary considerably depending on the level of economic and social

---

[1] Liew Woon Yin (LL.B, Singapore) is currently the Director-General of the Intellectual Property Office of Singapore (IPOS). She began her career as Deputy Registrar of Trade Marks & Patents at the Registry of Trade Marks & Patents, Ministry of Law. Liew then spent several years working at the headquarter of the Ministry of the Environment as a Legal Officer and as a Deputy Public Prosecutor. Subsequently, she returned to the Registry of Trade Marks & Patents and was appointed the Registrar a year later. When the Registry was converted into a statutory board in 2001, she became its Director-General. As Director-General, she is responsible for promoting the importance of intellectual property in Singapore and for improving and strengthening the legal framework of IPOS. Under her direction, a number of key intellectual property laws such as the Patents Act and the Trade Marks Act were reviewed and amended. Liew was also instrumental in the enactment of new Intellectual Property legislation such as the Geographical Indications Act and the Registered Designs Act. All the Intellectual Property legislations are now under the purview of IPOS. Liew implemented the Trade Mark computerised system, and the computerised patent system. She is a frequent speaker at overseas seminars and conferences and has been representing Singapore in a number of international trade and industry meetings such as Free Trade Agreement discussions. She is also the key driver behind several important partnerships with international and foreign organisations such as FICPI, EPO and JPO. The views expressed in this article are those of the author and do not necessarily represent the position of the Singapore Government.

development of the country concerned. In the short-term, the costs to developing countries, which may as yet be unable to fully exploit the international IP system for their own benefits, can be substantial.

In recent decades, IP has become a hotly debated issue in public and policy fora, arising from its rapid growth in scope and application. The World Trade Organization (WTO) Agreement on Trade-Related Aspects of Intellectual Property Rights (WTO-TRIPS) negotiated in the 1986-94 Uruguay Round of the global trade negotiations was a key catalyst. For the first time, intellectual property rules were introduced into the multilateral trading system.

Singapore is in a unique position, having a relatively young IP regime[2] and yet what some consider a developed industrial and technological base. However, Singapore is an economy transiting from an old order grounded in tangible assets to one that has started to apply intangible assets for economic growth. The local industry was, in the past, highly dependent on and leveraging off the multi-nationals in Singapore. They now realise that they have to compete in global playing fields. Measures have been put into place to ensure that Singapore remains competitive in the new global knowledge economy, to foster local creativity and entrepreneurship, and to move our local industry up the value chain.

In order to do so, Singapore needs to keep pace with the growing strength of the IP regimes in the developed countries. This is in spite of the fact that Singapore is still a net user of IP, with a relatively low level of local innovation (as evidenced by the low levels of local patenting activity).

In addition to this national development role, it is imperative that we, as a trade-dependent economy, assure our trading partners that their IP rights are safeguarded. The security in knowing that their

---

[2] Singapore's independent patent system was established only in 1995 (previously having had a re-registration system based on the UK's) and the Industrial Design registration system in 2000.

rights are well protected could be a factor in U.S. businesses deciding to base the creative and more value-added sectors of their businesses here.

THE INTERNATIONAL PLAYING FIELD

Singapore is party to the WTO and became TRIPS-compliant in 1999. TRIPS cover five broad issues: how basic principles of the trading system and other international intellectual property agreements should be applied; how to give adequate protection to intellectual property rights; how countries should enforce those rights adequately in their own territories; how to settle disputes on intellectual property between members of the WTO; and special transitional arrangements during the period when the new system is being introduced. The areas covered under the TRIPS agreement are: copyright and related rights; trademarks, including service marks; geographical indications; industrial designs; patents; layout-designs (topographies) of integrated circuits; and undisclosed information, including trade secrets.

Although comprehensive in its scope, it sets minimum standards of compliance. Already these standards are said to be insufficient to match the increasing importance intangible assets have in trade and business, as well as the leaps in technological developments. These standards are being stretched through the efforts of developed countries and industry lobby groups through bilateral and multilateral agreements.

The USSFTA is an example of an agreement that stretches the boundaries of these standards.

CHANGING THE RULES OF THE GAME

Both the U.S. and Singapore are party to the WTO-TRIPS. This was useful because it meant that we were starting from a common position. Why did we agree to the raising of these standards?

First, the IP issues were a key priority for the United States. As the world's leader in innovation, they wanted to ensure that IPR for their goods and services were adequately protected. The U.S. position was to further promote the adequate and effective protection of IPR on a global basis.

Second, the USSFTA was intended to set a model for others to follow. Many Asian countries are still developing their IP regimes. Not all are TRIPS-compliant as yet because of implementation concerns and their impact on social and economic development. Thus the USSFTA was intended to be used as a template for future Asian FTAs with the United States.

Third, the FTA negotiation was also an opportunity for us to improve the current rules and to ensure that the standards of protection and enforcement keep pace with the rapid changes in technology. This is important to our new economic emphasis in the creative industries and the innovation aspect of technology. Although Singapore's regime is regularly reviewed to ensure its continued relevancy, the USSFTA accelerated the process. It is now no longer a question of the regime keeping pace with technological and business developments, but of ensuring that our economy can make the move to the big league.

THE PLAYERS

IP is a horizontal issue cutting across many vertical interest groups. As anticipated, arriving at such a landmark chapter was never an easy task. As with the other chapters, there were multiple interests at stake.

One key concern was the enforcement of these provisions. How can we ensure surveillance and enforcement, especially at a time when technology makes IP infringement harder to track and detect? How can we have comprehensive surveillance without impeding efficiency and other trade channels?

In addition, the negotiators had to consider the impact of IP on local consumers and businesses. The cost of IP protection should not translate into limiting access to products. Two issues which had the potential effect of limiting access concerned parallel imports and protection of anti-circumvention measures.

The negotiators had also to consider the effect a more stringent regime would have on our local industry and consumers. Singapore is not as yet an IP-savvy nation. More often than not, the local industry view IP rights as an unjustified cost rather than the protection of an asset. The public at large, has not yet fully grasped the concept of rights and ownership to something as intangible as an intellectual creation. The U.S.'s strong stance on piracy and holding consumers accountable were therefore challenging.

Quite obviously business interests influenced negotiations. One interesting aspect of this was the level of influence that the U.S. businesses had on their policy makers and policy. One should never underestimate it. In the IP negotiations, strong U.S. lobby groups were from the pharmaceutical industry pushing for a longer term of patent protection, and the media/entertainment industries reacting against piracy and online distributors.

THE CARDS ON THE TABLE

The components of the IP chapter covered a broad range of IP areas: trademarks; domain names on the internet; copyright obligations; pharmaceutical patents; plant protection; IP enforcement; and anti-piracy. Most of these provisions were agreed upon relatively easily with the U.S. as there was some common ground in both countries wanting to ensure high standards of protection.

However, there were some tough issues — issues that we felt would have considerable repercussions on our local industry and the general public.

Anti-circumvention Measures

Technological protection measures are measures that are put in place to permit or deny certain uses of the work. These can be in the form of encryption, passwords, pay-per-use mechanisms, etc. They are tools that the rights-holders use to more effectively protect their works against illegitimate use. However, these tools can be bypassed or "circumvented" to gain access to the works. There is currently no provision in Singapore's Copyright Act against such acts of circumvention. There is also no deterrent against the unauthorised development and distribution of such circumvention technologies.

However, beyond protecting their works against infringement, protection focused on technical protection measures may affect legitimate access to works for fair use. In some instances, the technical measures may be tied up with monopolistic practices, in which case, protection for the measures may call into question its justification in IP laws. These were some of the issues we had to grapple with.

Ultimately, anti-circumvention legislation is necessary, as in the face of more sophisticated forms of piracy, copyright owners are increasingly introducing technological protection measures in order to protect their works. These measures provide greater security and hence incentive for rights owners in using electronic platforms. They also provide a means for the development of different distribution and usage methods and systems, allowing permutations of business models on the web.

Hence, it was agreed that Singapore will implement legislation to provide that it is unlawful to knowingly circumvent or get-around effective technological measures that control access, to use the protected copyright works. It will also be unlawful to manufacture, provide or deal in technologies that are primarily designed, or marketed for the purpose of circumvention, or which have no other significant purpose than to circumvent the effective technological measures. These acts would attract liability, both civil and criminal, by themselves in addition to any liability for copyright infringement.

Criminalisation of End-user Infringement

Our current laws already provide for criminal penalties for the manufacture, distribution or sale of infringing articles. Presently, a person can be fined S$10,000 for each infringing article up to a maximum of S$100,000 or a maximum of five years' imprisonment.

With rapid technological developments resulting in on-line distribution of software, music, publications and other media, and the increasing ease of replication, the entertainment and media industries are striving hard to overcome the escalating problem of piracy of their copyright material.

Hence there was a substantial industry lobby to stop the "pirates", come what may. The problem was defining who these "pirates" are! Theft is theft, and as a single pickpocket is as liable for theft as say an organised gang, the question was whether it would be effective or even feasible to target the single, individual end-user who downloads what he considers "free" stuff from the web.

The final text covers "significant wilful infringements of copyright" and "wilful infringements for the purpose of commercial advantage or financial gain" by anyone. This allows some refinement in the practical enforcement to focus efforts and resources on clamping down on the more egregious infringements and infringers.

Parallel imports

It is a common practice for companies to supply products, at different prices, to different countries, and at times, of different standards. Such market segmentation is practised in the pharmaceutical industry and is enforced through a set of exclusive licensing arrangements, such that each licensed distributor or manufacturer can supply only to a particular territory at a particular price. There can be a fine line between such market segmentation and anti-competitive behaviour. Parallel imports act as a check against these exclusive arrangements.

This became a sticking point between us and the U.S. with respect to the parallel imports of pharmaceuticals. The industry was recognised as a specialised one by both sides due to the exceedingly high costs and risks involved. Industry sources cite an average of 10–15 years and US$800 million to bring a new medicine to the market.

Currently, the size of our parallel import market for patented pharmaceutical products is small. However, because we are small buyers with little negotiating muscle, parallel importation is a useful safeguard mechanism against anti-competitive pricing.

The U.S. pressed strongly for restrictions on parallel imports on behalf of their pharmaceutical industry. We were sympathetic as the biomedical sciences and pharmaceutical industries have become a key area of growth for Singapore. Strengthening protection for pharmaceuticals helps support Singapore's drive as a choice location for value-added activities such as R&D, clinical development and headquarter activities.

Singapore already has a common legal action of inducing a breach of contract to allow the IP owner to sue a Singapore parallel importer who knowingly and intentionally induces a breach of contract between the IP owner and his licensed distributor. However, this was insufficient for the U.S. who wanted to lower the hurdle to prove inducement of a breach of contract. This remained a bone of contention until the last day of negotiations with both sides tuning and retuning the wordings.

The final agreed text allows the prevention of the purchase of any patented pharmaceutical product which, the purchaser *knows or has reason to know*, has been distributed in breach of a license agreement.[3]

---

[3] Refer to footnotes 16–10 of the USSFTA — A Party may limit such cause of action to cases where the product has been sold or distributed only outside the Party's territory before its procurement inside the Party's territory.

Self-Help for IP Owners: Maintaining the Co-operative Approach for Singapore

Singapore has always felt strongly that IPR enforcement is the shared responsibility of the authorities and the owners where both sides combine resources to curb piracy. Our legal system provides both civil and criminal avenues for the enforcement of rights by IPR owners. In respect of criminal avenues, owners can obtain a search warrant and work together with the police in the raid of premises used for infringing activities. They can then initiate criminal proceedings against the offenders by way of fiats issued by the Attorney-General's Chambers.

The U.S. felt that enforcement should be the sole responsibility of the authorities, citing costs to the owner in such a mechanism. However, the facts held out — that this co-operative system *is* working for Singapore, allowing our authorities to prioritise their enforcement efforts on major syndicates and upstream infringing activities, while at the same time giving right-holders the option to initiate criminal proceedings on their own where it is more efficient for them to do so.

A LOOK BACK

The recognition of IP as an important engine of Singapore's continued growth grew gradually over the past 20 years. Although there were no fundamental differences between the two sides, we were nevertheless surprised by how tough the U.S. demands were. It was apparent that for the U.S., IP was one of the critical issues of the FTA.

Through the gruelling two years, our negotiators developed a better understanding of the role the IP regime plays in a developed country.

The IP Provisions in a Nutshell

The IP Chapter in the USSFTA is part of Singapore's efforts to ensure that it has the advanced regulatory infrastructure to support Singapore's growing knowledge economy. The USSFTA legislation provides a boost for industries where IP plays an important role, particularly in IT, pharmaceuticals, high technology, science and creative industries.

The Agreement incorporates all the obligations set forth in the World Intellectual Property Organization (WIPO) Copyright Treaty (WCT) and the WIPO Performances and Phonograms Treaty (WPPT).

The key provisions include:

- The term of copyright will be increased to the "life of the author" plus 70 years or 70 years after first publication, broadcast or performance.
- It will now be a criminal offence to knowingly remove or alter rights management information (RMI), or distribute, import for distribution, broadcast, communicate, and make available works with altered RMI without approval.
- The framework for ISPs will be enhanced to provide legal incentives for ISPs to co-operate with copyright owners in deterring unauthorised storage and transmission of copyrighted materials.
- As an alternative to proving damages, a range of damages will be set for the Courts to make an appropriate order as to the sum to be paid without the need to prove actual amount of damages suffered.
- The term of a patent will be extended to compensate the patent owner for unreasonable delays from the patent office in granting a patent. For pharmaceuticals, there will also be available an extended patent term of protection for a limited time (maximum five years from the end of term), to

compensate for unreasonable delays in marketing approvals from the Health Sciences Authority.

- Compulsory licensing will only be allowed if it is to remedy an anti-competitive practice or in a case of public non-commercial use, national emergency or extreme urgency.
- Registration of non-visually perceptible marks including sounds and scents will be allowed.
- The Trade Marks Act will include provisions to protect well-known marks against dilution.[4]
- Singapore will accede to the International Union for the Protection of New Varieties of Plants (UPOV) convention bringing with it a new right — the Plant Variety Right to Singapore.

A strong IP regime provides an incentive for research and development and a ladder on which industry can climb up the value-chain. While there is always the risk of either over-protection or under-protection, what the law must do is to seek a balance between granting exclusivity and allowing for the free flow of ideas and knowledge sharing. The amendments are far ranging but considerably more needs to be done to ensure that a balance of interests is maintained.

THE ROAD AHEAD

Our work is not over. For us, we will need to amend the IP legislation so that we are compliant with the USSFTA. 2004 will see a series of amendments to our IP regime — with amendments made not only to cater for the USSFTA but our own review of the legislation to make it more industry-relevant and to keep pace with the latest developments.

---

[4] Dilution occurs when a mark is used in a way which tends to blur its distinctiveness or tarnish its image. Dilution reduces the public's perception that the mark signifies something unique, singular or particular.

It might be a bumpy road ahead for some, as consumers and industry adjust to the higher standards demanded for a developed nation where IP is a critical business asset. Already we have established ties to key industry associations to buffer the effect on the local industry. The publicity and education machine is preparing to launch campaigns and programmes to educate the public and industry on the upcoming developments.

13 Labour

ONG Yen Her[1]

SIGNIFICANCE AND OBJECTIVE OF THE USSFTA LABOUR CHAPTER

The U.S.-Singapore Free Trade Agreement is the first bilateral trade agreement between the U.S. and a country in Asia. One significant feature of the agreement is the inclusion of a Labour chapter to safeguard, promote and enhance workers' interests and rights as well as to ensure that the benefits of economic integration are broadly shared with the workforce.

To this end, both Singapore and the U.S. reaffirmed their commitment as members of the International Labour Organisation (ILO) to observe the labour principles and rights as embodied in the ILO Declaration on Fundamental Principles and Rights at Work under the USSFTA. These labour principles cover freedom of association and collective bargaining, the abolition of forced and child labour and ensure acceptable conditions of work including minimum age and the elimination of employment discrimination.

---

[1] Lead negotiator for the U.S.-Singapore Free Trade Agreement (USSFTA). Mr. Ong worked for the Singapore National Trades Union Congress (SNTUC) from 1979 to 1984. He joined the Ministry of Labour in 1985 as the Director of Labour Relations. Since 1998, he has been holding the position of Divisional Director, Labour Relations and Welfare in the Ministry of Manpower. His areas of responsibility in the Ministry include industrial relations, labour standards, wages, trade unions, international labour affairs, human resource development and practices. The views expressed in this article are those of the author and do not necessarily represent the views of the Singapore Government.

While the principal objective of the Labour chapter is to promote and protect workers' welfare, the two countries also recognise that labour standards should not be used for protectionist trade purposes.

Under the Labour chapter, both countries further committed themselves to ensuring that their respective domestic laws are effectively enforced, so that workers' interests and rights could be well safeguarded. Singapore and the U.S. also recognised that cooperation between the two countries provides enhanced opportunities to improve labour standards and the well-being of workers. A comprehensive Labour Cooperation Mechanism was therefore incorporated into the Labour chapter of the USSFTA. Included in the Mechanism are joint cooperative activities that could be undertaken by both countries that would help strengthen bilateral ties in the field of labour.

CONTRIBUTORY FACTORS TO SUCCESSFUL CONCLUSION OF LABOUR CHAPTER

In some trade negotiations, labour concerns have been a thorny issue and have, in fact, stalled the progress and conclusion of the negotiations. Against this backdrop and given the obvious differences between the labour regimes of Singapore and the U.S. there were initial apprehensions when negotiations commenced. However, as we proceeded with our work, we were gratified that we were able to conduct the negotiations in a cordial atmosphere and arrive at mutually satisfactory solutions.

Right from the start, labour negotiators from both countries were able to share the common objective to promote labour standards as well as to enhance and safeguard workers' interests through the USSFTA. But, the more important factor contributing to the successful conclusion of the agreement is that Singapore and the U.S. acknowledged that both countries have high labour standards, effective enforcement of domestic labour laws and have generally no difficulties in observing the principles and rights under the ILO Declaration.

Another important factor contributing to the smooth conclusion of the USSFTA was that the two lead labour negotiators were equally attuned to labour issues and aspirations, given their common background of having served for some time in their respective labour movements, namely, the Singapore National Trades Union Congress (SNTUC) and American Federation of Labour-Congress of Industrial Organizations (AFL-CIO) respectively. We shared a common viewpoint and the values of the fundamental labour principles while appreciating the differences between our two countries.

SINGAPORE IN THE INTERNATIONAL ARENA

Singapore has been a member of the ILO since her independence in 1965 and has always taken a serious view of her obligations as an ILO member country. Compared to many other member states, Singapore's ratification record of ILO Conventions has put us in a favourable position. To date, Singapore has ratified a total of 22 ILO Conventions, of which four are core ILO Conventions that embody the ILO fundamental principles and rights at work. [2]

In the domestic arena, Singapore has an effective legislative framework to safeguard and promote the welfare of workers and to foster harmonious industrial relations through close labour-management cooperation and tripartite partnership. Key employment laws governing industrial relations in Singapore include the Employment Act and the Industrial Relations Act. These laws form

---

[2] There are a total of eight core Conventions that embody the four fundamental labour principles and rights at work. They are Convention 100 on Equal Remuneration; Convention 111 on Discrimination (Employment and Occupation); Convention 138 on Minimum Age; Convention 182 on Worst Forms of Child Labour; Convention 29 on Forced Labour; Convention 105 on Abolition of Forced Labour; Convention 87 on Freedom of Association and Protection of the Right to Organize, and Convention 98 on Right to Organize and Collective Bargaining.

the foundation for Singapore's harmonious industrial relations over the years. Industrial harmony has contributed to the growth of the economy and improvement in the economic and social well-being of all workers in Singapore.

Employment Act

The Employment Act is the main legislation governing the minimum terms and conditions of employment in Singapore. The Act helps to harmonise both the interests of employers and employees by spelling out their respective rights and obligations.

Industrial Relations Act

The Industrial Relations Act establishes a system for the prevention and settlement of trade disputes through collective bargaining between the employers and trade unions, conciliation by the government (through the Ministry of Manpower) and arbitration by the Industrial Arbitration Court. This dispute settlement system has contributed significantly to the development of Singapore's harmonious industrial relations and is a cornerstone of our tripartite partnership.

Tripartism in Singapore

Beyond protecting workers' rights through legislation, it is a long-standing policy of the Singapore government to promote tripartite cooperation among the three social partners comprising employers, trade unions and the government to achieve Singapore's economic and social progress and to enhance the interests of all parties.

The SNTUC and the Singapore National Employers Federation (SNEF) are the Singapore government's social partners within the framework of tripartite cooperation. Constructive tripartite engagement amongst the government and its social partners has enhanced Singapore's ability to overcome economic adversity and to share the fruits of economic success in good times. The tripartite framework of cooperation has enabled the three social partners to participate in and contribute to the formulation of key employment and industrial relations policies. This has helped Singapore to more effectively tackle complex and difficult national issues that have long-term implications.

Although there was a high level of understanding between the negotiators and the atmosphere of the negotiations was always cordial, there were difficult issues that needed to be addressed and resolved. In the process of addressing these difficult issues, both parties had to take into account the differences between the U.S. and Singapore's labour frameworks and the need to ensure that workers' rights and protections were not undermined while working towards solutions that were acceptable to both countries. One example is the issue of minimum wage.

NO MINIMUM WAGE IN SINGAPORE

Unlike the U.S. which prescribes legally binding minimum wages to ensure that workers' interests are protected, wage increases in Singapore, particularly for the rank and file employees, are largely determined by the recommendations of the tripartite National Wages Council (NWC). The difference between the U.S.'s legislative approach and Singapore's tripartite consensual approach proved to be a sticky point during the USSFTA negotiations.

Although the wage regimes in our two countries are fundamentally different, both governments shared the same objective of ensuring that workers are equitably rewarded for their contributions to their companies and the economy.

Singapore believes that workers should be fairly remunerated. She has put in place a credible wage determination mechanism, through the tripartite NWC, which reviews and formulates national wage guidelines on an annual basis. The yearly guidelines will be gazetted under the Employment Act to provide a legal basis for employers and trade unions/ workers to negotiate for wage increases for the coming year, taking into consideration the performance of the company. In formulating the guidelines, the NWC, which comprises key representatives of the employers, trade unions and the government, takes into consideration factors such as domestic economic growth, productivity growth, domestic employment situation, inflation, Singapore's international competitiveness, and the regional/global economic outlook. The implementation of the guidelines is not mandatory, as the intention is to allow for flexibility in the negotiations of wage adjustments between the employer and the unions/workers to suit the particular circumstances of each company. However, the NWC has proven to be a robust system with the guidelines being widely followed, by virtue of the fact that these guidelines are relevant and are formulated by consensus involving the representatives of employees and employers.

The U.S. and Singapore were able to reach an agreement that while the U.S. has minimum wage laws, Singapore will not do so but continue to adopt the tripartite approach to achieve the same objective of ensuring that workers are fairly rewarded in line with economic and productivity growth.

POSITIVE OUTCOMES

Apart from economic benefits, the USSFTA also serves to advance mutual interests in the area of labour. Opportunities presented during the negotiations for Singapore and U.S. to better understand and appreciate each other's labour regimes do not cease with the conclusion of the USSFTA.

Opportunities for Exchange

In the course of the negotiations, Singapore and the U.S. were constantly seeking to better understand each other's labour system and legislation in order to facilitate the conclusion of a labour chapter that would be mutually beneficial. These exchanges, which included a two-day visit to Singapore by the U.S. labour negotiation team, [3] have enabled both parties to gain insights into and better appreciate each other's labour practices.

Interactions Went Beyond Those at the Governmental Level

The negotiations also afforded both the SNTUC and the AFL-CIO the opportunity to establish closer contacts and rapport as evidenced by their efforts to enunciate the goals they hoped to see achieved in the USSFTA through their joint statement.

JOINT STATEMENT SIGNED BETWEEN SNTUC AND AFL-CIO[4]

During the course of negotiations, civil society groups and labour unions in the U.S., particularly the AFL-CIO, had called for strong measures to be included in the free trade agreement to ensure that the rights of workers are not compromised in the process of trade liberalisation. The AFL-CIO has insisted that the FTA should ultimately lead to genuine and tangible benefits for workers.

The SNTUC shares the same concerns as the AFL-CIO and both unions jointly issued a statement to urge their respective governments to: affirm and implement their commitment to creating greater and better employment opportunities, and improving the

---

[3] The team was briefed on Singapore's labour legislation and was introduced to our social partners.

[4] See Appendix IV.

standard of living and quality of life for all workers; and honour their commitment towards the fulfilment of international labour standards and the effective enforcement of domestic labour legislation. The joint statement also called for both governments to subscribe to the principles of transparency and accountability in the process of bilateral trade and investment agreement negotiations.

An Established Platform for Cooperation

The USSFTA provides for a Labour Cooperation Mechanism annexed to the labour chapter. This Mechanism paves the way for continued exchanges between Singapore and the U.S. on ways to improve labour laws and practices in both countries through specific cooperative activities. This means that the conclusion of the USSFTA does not bring an end to Singapore-U.S. interactions in the area of labour. Rather, it marks the beginning of a new and meaningful collaborative relationship.

CONCLUDING OBSERVATIONS

The USSFTA negotiations have provided valuable lessons and experiences for Singapore and our labour negotiators.[5] Meaningful exchanges were established and these have allowed both the U.S. and Singapore to better appreciate each other's labour regimes and, at the same time, dispel some misperceptions along the way. Further, in the course of enhancing the interests of both countries, precious networking and personal friendships were also established with our U.S. labour counterparts. Such ties would undoubtedly further contribute towards the strengthening of our close relationship.

---

[5] Refer to Appendix XVII.

14 Environment

LOH Ah Tuan, KHOO Seow Poh, CHUA Yew Peng
and Fion TAN[1]

ENVIRONMENTAL PHILOSOPHY

Singapore believes that liberalised trade and protection of the environment are key components of sustainable development, and that trade and environmental policies can and should be mutually supportive.

Over the last 30 years since our independence, we have developed a robust environmental regime even as the economy took off on a trajectory of rapid growth. This stems from a firm belief that the objectives of environmental protection and economic development are equally important and mutually enhancing.

---

[1] Loh Ah Tuan is the lead negotiator on the Environment chapter for the USSFTA. He is also a leading member in negotiating the to-be-concluded Canada-Singapore Environmental Co-operation Agreement under the Canada-Singapore Free Trade Agreement. He is currently the Director-General of Environmental Protection of the National Environment Agency, Singapore. His responsibility is to ensure that Singaporeans continue to enjoy clean air, clean water and a healthy environment, and more importantly, the environmental sustainability of Singapore.

Khoo Seow Poh is the Director of Corporate Communications and International Relations at the Ministry of the Environment and Press Secretary to the Minister for the Environment. He joined the Ministry's Headquarters in 1990 and was appointed to head the then International Environment and Policy Department in 1994. He also concurrently assumed the role of Press Secretary to the Minister. Khoo has represented the Ministry and the Singapore in many international forums. In May 2001, He was appointed Director for the newly formed Corporate Communications and International Relations Division. The Directorate oversees and co-ordinates the Ministry's communications policies as well as policies relating to bilateral, regional and international environmental co-operation.

Singapore is a small island city-state with an area of only about 680 sq km and a population of four million — about the same population as that of Rhode Island. It is highly urbanised and industrialised. Given these conditions, Singapore has a very small margin for error where environmental protection is concerned. Hence, sound environmental management has always been one of the pillars of our development and will continue to be so.

The Singapore economy is fully open to the world, both in the areas of trade and investment. This open economy is the result of both a policy of choice and an invention of necessity because of our small size and limited resources. Singapore is a major trading hub, with trade accounting for about 2.7 times of its GDP — the highest in the world. For a small city-state such as Singapore, effective environmental protection and management is of paramount importance as our very survival depends on the existence and maintenance of a safe and sustainable environment.

Singapore believes, and this belief is borne out by her experience, that environmental problems can be prevented through judicious forward planning and the imposition of appropriate controls, and that local problems are best addressed by policies and measures tailored to meet the specific requirements of the local conditions.

Chua Yew Peng is currently the Deputy Director for International Relations with the Ministry of the Environment. He has been involved in international relations and policy work since 1994. In his 20 years with the Ministry, Chua has served a ten-year stint in the engineering division. With the International Relations Department, he has represented the Ministry and Singapore in other international forums and Free Trade Agreements negotiations with environmental co-operation elements, such as the Canada-Singapore Environmental Co-operative Agreement.

Fion Tan is Assistant Director for International Relations of the Ministry of the Environment. She has been involved in international relations and policy work since 2001. Her responsibilities include Trade and Environment matters and she is also involved in other FTA negotiations such as the Canada-Singapore Environment Co-operative Agreement.

The views expressed in this article are those of the authors and do not necessarily represent the views of the Singapore Government.

ENVIRONMENTAL NEGOTIATIONS

Negotiating the Environment chapter of the United States-Singapore Free Trade Agreement (USSFTA) was not as difficult as originally envisaged. Using the sea as a metaphor, we did encounter some rough waters initially, riding the usual crests and troughs at the early stages of the negotiations. However, with common sense and a willingness to respect each other's points of views we were able to avoid the tsunamis, hurricane-force winds and waves, which could have sunk the negotiations. Our two-year voyage of negotiations not only enabled us to better understand world trade but also to view it from different perspectives. It was an edifying experience.

For the Singapore Environment Team, negotiating the Environment chapter in the USSFTA was like navigating in uncharted waters. We had never done one before and had no Asian precedent to use as a guide as it was also the first time an Asian country embarked on a course to sign a Free Trade Agreement with the United States. In Asia, the traditional practice in regional and bilateral environmental negotiations is to take a co-operative and non-litigious approach. Agreements reached through such an approach provide a mechanism for general cooperation while specific aspects of implementation at the national level are largely left to the discretion of the individual country, taking into consideration its domestic conditions. Our team studied the few precedents available and found that none could adequately cater to the unique set of circumstances facing us. We had to put together a new approach to meet our needs.

At the beginning of the negotiations, both U.S. and Singapore acknowledged that both countries had high environmental standards and were also strong proponents of free trade. This acknowledgement served as the cornerstone of our negotiations as it guided both sides on a wide range of issues relevant to the negotiations.

INHERENT CHALLENGES

When the negotiations started, the Singapore team felt that both sides needed a comprehensive understanding of each other's environmental management regimes. The need was borne out by the realisation that both negotiation teams did not fully understand each other's environmental management strategies and philosophies, and there were members on the U.S. team who were not from the environment agencies. This problem was compounded by the fact that the two sides approached the negotiations from different cultural perspectives. Different cultures use different styles of negotiation and persuasion; some cultures focus on cultivating a close, trusting relationship with the other side, whereas some others prefer a more direct, explicit style of interaction based on reasoned arguments. Furthermore, it was inevitable that members of both negotiation teams brought to the negotiations their pre-conceived assumptions and other attitudinal baggage, which had been formed over time through personal experiences and exposure to the media. To bridge the knowledge and understanding gap, the Singapore team gave an hour-long briefing on Singapore's approach to environmental protection, including our environmental philosophy and core values to the U.S. team.

Notwithstanding the preparations made to bridge the differences, we realised as soon as we started negotiations that the negotiating styles adopted by both sides were quite different, each having been moulded by the culture, geography, history, and political system in our respective countries.

Both sides realised that in order to move forward in the negotiations, there was a need to take a step back and try to fully understand each other. A process of regular and open communication was then initiated through which both sides exchanged detailed information that was pertinent to the negotiations, such as additional details of our respective approaches to environmental management, enforcement regimes, policies and measures in place, and also unique concerns and circumstances. This open communication process and the mutual understanding and respect it generated proved crucial to the timely and successful conclusion of the negotiations, as there were many elements in the text document which were quite complex and needed the reconciliation of different points of view and policy priorities from both sides.

As the talks proceeded, it became increasingly clear that there was essentially no major difference between the respective approaches and concerns of both parties. Both sides accepted that neither had the right to interfere in the domestic environmental management regime of the other. Both sides also agreed that the right to enact environmental laws and regulations was inalienable and could not be compromised. There was also mutual recognition that either party had the right to exercise discretion in the development and execution of its environmental laws and regulations. Last but not least, there was also mutual recognition of the right of either party to exploit its own resources in accordance to its own environmental and development policies.

ENVIRONMENT CHAPTER

The Environment chapter of the USSFTA reflected both countries' commitment to enhance their respective capacities to protect the environment and promote sustainable development in concert with the strengthening of bilateral trade and investment relations. At the same time, it acknowledged the sovereign right of either party to establish its own level of domestic environmental protection and its own development policies.

In the chapter, both parties reiterated their commitment to actively and rigorously enforce their respective domestic laws relating to environment as well as pledged not to compromise the protection afforded by these laws when promoting trade and investment between the two countries.

The Chapter also encouraged both parties to consult and cooperate closely on environmental issues of mutual concern and interest. This subsequently led to an agreement to set up a working sub-committee, comprising government officials of both countries. Both parties also agreed to make available channels and mechanisms for public participation in the implementation of this Chapter.

As a way to facilitate the sharing of best practices and the development of innovative approaches, both parties agreed to sign a Memorandum Of Intent on Cooperation in Environmental Matters, which would focus on training and capacity building programs that protect the environment and promote sustainable development.

The Memorandum will provide a framework for the two parties to cooperate in promoting sustainable environmental policies, practices and measures. Bilateral co-operative activities envisaged include technical information sharing, exchange of experts, capacity-building training, and joint research projects in projects of mutual interest to both parties. Under the Memorandum, U.S. and Singapore also intend to cooperate on activities aimed at promoting regional exchange of information on environmental best practices and capacity building for third countries in Asia.

In such government-to-government cooperation, both sides can be expected to harness the support of corporate entities and non-government organisations in terms of providing views and recommendations. Singapore believes that it is only through the collective efforts and joint ownership of the environment by all three sectors, namely, the Public, the Private and the People sectors that we are able to forge an enduring and sustainable environment without compromising our social and economic progress.

LESSONS

Among the many invaluable lessons learnt from the two years of negotiating the Environment chapter, there were two particularly instructive ones that we would like to highlight. First, we learnt that one should always approach negotiations with an empathetic and open mind. Second, we learnt that it was counter productive to refuse compromise by doggedly sticking to one's original position. Both parties found that it was highly beneficial to clarify respective interests and concerns early in the discussions. With this done, a solution or a way forward would invariably become manifest.

For example, the various briefings conducted by us, sometimes impromptu, for our U.S. counterparts who were less familiar with Singapore's environmental regime, provided them with a better appreciation of Singapore's unique circumstances and constraints as a city-state. Similarly, through detailed clarifications by our U.S. counterparts, we too gained a deeper insight into the complexities of the U.S. consultation regime and process, often viewed as unnecessary encumbrances by other countries, which had conducted such negotiations with the United States. Such clarifications and explanations had helped to promote mutual understanding and respect between the U.S. and Singapore, thereby paving the way for the eventual resolution of several "thorny" issues that threatened to impede the progress of talks.

Members of the Singapore environment negotiation team feel privileged to have participated in the negotiations of the USSFTA. The successful conclusion of the environment talks was made possible through the solid support and assistance provided by the various agencies such as our legal advisors, Ministry of National Development and its agencies, etc. All the agencies worked together as a team, setting aside intra-agency differences to secure an outcome which would be in the best interest of Singapore.

15 The Role of Legal Counsel and Dispute Settlement

Sivakant TIWARI[1]

BIRTH OF A LEGAL TEAM

In mid-November 2000 I was asked to attend an urgent meeting at our Ministry of Trade and Industry, together with senior officials of various Ministries and agencies. We were told that, at a golf game in Brunei, President Clinton and Prime Minister Goh had agreed that the two countries would negotiate a Free Trade Agreement which was to be completed within the remainder of the term of the Clinton Administration, i.e., in the next two to three months.

We were informed that the U.S.-Singapore FTA (USSFTA) was the most important FTA for the Republic and I was to form and lead a team of legal officers to work on it. On my return to the office I

---

[1] S. Tiwari is the Principal Senior State Counsel of the International Affairs Division in the Attorney-General's Chambers, Singapore. He first served (on secondment from the Legal Service) in the Ministry of Defence and was the Head of its Legal Department. He then became the Head of the Civil Division in the Chambers from 1987–Jun 1995, after which took over as the Principal Senior State Counsel of the International Affairs Division. He has led many bilateral and multilateral negotiations on behalf of Singapore, including that involving the Singapore-Johore Boundary Agreement and the Singapore-Malaysia dispute over Pedra Branca. He was the Legal Adviser to the Singapore delegation to the Uruguay Round negotiations and the USSFTA negotiations and has represented Singapore in the negotiations for the WTO Agreement on the Trade-Related Aspects of Intellectual Property Rights and at many ASEAN negotiations and meetings. He was a member of the Singapore delegation for the UNCLOS negotiations. The views expressed in this article are those of the author and do not necessarily represent the views of the Singapore Government.

decided to include Ms. Deena Bajrai[2] and Mr. Daren Tang[3] in the team and told them to cancel any holiday plans they had for the December period as we would be working non-stop throughout the 1 November to December 2000 and January 2001 period.

THE LONG JOURNEY — THE WORK BEGINS

The first round of negotiations began in Washington in December 2000. It was bitterly cold with snow everywhere — the only consolation being the free flow of hot coffee at the Georgetown Suites, where we stayed, and the Vietnamese restaurant round the corner.

For the legal team, the work which started in December 2000 did not end until the "legal scrubbing" work ended the night before the signing of the FTA by President Bush and Prime Minister Goh at the White House on 6 May 2003. In some respects, the "legal scrubbing" work became as difficult as the substantive negotiations as the lawyers for both sides pored over every sentence of the USSFTA text to ensure that errors, inconsistencies and ambiguities were corrected and unfinished text resolved in consultation with the negotiators of both sides.

For the period 1 May 2003 to 5 May 2003, both the U.S. and Singapore legal teams hardly had any sleep as we sorted out the FTA text with our U.S. counterparts during the day and our officials at home at night in view of the 12-hour time difference between Washington and Singapore. The USTR office in Washington became our home and we adapted to American style work habits with sandwiches and coffee for lunch and dinner. I found it a pleasure to work with my counterpart, Will Martyn.

---

[2] Deena Bajrai is State Counsel, International Affairs Division, Attorney-General's Chambers.

[3] Daren Tang is State Counsel, International Affairs Division, Attorney-General's Chambers.

I am proud of my two officers. We worked well as a team and they performed splendidly. With 21 negotiating groups[4] — one for each chapter of the FTA — the work as legal advisers was not easy as we rushed from one negotiating group to another. In addition I also had to be the lead negotiator for the very difficult Intellectual Property chapter and the following other chapters of the FTA: Dispute Settlement, Final Clauses and Establishment of a Free Trade Area and Definitions. Daren Tang assisted with the Services chapter negotiations. We did our best and saw the FTA through.

NO RESPITE — THE WORK CONTINUES

Negotiating an FTA — especially one of the complexity and broad-ranging nature as the USSFTA — is a time-consuming and tough job. However, the work does not end on the signing of the FTA. Once, the FTA has been signed, the two sides need to work out its implementation within the agreed time-frame.

On the Singapore side, I was landed the job of overseeing the implementation work as Chairman of the USSFTA Inter-Ministry Committee on Implementation (USSFTA IMC on Implementation). We completed the non-IPR implementation work by 31 December 2003 in time for the USSFTA to enter into force on 1 January 2004.

The implementation work for the IPR chapter is massive and requires a change to much of our IPR legislation, additional legislation in new areas and new enforcement arrangements. I am currently chairing a separate inter-ministry committee (USSFTA IMC on Implementation — IPR) to complete this aspect of the work — part of which must be completed by 1 July 2004 and the remainder by 1 January 2005.

---

[4] Refer to Appendix VI for a list of the groups.

HOW DO WE ENSURE COMPLIANCE?

Both the U.S. and Singapore have undertaken a variety of obligations under the USSFTA. Each side expects the other to live up to its commitments. If we are to achieve this, there needs to be a common understanding of what the commitments require, a process to pre-empt and facilitate any problems and a mechanism to deal with situations where efforts at avoidance of a dispute have been unsuccessful and one side seeks a remedy for damages to its trade interests arising from the acts or omissions of the other.

THE JOINT COMMITTEE

A Joint Committee of government officials, chaired by the United States Trade Representative and Singapore's Minister for Trade and Industry, or their designated representatives, is set up under the USSFTA. It has the broad mandate to review the trade relationship between the parties. Specifically, it can, *inter alia*, review the general functioning of the FTA, issue interpretations in relation to it and facilitate the avoidance and settlement of disputes under it. Hopefully, the Committee will be able to assist in sorting out problems and avoid their developing into disputes.

THE DISPUTE SETTLEMENT PROCESS

What happens if the efforts of the Joint Committee at avoiding a dispute do not succeed? The dispute settlement process has then to be resorted to. This is discussed below.

Disputes to which the Dispute Settlement Mechanism Applies

The dispute settlement mechanism under Chapter 20 of the USSFTA will apply[5] to the following kinds of disputes:

   a. a measure inconsistent with the obligations under the USSFTA is sought to be implemented;

   b. one side has otherwise failed to carry out its obligations;

   c. a benefit which one party[6] could have expected to accrue to it under certain chapters of the USSFTA is being "nullified or impaired" as a result of a measure that is inconsistent with the USSFTA.

It will be noted that the circumstances in which the dispute settlement process can be resorted to are broad — the objective being to cover all possible situations. However, the basic idea is that the process can be used if there is a breach of an obligation ("violation") or the loss of a reasonably expected benefit ("non-violation").

Where a fact situation gives rise to a dispute which can fall under the USSFTA, the World Trade Organization (WTO) Agreement or any other agreement to which both countries are parties, the complaining country has the option to select the forum in which to settle the dispute. Once selected, the forum selected is to be used to the exclusion of other possible fora.

---

[5] The dispute settlement mechanism under Chapter 20 will apply to the chapter on Financial Services (Chapter 10) and the chapter on the Temporary Entry of Business Persons (Chapter 11) as modified by those chapters (see Arts 10.8, 10.9 and 11.8 of the USSFTA).

[6] The term "party" is used in this article to refer to Singapore or the U.S. Sometimes the inter-changeable term "country" is used. The term "parties" refers to both countries jointly.

Consultations

The first step in resolving a dispute is for the parties to do so through consultations. Under the USSFTA the consultation process can be used not only to settle a dispute but also in relation to any matter which a party considers might affect the operation of the USSFTA. Consultations are to be initiated by the delivery of a written notification to the designated office of the other side.

Each party is to respond, without delay, to requests for consultations and afford adequate opportunity for it. Consultations are to be entered into in good faith and each side is to maintain the confidentiality of any documents exchanged during the consultations. Businesses would find this reassuring when they are connected with a dispute which involves confidential information. If the consultations are successful, the dispute can be taken to have been resolved.

The Joint Committee's Assistance

In the event that the consultations do not succeed in resolving the dispute within 60 days of the delivery of the request for consultations, either party may, through a written notification, refer the dispute to the Joint Committee. The Joint Committee has to try its best to find a solution.

The reference of a dispute to the Joint Committee provides a second opportunity for the parties to attempt to resolve the dispute directly and informally in an amiable fashion.

Public Views

Trade issues do not only involve the Government. They also impact on businesses, the livelihood of workers and the public in general. Accordingly, the USSFTA requires both sides to seek and consider the views of members of the public when a request for consultations is made or received. There is also provision for requests from non-governmental bodies to provide written views during the hearing by a panel. The idea is to take into account the views of all those affected and draw upon a broad range of perspectives in arriving at a solution.

Dispute Settlement Panel

If the Joint Committee does not resolve a dispute within 60 days of the referral of the dispute to it or within any extended period agreed upon by the parties, the complaining party may refer the dispute to a dispute settlement panel of three members.

Each party is to appoint one member of the panel within 30 days of a matter that has been referred to a panel. The chairman of the panel is to be appointed by agreement of the parties.

If a party fails to appoint a panelist or the parties are unable to agree on a chairman within 30 days after the date on which the second panelist has been appointed, the panelist or a chairman, as the case may be, shall be selected by lot from a contingent list. The contingent list consists of a list of individuals, agreed upon by the two countries, who are willing and able to serve as panelists or chairpersons.

An effective dispute settlement mechanism requires competent and impartial adjudicators. The USSFTA seeks to achieve this objective by requiring panelists and chairpersons to: have the expertise or experience in law, international trade or the resolution of disputes arising under international trade agreements; and be independent of and not be affiliated with or take instructions from either country and comply with a code of conduct to be established by the Joint Committee.

Report of Panel

A dispute settlement panel is to complete its initial report containing findings of fact and the determination of the question referred to it within 150 days (unless the parties have otherwise agreed) after the chairman has been appointed. The panel may also, at the request of the parties, make recommendations for the resolution of the dispute.

After considering any written comments by either side on the initial report, the panel may modify its report and make any further examination it considers appropriate. The panel is to provide the final report to the parties within 45 days of presentation of the initial report, unless the parties have agreed otherwise. Shortly thereafter, the final report is to be released to the public, subject to the protection of confidential information.

Implementation of Report

On receipt of a panel's final report the parties are to agree on the resolution of the dispute. This will normally involve conforming with the determinations and recommendations, if any, of the panel. In the event that a determination is that a party is not conforming to its obligation or its measure is causing nullification or impairment, the resolution, wherever possible, will be to eliminate the non-conformity or the nullification or impairment.

Non-Implementation : Compensation and Retaliation

If the two sides are unable to reach an agreement on a resolution of the dispute by eliminating the non-conformity or the nullification or impairment, the party complained against is to enter into negotiations with a view to developing mutually acceptable compensation. If it has not been possible to agree on compensation or if the complaining party considers that the other party has failed to observe the agreed terms of a resolution of the dispute, the complaining party may, following a 30-day notice to the other side that it intends to do so, retaliate by suspending benefits of equivalent effect to the other party.

Benefits are not to be suspended if the party complained against provides written notice of its intent that it will pay an annual monetary assessment. If the parties are unable to reach an agreement on the amount of assessment, it will be set at a level, in U.S. dollars, equal to 50 percent of the level of benefits determined by the panel to be of equivalent effect, or if the panel has not determined the level, 50 percent of the level that the complaining party has proposed to suspend.

Non-Implementation in Labour and Environmental Matters

Suspension of benefits will not apply in cases of non-conformity as to regards the application and enforcement of labour and environmental laws. In such cases, if the parties are unable to reach an agreement on a resolution of the dispute following a panel determination or have agreed on resolution but the complaining party considers that the other side has failed to observe the terms of the agreement, the complaining party may request the reconvening of the panel to impose an annual monetary assessment on the other party.

Assessments are to be paid into a fund established by the Joint Committee and are to be expended, at the direction of the Joint Committee, for appropriate labour and environmental initiatives. If the party complained against fails to pay a monetary assessment, it may be recovered from its escrow account failing which the complaining party may take other steps, including suspending tariff benefits, as necessary, to collect the assessment.

Compliance Review

If a party complained against considers that it has eliminated the non-conformity or the nullification of impairment that a panel has found, it may refer the matter to the relevant panel. If the panel agrees with the position of the party complained against, the complaining party must immediately reinstate any benefits it has suspended and the party complained against shall no longer be required to pay any monetary compensation.

Section III
Getting the FTA through Congress

16 Lobbying for the United States-Singapore Free Trade Agreement

CHAN Heng Chee[1]

There are essentially three benchmark phases in the successful completion of a comprehensive bilateral Free Trade Agreement (FTA) with the United States. The crucial first step is the indispensable political decision by the two countries to negotiate a FTA. For the United States-Singapore Free Trade Agreement (USSFTA), that decision came surprisingly and swiftly, at a golf game between United States President William Clinton and Singapore Prime Minister Goh Chok Tong, on the margins of the APEC Summit in Bandar Seri Begawan, Brunei on 15 November 2000. President George W. Bush took up the project shortly after he came into office. Many countries invest enormous energy and time to convince the United States to buy into the concept. It may take years or a major political event to focus attention and priority on the issue. The United States as a country is not predisposed to signing

---

[1] Chan Heng Chee is Singapore's Ambassador to the United States. She has served as Permanent Representative to the United Nations and concurrently as High Commissioner to Canada and Ambassador to Mexico. She took up her post as Ambassador to the United States in July 1996. Ambassador Chan was Founder Director of the Insititute of Policy Studies and Director of the Institute of Southeast Asian Studies. She was also Founder Executive Director of the Singapore International Foundation. Ambassador Chan served as a Member of the International Advisory Board of the Council of Foreign Relations, New York; the Council of International Institute for Strategic Studies (IISS), London; and the International Council of the Asia Society. She is an author of several articles and books on politics in Singapore, Southeast Asia and international security. The views expressed in this article are those of the author and do not necessarily represent the views of the Singapore Government.

bilateral free trade agreements. Until the year 2000, the United States had signed only two Free Trade Agreements, one being North American Free Trade Agreement (NAFTA) and the other was the U.S.-Israel Free Trade Agreement. The second step is the negotiations phase which could take many rounds of trade talks. For the USSFTA, there were 11 rounds of talks and several intersessional meetings and video conferencing. The eleventh and final round concluded on 11–19 November 2002 in Singapore. Negotiations on the last sticking issue — capital controls — carried on through December and January 2003. President Bush sent a letter to the House of Representatives and Senate on 30 January 2003 informing Congress of his intention to sign the Agreement, thus signalling the end of the formal negotiations. Thus began the third and final phase, which was lobbying for the passage of the USSFTA in the House of Representatives and the Senate.

Lobbying is "Made in America" and a finely developed art. It is a political activity born of necessity because of the structure of the American political system. The American political system is built on the principle of "separation of powers" and the philosophical premise that the foundation of democratic governance is the arbitration of competing interests. *The Federalist Papers*[2] did not contain the term "lobby", but James Madison in Federalist No. 10 recognised the existence of interests and their interplay as self-checking. Federalist No. 43 described the legislative task as providing "umpires" for clashing disputes. The term "lobby agent" was British and used to refer to men who hung outside the public

---

[2] *The Federalist Papers* is a series of 85 essays written by Alexander Hamilton, John Jay, and James Madison between October 1787 and May 1788. The essays were published anonymously. These papers were written and published to urge New Yorkers to ratify the proposed United States Constitution, which was drafted in Philadelphia in the summer of 1787. In lobbying for adoption of the Constitution over the existing Articles of Confederation, the essays explain particular provisions of the Constitution in detail. *The Federalist Papers* are often used today to help interpret the intentions of those drafting the Constitution. See http://memory.loc.gov/const/fed/abt_fedpapers.html.

room in Parliament. It was first used in 1820 in the New York State. But lobbying became something totally expanded and different in the United States. With the separation of powers between Congress and the Executive, it was necessary to ensure that support existed in both branches of the government to pass a bill. Congressmen and Senators in the United States enjoy total autonomy and independence, as America's government is not based on a Cabinet Government or Party Government of the Westminster model. The concept of party discipline or party responsibility is weak when it comes to the legislative process. Elected representatives are more inclined to vote according to constituency interests and personal principles than by what the party leader or party whip recommends. In a highly partisan Washington today and during tight votes, party leaders and whips apply persuasion and pressure and horse-trade for greater party discipline. To "lobby" for those not familiar with the system is to make one's case with people who have the authority of power to affect the issue of your concern. In the United States, they could be members of the Administration, Congress, Business and Media.

If the responsibility for the trade negotiations lay primarily in the hands of the negotiating team in Singapore led by Chief Negotiator Ambassador Tommy Koh, lobbying was the primary responsibility of the Singapore Embassy in Washington. Where there were bottlenecks, it was often necessary for the Embassy to help clear the path and try out the compromises that both sides could agree on — e.g., chewing gum, capital controls and competition. Similarly, complementary lobbying was mounted from Singapore by Ministers and members of the negotiating team when relevant American players visited the Republic.

GETTING THE ELEMENTS IN PLACE

In preparation for the lobbying phase of the FTA, the Singapore Embassy in Washington in a USSFTA lobby strategy paper drafted in January 2002 recognised, right from the start, the importance of a Business Coalition mobilising support for the FTA and identifying a group of Singapore supporters in Congress for the ultimate purpose of Congressional lobbying. It would be important to establish a USSFTA Business Coalition and a Singapore Congressional Caucus. The paper also recommended promoting visits of Congressmen, Senators and Staffers to Singapore to help them to understand Singapore's situation. The Business Coalition and the Congressional Caucus were to be the main pillars of the lobby plan. They are natural advocates with Congress and the Administration. Business is a natural ally of free trade, although there are some who oppose free trade. In the U.S. political system, American corporations, small and medium businesses, trade associations and business associations have enormous experience and are repositories of knowledge on the mood of Congress and the legislative predispositions of individual Congressmen and Senators. They have the ear of elected representatives because these are businesses operating in their electoral districts or state and they provide jobs for the people. They may also be financial contributors to the elected representative's election campaign. Business Coalitions have been formed to fight for the North American Free Trade Agreement (NAFTA) and Permanent Normal Trading Relations (PNTR). Business swung into action to support Trade Promotion Authority (TPA). Business Coalitions are independent and they act in their own interests, but they work closely with Embassies.

The Singapore Embassy took the initiative to invite a few leading American corporations with a presence in Singapore and business interest in Southeast Asia to a brainstorming discussion on the formation of a USSFTA Business Coalition. The American companies embraced the idea immediately and chose from among themselves three co-Chairs — Boeing, ExxonMobil and UPS — to lead the Coalition. It was their job to recruit other U.S. companies with an interest in Singapore and the bilateral FTA into the coalition. In the first year of the USSFTA Business Coalition, it signed on over

50 U.S. multinational companies (MNCs) and smaller firms. By the time the FTA was completed in December 2003, the Coalition grew to over 114 companies, industry associations and other organisations. (See Appendix III.)

The U.S.-ASEAN Business Council (USABC) and the United States Chamber of Commerce signed on as members of the Business Coalition. The USABC represents American Fortune 500 MNCs with interests in Southeast Asia and has taken the lead in promoting the ASEAN countries in Washington. It was appointed the Secretariat of the Business Coalition. The strength of the U.S. Chamber of Commerce lay in its network of Chambers of Commerce throughout the United States. The Chamber played a major role in NAFTA and in the annual rounds of fights for MFN status — later NTR and PNTR — for China. USABC has a close relationship with the major MNCs and the Administration. The Chamber works the Hill.

The advice and support of the USSFTA Business Coalition was invaluable to our negotiations and lobbying efforts. A dynamic relationship with the Business Coalition contributed to arriving at a better agreement. Frequently, they helped to untie some of the knots produced in the trade negotiations. When U.S. trade negotiators pushed a trade principle in the interest of purity or ideology, the Business Coalition's practical reactions gave a sense of what the market would bear. More importantly, the Administration was more likely to give in to their demands than to the Singapore negotiators. Their interventions at certain critical moments helped to resolve some sticking points. Their role in the lobbying efforts in the final months with Congress was absolutely crucial and will be dealt with later.

The establishment of the Congressional Caucus was made easier when Congressmen Solomon Ortiz, a Democrat for Texas, on a Congressional Delegation (CODEL) visit to Singapore told PM Goh Chok Tong that he was quite amenable to convening a Singapore Caucus as he believed in the USSFTA and appreciated Singapore's strong defence co-operation with the United States. Ortiz had come to know Singapore as a member of the House Armed Services Committee. His interest in Singapore stemmed from Singapore Technologies and Keppel-FELS' significant investments in his district which provided jobs for his constituents. Ortiz asked Curt Weldon, a Republican Congressman from Pennsylvania, to take on the role of the Republican Co-Chair in the Caucus. Once the two men agreed, Ortiz's office helped to recruit Congressmen as members of the Caucus. The Embassy made calls on Congressmen and staffers to urge them to sign on as Caucus members. The official launch of the Congressional Caucus took place in the Capitol on 8 October 2002. The Caucus as conceived was not trade-specific and was expected to last beyond the USSFTA. At the time of the launch more than 30 Congressmen from the House of Representatives had signed on. There were more Democrats than Republicans on the list, but that was not troubling because traditionally, it was more difficult to get Democrats to vote for trade. Recruiting Democrats early could be helpful. Approaching the Congressmen to join the Caucus gave us an opportunity to speak to them or their staffers on the FTA in progress. We were fortuitous in picking the right Co-Chair in Solomon Ortiz whose office worked tirelessly to build the Caucus. By January 2004 the Caucus had grown to 56 members, an astonishing large number for a small country. (See Appendix II.) A USSFTA Task Force was created within Congress headed by Congressman Pete Sessions (Republican-Texas) and Solomon Ortiz. Sessions and Ortiz were picked by the House Republican and House Democratic leaderships to see through the FTA. It was a good sign, especially on the Democratic side as it was an early signal that the Democrats would not fight the vote.

The Caucus aside, it was crucial to keep Congressional staff and Congressmen and Senators briefed on the developments in the FTA negotiations throughout. No one likes surprises and Congress expects to be briefed. Failure to maintain this process could end up with the FTA mired in the Committee or a negative vote because concerns were not addressed along the way. The most important players in Congress for the USSFTA were the staff and elected members of the House Ways and Means Committee which handles trade matters and introduces trade legislation. The Subcommittee on Trade in the Ways and Means Committee clears the first hurdle by examining the FTA and amending it for passage before sending it before the full Committee for passage. Only then is the bill introduced before the House. We maintained a good relationship with the Republican Chairman of the Ways and Means Committee William Thomas and the Democratic Ranking Member Charlie Rangel. Within the Trade Subcommittee we met with Republican Congressman Phil Crane and Democratic Congressman Sander Levin regularly. The Senate Finance Committee and its Subcommittee on International Trade were directly involved in the FTA. Republican Senator Chuck Grassley from Iowa was supportive of trade as was Ranking Democratic Senator Max Baucus. The Embassy enjoys a warm relationship with both Senators and their staff. In addition to these key committees in the House and Senate, there were others which impacted on the passage of the FTA. In the House, the Rules Committee played a critical role in timing the introduction of the FTA bill on the House Legislative Agenda. The House Energy and Commerce Committee and the House Judiciary Committee were also important players as each examined areas of the FTA which impinged on their jurisdiction. In the Senate, their equivalent committees, the Senate Commerce, Science and Transportation Committee and the Judiciary Committee took an active interest in the FTA. In fact, every committee in the House and the Senate took up sections of the FTA of relevance to their committee. We found that Members might hold intersecting Committee memberships. For example, a Member might be a member of the Financial Services Committee and the Armed Services or International Relations Committee Membership. Reaching out to appeal to their defence and foreign policy responsibilities and interests may positively colour their perception of the FTA from the Financial Services perspectives. Hence our lobbying effort was both extensive and intensive.

Starting in 2001, the Singapore Embassy stepped up efforts to arrange CODEL and Staffers' Delegation (STAFFDEL) visits to Singapore. CODELs are paid for by the United States Government to bring Congressmen and Senators to a foreign country. CODELs are targetted and issue-related. Elected Members who seek clarification on a specific issue in the FTA would be interested in taking the trip. Sometimes it helps a Congressman or Senator explain to his/her constituency why he/she is supporting the USSFTA. As explained earlier, CODELs need not be related to trade to win congressional support. Singapore's strong defence and security co-operation with the U.S. brought the Senate and Home Armed Services Committee members to see the facilities for themselves. Some had an interest in counter-terrorism and chose to come to Singapore. In addition to CODELs, Singapore think-tanks and the Singapore International Foundation sponsored visits of the American legislators. The same was true of STAFFDELs which are visits by the staffers who work for the Congressmen or Senators. Visits by staffers are particularly useful as they prepare position papers for their principals. The Embassy targeted Congressmen and Senators from the key committees. Interest in such visits peaked in 2002 and 2003 when the FTA was in its final rounds and just before the vote. Of the seven Congressmen who split their votes on the Singapore and Chile FTAs in favour of Singapore, three had visited Singapore — Congressman Paul Gillmor (Republican-Ohio), Congressman Cliff Sterns (Republican-Florida) and Congressman Lloyd Dogget (Democrat-Texas).

One of the issues we had to decide on early was whether for the lobbying exercise, Singapore would employ a lobbying firm. Lobbyists are ubiquitous in Washington and are a feature of the political process. The Singapore Embassy decided in the end to hire a boutique firm rather than approach one of the major big name lobby firms. We had done most of the work of forming the Business Coalition and the Congressional Caucus, and all the members of the Embassy from the Ambassador to Deputy Chief of Mission to every

First Secretary had been keeping good contact with Congress. We are generally a Do-It-Yourself (DIY) Embassy. A boutique firm met our requirements with a right price, close contact and access. Fontheim Associates was useful in the process, helping us interpret arcane trade legislation and introducing us to the leaders of the Blue Dog Democrats, or trade friendly Democrats.

LOBBYING FOR THE FTA

Once USTR put out a Federal Register notice in 2001 to invite interested parties to provide inputs on the USSFTA, we strongly encouraged industry and business contacts to write in support of the FTA. We were fully expecting negative letters from the usual anti-trade quarters. American MNCs operating in Singapore was one of our most enthusiastic sources of support. American Corporations based in the United States were also supportive. Unexpectedly we were successful in securing letters of support from Governor Frank O'Bannon of Indiana, Governor Gary Locke of Washington state, Governor Mike Johanns of Nebraska, Governor Mike Easley of North Carolina, Governor Michael Leavitt of Utah and Governor Linda Lingle of Hawaii. The Secretary of Commerce of California under Governor Gray Davies, Lon Hatamiya, wrote to USTR declaring California's support.

The laser beam focus came in the second half of 2002 and remained in place till the passage of the FTA. Early in 2002 we drew up a Congressional Map and systematically assigned each of our diplomatic officers to contact different staffers to ascertain their concerns and their likely voting positions. I had the task of reaching out to Congressmen and Senators. We returned to the Map to check and correct the information as we updated their positions over the months running up to the vote. There are 100 Senators and 435 Congressmen. Ideally, we should touch base with every elected representative. It was, however, possible to leave aside Congressmen and Senators who never supported a trade vote in their entire careers because of the district or state they represent. The energy spent on rallying for their support would be wasted. Elected representatives with strong unions in their states or districts do not vote for trade because unions and workers associate free trade with a loss of jobs for Americans. Sensitive sectors in the U.S. such as textiles and steel also force their representatives to become protectionist and reject FTAs.

Our lobbying was not simply targetted at the Hill. It was multi pronged and directed at the strategic players in industry, business and media and the think-tanks at the same time. MTI sent an officer who was one of the negotiators during the 11 rounds to join the Embassy team. With the staff from International Enterprise Singapore (IES) in Washington, they met American trade and industry associations to brief them on the provisions of the FTA and the merits of the agreement pertaining to their specific interests. Altogether they conducted 20 briefing sessions in the east and west coast of the United States and the mid-west. Media represented by the main trade journals and newspapers such as *Journal of Commerce*, *Washington Trade Daily* and *Inside USA Trade*, and Hill publications such as the *National Journal* were useful channels for our views and gave the FTA publicity. The news agencies were given full briefings at different stages of the closing negotiations. Every speaking opportunity, seminar and forum was made use of, at think-tanks such as Centre of Strategic and International Studies (CSIS) and the Institute for International Economics (IIE), the Chamber of Commerce, the USABC and Progressive Policy Institute.

Singapore's political leaders played their part too. Prime Minister Goh Chok Tong who started the ball rolling in 2000, in his visit to the Oval Office to meet President Bush in May 2001, gently nudged the FTA along. He tabled our interest and sought support from the House and Senate members. Deputy Prime Minister Lee Hsien Loong and Deputy Prime Minister Tony Tan in their visits to Washington kept the subject at the front and centre of their meetings with Hill members and business leaders. Minister of Trade and

Industry George Yeo made regular visits in 2001, 2002 and 2003 to speak about the USSFTA. He met with the Administration and dealt with USTR Robert Zoellick. They talked over the broader approaches and how to deal with the really difficult issues. He also met often with House Ways and Means members and especially the Trade Subcommittee and the Senate Finance Committee. The high level lobbying by the Ministers was particularly important. It registered with Congressional members that we took their views and concerns seriously and our political leaders would take the trouble to come to Washington personally to meet with them.

Interest in the FTA picked up rapidly once the negotiations concluded and President Bush notified Congress of his intention to sign the Agreement. Then Congress, business, industry, the NGOs and labour were eager to find out more about the provisions. We needed to get our perspectives and explanations across. The reality of Washington is the competition for the attention of the lawmakers and everyone else. This time it was the impending Iraq war. Fortunately trade staffers were not the same individuals handling foreign policy and security. Embassy resources were stretched covering the Iraq war, as every Embassy in the capital was compelled to do, as well as pumping up support for the FTA.

The most intensive lobbying took place from May to July 2003. It was impossible to tell with certainty when the USSFTA vote would be scheduled in the House and Senate. There were educated guesses dependent on the timing of Committee hearings. Eventually the House of Representatives voted on 24 July. The USSFTA was passed with a 272–155 votes. Senate voted on 31 July and the USSFTA was passed by a comfortable 66–31 votes. The votes were considered to be very significant support for the FTA given that trade votes are generally tight. NAFTA was passed by 234–200 in the House. The Senate vote was 61–38. PNTR for China (May 2000) was passed 237–197 in the House and 83-15 in the Senate (September 2000). The TPA vote (July 2002) was 215–212 in the House and 63–34 in the Senate (August 2002).

WHY WERE THE RESULTS SO POSITIVE?

The answer is simple. Firstly, we had a high-standard trade agreement, a good product to sell. Singapore is also considered a country with high standards of transparency, openness, rule of law and high labour standards. This was an important point and it came up in our conversations with the legislators and with the business support. NGOs did not seem as hard on us. Secondly, the lobbying exercise was effective.

Our lobbying was effective because firstly, it was a comprehensive and well-coordinated strategy, and the Embassy was a well-coordinated team. The Ambassador was in overall charge providing the broad directions. The Deputy Chief of Mission was responsible for the nuts and bolts coordination. Every member of the Embassy team added his or her insights and knowledge to build up a winning game plan. Our strategy covered all players at all levels — the Administration and its different agencies (which may have different views from USTR), the Senate, the House of Representatives, State Governors, industry, business, NGOs, media, think-tanks, labour unions and the exporting states to Singapore, a recognition of the pluralism and diffusion of power and influence in the American political process. Critical to our success was the seamless coordination with the Business Coalition. Where we could not gain access, we asked them to knock on the doors of the lawmaker. Where they thought the Ambassador's call would make a difference, they pushed us in that direction. The Business Coalition had been in this game before. They knew what to do.

Secondly, our outreach was early, deep and wide. The Embassy tried to reach as many of the legislators as we possibly could even during the negotiation stage. In the end the Embassy team on our own met personally with 353 of the 435 members of the House of Representatives or their staff and 78 of the 100 Senators or their staff. The Ambassador invited Congressmen and Senators to dinners and lunches at the residence in groups of five or six at a time, sometimes larger, to discuss the FTA in depth. When Cabinet Ministers visited Washington, they too engaged in this gentle lobbying over a social meal. Similar dinners were hosted for staffers to enable them to raise key issues with us.

Thirdly, the message was important, so was the messenger. Visits to the offices of the Senators and House of Representatives proved absolutely essential. The House is more unpredictable. Senators generally are more supportive of trade. We learnt that it was important to address the specific concerns of the Congressmen and Senators, and the manner of communication could win or lose the vote.

Fourthly, we defused issues early to avoid their emergence as major road blocks for the Agreement. The issues could emerge from anywhere. It could come from the think-tanks, NGOs, industry or Congress. This happened in the case of Integrated Sourcing Initiative (ISI), chewing gum, services, labour and environment, to name a few examples. The Embassy was pro-active early to explain the Singapore situation to potential detractors. For instance, our early engagement of the AFL-CIO was important. Minister of Trade and Industry George Yeo and the Ambassador met with John Sweeney. With our mix of a good environment and labour track record, no textiles and no steel, and strong Congressional support, AFL-CIO did not fight the USSFTA as hard as they normally would do.

Fifthly, we learned that where there was opposition to the USSFTA from Senators or Congressmen, the reason could have nothing to do with Singapore but arose from partisan politics, or a matter of principled disagreement. Some Democratic Congressmen and Senators told us that they were disinclined to support the FTA because the Administration had not consulted with Congress sufficiently over many issues. Senator Diane Feinstein (Democrat-California), a pro-trade senator who is supportive of Singapore, generally did not vote for the FTA because she objected to the fact that USTR "slipped" in the 5,400 H1-B visas into the Agreement. She argued that immigration issues was the Senate's prerogative and the visa issue was an usurpation of the Senate's power. There were also many Congressmen and Senators who had wanted labour and environment to be made more central to the free trade agreement, such as introducing trade sanctions for violations of labour and environment standards. In such instances, we accepted their positions and asked them to add in their Debate Statements that they supported Singapore but not the FTA for their principled reasons. Quite a few graciously did that.

Lobbying for the USSFTA took place at a time of the strongest bilateral ties between the United States and Singapore. It was never more evident than at this crunch time that Singapore's brand name, so carefully and assiduously grown during the country's short history, was a helpful and powerful selling point.

17 What I Learnt from the U.S. Business Community

NEO Gim Huay[1]

ADVOCATES FOR THE ECONOMICS OF FREER TRADE

The U.S. business community was one of the first to respond when news emanated on 16 November 2000 from Brunei Darussalam, host for the 8th APEC Economic Leaders' Meeting, that U.S. President Bill Clinton and Singapore Prime Minister Goh Chok Tong had agreed to launch negotiations for a U.S.-Singapore Free Trade Agreement (USSFTA).

Sixteen business associations including the U.S.-ASEAN Business Council, the National Association of Manufacturers and the Business Roundtable, signed a letter to President Clinton two weeks later, on 29 November 2000 to support the President's decision to launch negotiations on an FTA with Singapore. However, at the same time, it exhorted the Administration to

---

[1] During the USSFTA negotiations, Neo Gim Huay was the Deputy Director for Trade in the Ministry of Trade and Industry. She coordinated the negotiations among the Singapore agencies and worked with the Chief Negotiator Tommy Koh and his deputy Ong Ye Kung to resolve the key policy issues under the USSFTA. When the negotiations were concluded in December 2002, Neo was posted to the Singapore Embassy in Washington D.C. to assist Ambassador Chan Heng Chee and her embassy officials to build support among the U.S. businesses and Congress for the USSFTA. Prior to her posting in the Ministry of Trade and Industry, Neo worked in the Scenario Planning Office of the Prime Minister's Office and Singapore Airlines Pte Ltd. She is currently with the Ministry of Finance. The views expressed in this article are those of the author and do not necessarily represent the views of the Singapore Government.

"undertake meaningful efforts to dialogue regularly with interested parties as the talks unfold", urged the officials not to be "distracted by an artificial time constraint of one month" — the Singapore and U.S. governments had agreed to endeavour to conclude negotiations before the end of the year — and to "focus on the content of this important agreement".

It was a cautionary note from the business community that politics ought not to override the substance in the FTA negotiations — that while the former may have been the catalyst, economic substance had to be the driver. It was an important piece of advice that negotiators on both sides took heed to. And fortunately so — without which we would have lost a valuable opportunity to push the envelope of trade liberalisation in our respective regimes and reap concrete benefits for our businesses.

PURSUING COMMERCIAL AND STRATEGIC INTERESTS

U.S. business interests in the FTA were very much driven by both commercial and strategic considerations. Although Singapore's tariffs on U.S. products are already zero with very few exceptions, the USSFTA was an opportunity for the U.S. business community to enhance market access in Singapore in the area of services, particularly the financial and professional services, as well as to strengthen Singapore's policies in the areas of transparency and competition. U.S. business interests in Singapore are not trivial. Unknown to many, despite its small size, Singapore is the 11th largest trading partner of the U.S. Outside of Mexico and Canada, bilateral trade between Singapore and the U.S. exceeds the U.S.'s trade with all its present FTA partners, such as Central America, Australia and Chile. Singapore is also the largest services market for the U.S. in Southeast Asia and the 6th largest in the whole of Asia.

The U.S. business community also seized the opportunity of the FTA to remove barriers in their own home market. 62 percent of U.S.-Singapore trade comprises of intra-MNC trade, which means that much of the tariff savings that the U.S. will offer under the FTA will accrue to the U.S. companies based in Singapore. The outcome of the FTA is thus a win-win. It creates a home away from home in Singapore for U.S. companies who wish to internationalise or outsource their operations to the Asian region. At the same time, it strengthens Singapore's attractiveness as a manufacturing and investment base for U.S. companies.

Strategically, some businesses also saw the USSFTA as a potential pathfinder in forging consensus in emerging areas of trade, such as e-commerce and intellectual property protection. Prior to Singapore, the first as well as the only substantial FTA that the U.S. had negotiated was under the framework of the North American Free Trade Area (NAFTA) with Mexico and Canada more than ten years ago (the other FTAs that the U.S. has entered into are with Israel and Jordan). There have been many changes in the global trade front since then, as a result of technology and globalisation developments, that NAFTA did not address.

Tactically, re-opening discussions in NAFTA was not a preferred choice for these businesses because it might have opened old wounds, unsettling the carefully balanced consensus that had been struck among the three governments — Canada, Mexico and the U.S. — and their huge and diverse base of constituencies. With 146 members and the need to take into account the differing needs, political interests and stages of development of each of its member economies, the World Trade Organization (WTO) was also inappropriate as a forum to address new issues. Rather, it was more effective to form caucuses of like-minded economies through bilateral and regional trade agreements to advance the global trade liberalisation agenda.

To them, Singapore was an ideal partner to examine these issues in greater detail — with a domestic polity that enjoys strong consensus on liberal economic policies and bureaucrats known for their hard-headed analysis and careful deliberations in policy making. The Singapore economy, a relatively advanced economy in transition from a developing to a developed economy, would also be appropriate as a test bed for policy innovations in the New Economy. For certain U.S. businesses, their longer-term strategic goal was to duplicate and adapt the FTA template to be forged between Singapore and the U.S. to other regional and multilateral fora, such as APEC and the WTO. This ambitious order from the U.S. business community became the negotiating backdrop for the officials in the two-year long FTA discussions.

ACTIVE PLAYERS IN THE NEGOTIATIONS

The U.S. business community played a very active role in the negotiations. They sought regular briefings from both U.S. and Singapore officials and monitored progress closely, constantly adding pressure on both sides to expedite the negotiations. During one of my trips to Washington mid-way through the negotiations, my colleagues from International Enterprise Singapore (IE Singapore) arranged for me to meet with Bob Vastine, President of the Coalition of Service Industries. Vastine asked me about the progress of the financial services negotiations. At that time, we had not made much progress and I stated so matter-of-factly — the U.S. was taking time with its inter-agency consultations and had yet to put forward its proposal. Not long after, my colleague in the Monetary Authority of Singapore (MAS) told me that the U.S. had forwarded its proposal to Singapore. I have not had the opportunity to verify this, but I half suspect that my meeting with Vastine had something to do with it.

Besides pacing the progress of the negotiations, the U.S. business community was invaluable in contributing to the richness of the discussions and the robustness of the eventual agreement. They effectively advocated their industry interests and actively lobbied the governments from both sides on their positions. I was once asked to comment on and compare the negotiating skills of the U.S. and Singapore officials. My reply was that the best negotiators are in neither the U.S. nor Singapore governments. They reside with the U.S. business representatives in Washington D.C.!

Indeed, many of these business representatives have had many years of experience — lobbying their own governments as well as foreign governments, persuading think-tanks and other non-governmental organizations to their positions and sparring with industry partners on issues where their interests do not coincide. U.S. businesses are not homogeneous. Their interests vary and sometimes oppose one another. For example, within the U.S. textiles industry, while the manufacturers may advocate more restrictive rules of origin (this refers to the rules that determine whether a good is made in Singapore and can enjoy preferential tariff treatment under the USSFTA) to shield itself from foreign competition, the retailers would inevitably favour more liberal rules of origin and the removal of barriers in the U.S. market to facilitate their sourcing and importing of goods from Singapore.

PROFESSIONALS IN THE BUSINESS OF NEGOTIATIONS

For the negotiations, the U.S. business representatives were not shy in expressing their business interests to the officials. Rather, they lobbied both governments, hired consultants to champion their interests and where possible, forged allies to strengthen their positions. Singapore soon learned the art of the game and, with the help of our embassy in Washington D.C., joined hands with the U.S. business groups, whose interests were aligned to ours, to help persuade the U.S. officials to our point of view.

In many ways, negotiating an FTA is not different from policy making — one needs to balance and accommodate the interests of different groups, while bearing in mind the larger objective, which is, in the case of the FTA, that of driving towards higher trade liberalisation and facilitation standards. However, the FTA process can be very much more complicated than domestic policy making because you have to understand, balance and address the needs of not just your own constituencies but that of your partner's as well. Once two countries agree to negotiate an FTA, it is almost akin to two individuals agreeing to partner each other in a three-legged race. You watch the pace of your partner and prod him along, in order to help yourself move forward.

Trust and understanding are, in my view, the most critical elements in any successful negotiation. They affect and determine how willing the other party is prepared to accommodate your sensitivities and needs and to moderate his positions for a win-win outcome. For the U.S. negotiations, we had to negotiate not just with U.S. officials, but also with its businesses and non-government associations. This means that Singapore had to establish trust and understanding with U.S. officials as well as with its constituencies. Our close relations with the U.S. business community was not formed overnight but had been built up over time and carefully nurtured, through regular meetings, informal gatherings and casual meals. Our embassy in Washington D.C. and our economic agencies based in the U.S. were instrumental in laying this foundation.

In my various trips to Washington D.C., I have always found my interactions with U.S. business representatives an enjoyable affair. In my view, they are professionals in the business of negotiations — they scrutinise every development, understand their own interests and are relentless in pursuing them. Equally, they are also always prepared to listen and to understand the constraints of their counterpart and to propose creative solutions for which both sides may have their specific needs addressed.

The issue of illegal transhipments through the Singapore port to the U.S. was one of the hotly debated subjects in the FTA. One of the strongest advocates for tighter port control came from Eric Smith, President of the International Intellectual Property Alliance. At a meeting I had with him in Washington D.C., Smith recalled how the intellectual property companies were suffering huge losses from pirated products that had been illegally shipped into the United States. Given that Singapore was one of the world's biggest transhipment ports, could we do something about it? I explained the constraints of our port operations and how the sheer volume of transhipment cargo passing through would make physical inspection difficult, if not impossible. The wrong enforcement approach would impede legitimate trade and force the shippers elsewhere. Singapore understood the concerns of the industry and hence was proposing to work out an information exchange arrangement under the FTA, to facilitate enforcement efforts by the U.S. authorities. Smith persuaded and tried to convince me to his point of view. I did the same. Towards the end of the conversation, Smith noted that while the industry may be prepared to accept Singapore's proposed compromise for the moment, he would continue to exert pressure so that Singapore would continue to strive towards a more rigorous enforcement regime. Smith had relented and compromised because he believed that Singapore had genuine constraints and trusted that Singapore would always think and act in the best interests of the businesses.

EFFECTIVE LOBBYING PARTNERS FOR THE USSFTA

No doubt the U.S. business community was critical to the successful conclusion of the USSFTA. However, their contributions did not stop when the negotiations ended. In fact, the intensity of their activism and involvement increased during the lobbying phase as they sought to ensure that the USSFTA could be ratified by the U.S. Congress early, to enable them to reap the benefits. We had been warned by those familiar with the complex politics in Congress that if not handled properly, the approval of the USSFTA legislative bill could be delayed indefinitely, or worse, torpedoed entirely. Like Singapore, the U.S. business community did not want to take such a chance.

Canvassing for support from members of the U.S. business community for the USSFTA was, fortunately, not as difficult as having to negotiate with them on the specifics of the agreement. Our interests were aligned and we shared the same goal of seeing the USSFTA through Congress as early as possible. This strategic alliance was forged early on in late 2002 between the Singapore Embassy and the U.S. business community, under the USSFTA Business Coalition, as we neared the conclusion of the FTA negotiations. The Coalition was co-chaired by three friends of Singapore — ExxonMobil, United Parcel Services and Boeing — with secretariat support from the U.S. Chamber of Commerce and the U.S.-ASEAN Business Council.

Much credit must also go to the office of the U.S. Trade Representative and the various U.S. agencies for having kept their business stakeholders in the loop at every stage of the negotiations. As a result, there was strong ownership of the negotiating outcomes and the business community was able to conduct its lobbying efforts effectively. In fact, some of the U.S. business representatives that I met in Washington D.C. were more familiar than I was in the specifics of the final negotiating text. I recall a briefing that I conducted with some business representatives from the intellectual property protection community. They quizzed me on why certain positions had been worded as such. With due diligence, I explained the history and why Singapore had negotiated for certain textual changes in the negotiations. I realised subsequently that they had already been briefed by the U.S. officials, and had only wanted to verify my stories against what they had heard — just to be absolutely sure!

It was also fortunate that the Singapore Embassy enjoyed a close relationship with many of these businesses, who saw Singapore not just as a commercial partner, but also a worthy friend. The reality in Washington D.C. is that the business associations and representatives have limited financial resources and time. At the end of the day, how much time and money they would decide to allocate to advocate the USSFTA cause were dependent as much on the concrete benefits they could reap as on the value they placed in their relations with Singapore and Singaporeans.

When the International Trade Commission (ITC), an independent U.S. federal agency, conducted a public hearing to evaluate and assess the economic impact of the USSFTA on the U.S. economy, prior to Congressional consideration of the USSFTA Bill, more than 15 different businesses and associations submitted a testimony or showed up in person to support Singapore and the FTA. This included the Coalition of Service Industries, the Pharmaceutical Research and Manufacturers of America (PhRMA), the U.S. Chamber of Commerce, the Entertainment Industry Coalition for Free Trade, the Semiconductor Industry Association, Wal-Mart and Citigroup. One of the officials from the ITC remarked to me that this was an unusual phenomenon, because the ITC was more often than not used by aggrieved businesses to seek domestic protection against foreign competition! While they did not anticipate much controversy on the USSFTA, the ITC certainly did not expect so many businesses to turn up to demonstrate support. It was the best endorsement we could seek for the FTA!

MULTI-FACETED STRENGTHS OF THE BUSINESS COMMUNITY

The USSFTA negotiations as well as the subsequent lobbying in Congress provided me with an inner glimpse into the workings of the U.S. business community in Washington D.C. I took away a number of lessons on why, perhaps, U.S. businesses compete so successfully globally.

The U.S. business community uses its own initiative, operates swiftly and takes pride that it exists as an independent institution in Washington circles. Despite the close partnership between the Singapore Embassy and the business community during the lobbying phase of the FTA, the community made a conscious effort to maintain its independence from the embassy. So while the embassy provided information and background briefs on the specifics of the agreement, the community referred to these only as inputs and prepared their own publicity and communication packages. And while the Singapore Embassy may have had its strategy of lobbying Congress, the businesses generated their own ideas to garner votes. In retrospect, the multi-pronged approach that the various stakeholders took for the USSFTA lobbying was probably more effective than if the embassy and the businesses had coordinated every step of the way.

Having lobbied on various issues, the businesses were very familiar with the workings of Congress and deployed creative means to win votes. Their sense of independence, combined with an attitude of self-reliance, brought many merits — it lent credibility to what they had to say as they spoke in their own capacity and for their own interests, not someone else's; it also made them highly resourceful in getting what they needed, and doing what they could, to pursue their objectives. As we progressed closer to the actual vote of the USSFTA Bill in the House, the USSFTA Business Coalition started to distribute buttons in Congress, which said, "Vote 'yes' for the USSFTA". It was an excellent idea, timely executed. The buttons gave profile to the FTA and more importantly, it was a visual demonstration of the broad-based support that the FTA had in Congress.

Another memorable experience took place at a meeting with the House of Representatives Hispanic caucus. The embassy had received word that a group of Congressmen were having a meeting and there would be an opportunity to intercept and lobby them on the FTA after the meeting. Upon arrival, we met our business colleagues who were also there to lobby the Congressmen on both the Singapore as well as Chile FTAs. Alas, after an hour's wait, I was given a minute to say my piece and was forced to rush through my presentation. When his turn came, Bill Lane from Caterpillar, a seasoned lobbyist, took out a model of a Caterpillar truck and said, "this truck levels the playing field. Because of the U.S.-Chile FTA, Caterpillar will no longer be disadvantaged by European companies, who already have a Chile-EU FTA, because it will now enjoy equal access to the Chilean market." He took 30 seconds and achieved maximum effect. Even today, one year after, I still remember what he had said.

I used to think that only Asians work hard. My stint in Washington D.C. corrected this misperception. In retrospect, it was naïve of me to have subscribed to such a belief. In fact, I was very much humbled when I compared the work ethics of the Americans I had met in Washington D.C. with my own. In Washington, it is not uncommon for people to start networking as early as 7:30am over breakfast — exchanging information, influencing opinions and making new contacts. The activities will continue throughout the day, right through lunch and sometimes only ending at 10pm after dinner. I concluded, after my stint in Washington D.C., that Ambassador Tommy Koh's "makan diplomacy"[2] is a virtue that can be applied universally and those who can eat and stay slim, like Ambassador Chan Heng Chee, make the best ambassadors!

The U.S. business community form an integral part of the Washington network comprising business representatives, government and embassy officials, Congressional staffers, media personnel as well as scholars from the think-tanks. It is a dynamic network where existing contacts are continually strengthened, old contacts renewed and new contacts made. To exert influence and to be in the know, one must be part of this network. When I first arrived, Stanley Loh, Deputy Chief of Mission of the Singapore Embassy gave me a valuable piece of advice — do not promise what you cannot deliver and if you promise to deliver, do so immediately. That is the best means by which you can establish trust and build a relationship with your partners. Stanley had spoken the unspoken

---

[2] Dining diplomacy

code of behaviour in Washington. Promises made are almost always fulfilled. And because of their busy schedule, these business representatives will always deliver what they had promised you immediately — lest they forget, I was told. They expect the same of you. Because of how quickly events may unfold in Congress, there is a strong sense of urgency and a heightened consciousness that any delay may mean an opportunity lost.

I find Washington D.C. an interesting place because it is constantly abuzz with competitive activity. People are always eager to hear the latest gossip in town and to learn about new developments. When my colleagues from IE Singapore and I offered to conduct briefings among the various business associations to explain the key provisions of the FTA, we never had difficulty finding a ready audience. I was constantly impressed with the level of knowledge and awareness among the participants and their eagerness to understand the FTA better to see if there are new business opportunities that could be seized. In the U.S., many businesses see their interests as closely intertwined with that of government policies. Hence, many dedicate special resources to ensure a voice and influence in the Administration and in Congress. The bigger companies would have employees specialised in government relations stationed in Washington D.C. to exert a presence, while the smaller ones would see that their interests are being represented through lawyers, private lobbyists, business associations and trade bodies.

CONCLUSION

The USSFTA provided a means by which Singapore connected itself intimately to the Washington process. It gave us a window from which we could observe the workings of Congress and an avenue by which we could actively engage the business associations, the think-tanks and other institutions. In fact, the USSFTA legislative bill was the first time an issue directly concerning Singapore was debated in the U.S. Congress. I was fortunate to have been a part of this process.

Both the U.S. and Singapore will benefit from the FTA. It will bring substantial economic benefits to businesses from both sides. The FTA will be an anchor for the U.S. in South East Asia — important for the long term peace and security of the region. But more importantly, the FTA will be a bridge across the Pacific from which people, goods, services, capital, ideas, technology and opportunity may flow.

The FTA is a live document. Enshrined in the FTA is a provision that allows the trade ministers in Singapore and the U.S. to meet on a yearly basis to "supervise the implementation of the FTA and to review the trade relationship between the Parties". Whether or not the FTA will remain relevant and whether or not bilateral relations will strengthen year-on-year, is not guaranteed. Rather, while the seeds have been sown, whether we reap the fruits will depend on how both sides unleash the potential and harness the opportunities in the FTA. Businesses, on both sides of the Pacific, hold this key.

18 Lobbying the American Business Community in Singapore[1]

Jennifer CONLEY[2]

2000: EARLY BEGINNINGS

When President Clinton and Prime Minister Goh Chok Tong agreed to initiate negotiations on a U.S.-Singapore Free Trade Agreement (USSFTA) in Brunei in November 2000, The American Chamber of Commerce in Singapore (AmCham) began to tentatively drum up interest in the agreement.

---

[1] AmCham is one of the overseas chapters of the United States Chamber of Commerce. The U.S. Chamber was formed in 1912 as a unified body representing U.S. business interests of all sizes and from all sectors. The Chamber has grown to represent more than three million businesses with nearly 3000 state and local chambers, 830 Associations and over 90 American Chambers of Commerce abroad. The U.S. Chamber of Commerce, together with the U.S.-ASEAN Business Council, helped rally support from companies and the Congress in the U.S. while AmCham worked with their constituents in Singapore.

Serving the American business community in Singapore for 30 years, AmCham Singapore is one of the largest and most influential foreign business associations in the region. Its mission is to promote the interests of AmCham members in Singapore and the region by providing advocacy, business information and networking opportunities. With 1,500 members, including a majority of the Fortune 500 companies doing business in Singapore, AmCham represents over US$25 billion in investments in Singapore alone. The conclusion of a comprehensive U.S.-Singapore Free Trade Agreement became a major focus for AmCham from November 2000 until its ratification by Congress in July 2003.

[2] Jennifer Conley was Communications Manager at AmCham until January 2004. She came to AmCham in November 2000, the week when Prime Minister Goh and President Clinton played their celebrated golf game in Brunei and the USSFTA negotiations began. Prior to AmCham, Conley was public relations consultant for an Australian Government humanitarian aid project to clear landmines in Cambodia. Previously, she worked for *The Age* newspaper in Melbourne, as an editor and features writer. The views expressed in this article are those of the author and do not necessarily represent the views of AmCham.

The chamber surveyed members and initially the response was disappointing. It was a struggle to demonstrate that there could be direct benefits for business. Singapore was already an excellent place to do business and tariffs were virtually zero.

Early 2001, AmCham began a process of stimulating interest, engaging business people in regular discussions, researching major areas of concern and reporting those concerns to the negotiating teams. This took more than two years.

A Free Trade Taskforce was formed to determine the focus of AmCham efforts and a series of meetings were held with U.S. negotiators to explore competition policy issues, manpower and other related trade matters. AmCham had already released a press statement in support of the FTA, urging both sides to work towards creating a world-class agreement.

With the change in Administration, President Clinton's Administration transferred the unfinished task of concluding a trade agreement with Singapore to its successor. At the time, the then U.S. Trade Representative (USTR), Charlene Barshefsky, and Singapore Trade Minister George Yeo said "substantial progress" had been made but acknowledged that "much work remains to be done". There were fears in business circles that the agreement might languish.

On 23 January 2001, AmCham sent a letter to President Bush — still fresh from his inauguration on January 20 — urging the new Administration to kick off the third round of negotiations as soon as possible.

"The completion of a comprehensive FTA will increase the flow of trade and investment between the United States and Singapore and will promote an open and stable Asia-Pacific," the letter said. At the same time, the chamber launched a members' letter-writing campaign, calling on interested companies to fax their support to the President.

At his confirmation hearing in early February, the new USTR, Robert Zoellick, quickly went on record to support "market-opening" agreements with "willing and ready partners". He expressly named Singapore and by March the decision to resume negotiations had been announced.

AmCham continued to raise interest among its members and the wider business public. In April, the newly-appointed Executive Director of AmCham, Nicholas de Boursac, published an opinion piece in the *Straits Times*. The article robustly supported bilateral agreements and urged the case for a fully comprehensive agreement that would boost wider liberalisation.

"Curiosity has been growing steadily since the decision in Washington last month to resume negotiations ... but it is vital that the significance of this proposed pact continues to be asserted," he wrote. "The U.S.-Singapore Free Trade Agreement will be a milestone."

2001: THE WISH LIST

AmCham had begun the process of re-stimulating interest among its members. Negotiations were to resume in April 2001, and with the sudden realisation that this agreement might actually become a reality, there was a strong response to a further survey of the membership in March 2001.

Members identified a smorgasbord of issues. These included:

1. Anti-competitive or discriminatory behaviour by dominant players and the issue of government-linked companies having a perceived unfair advantage;
2. Liberalisation of professional services including legal, architecture and engineering;
3. Intellectual Property Rights and investment protection issues;
4. Increased transparency of valuation processes for excise duties on automobiles and
5. Liberalisation of financial services, in particular access to local Automated Teller Machines (ATM) networks and multi-branch banking.

Once the question had been asked, AmChamers began in earnest to draw up a "wish list" for this ambitious trade pact. They sought greater access to the Singapore market, a more transparent regulatory and licensing regime and a level playing field with local services companies. They wanted "to do business in Main Street".

American financial institutions, engineers and lawyers were among those seeking free access. In financial services, there was a push for quantitative limits to be removed on the number of U.S.-owned banks that could operate as fully-licensed retail banks.

Traditionally trade had involved moving goods across a country's borders but the development of new technologies and the global information economy has added a new element. American companies were not facing problems related to tangible goods travelling by plane or boat but to products that could move instantaneously around the world.

The entertainment and software industries saw the chance to put in place greater intellectual property protections in South East Asia. The proposed U.S.-Singapore Free Trade Agreement was an opportunity to develop world-class safeguards, they argued. Higher standards would encourage investment in Singapore and help to eliminate piracy and counterfeiting.

2001–2003: SEEKING THE SUPPORT OF WASHINGTON

While the Singapore and U.S. negotiating teams knuckled down to the detail of the agreement AmCham was among a number of business organizations that realised that whether or not the agreement was world-class, there was no guarantee of support for the agreement in the U.S. Congress. An unofficial campaign was launched. By 2002, this had taken the official form of the U.S.-Singapore FTA Coalition but until then, AmCham's leadership wasted no time in taking its case to Capitol Hill in Washington.

In June 2001, the annual delegation of AmCham members to the U.S. capital encouraged an open dialogue on the USSFTA. At nearly every meeting with Federal lawmakers, the agreement was the major subject of discussion.

"The overwhelming impression is that there is broad support for it [the FTA] in Washington; it is moving fast and Washington would like it to continue to move fast," de Boursac reported to the membership. Singapore was one of 21 AmChams in the Asia-Pacific region participating in the delegation that discussed a range of issues relevant to U.S. businesses in the region. The group, the Asia-Pacific Council of American Chambers of Commerce, represented an estimated US$40 billion of American investment in Asia-Pacific.

At the Washington delegation a year later, negotiations continued but a new element had entered the FTA discussion — the President's Trade Promotion Authority (TPA), formerly known as "fast track".

In 1994, for the first time in 20 years, Congress had refused to grant the President's fast track power, which had enabled his Administration to negotiate foreign trade agreements for Congressional approval on an up-or-down basis.

AmCham had long been a vocal supporter of TPA, arguing that with TPA in place, U.S. trade negotiations would receive a much-needed boost. The chamber's concern was that denying the President the authority to make trade deals that could not be altered by Congress — but could still be rejected — threatened to marginalise the United States at a time when other countries were forging important pacts. The U.S. had sat on the sidelines of trade talks during the mid to late 1990s while European and Asian countries concluded a number of beneficial agreements.

AmCham representatives again joined the Asia-Pacific AmCham delegation in stressing the importance of passing the TPA. The bill was the topic of heated debate over several weeks. In August 2002, it was finally passed. "We commend the House and Senate Members for voting for this important trade legislation. It will be instrumental in helping the U.S. forge important trade partnerships around the world," the 2001–2003 Chairman of AmCham, Landis Hicks, said in a statement at the time. "We are now one step closer to completing agreements like the U.S.-Singapore free trade agreement."

THE FACES OF TRADE

AmCham had issued a statement early in 2002 urging quality rather than speed in the negotiations. So there was no complaint from businesses when the 11th and final round of the USSFTA negotiations was still taking place as late as November 2002. A final issue concerning capital controls was resolved in January 2003 and the text of the agreement was sent to legal experts for review.

On 30 January, President Bush notified Congress of his intention to sign the agreement, beginning a 90-day process of review. The USTR, Robert Zoellick, in accordance with the Trade Act 2002, requested the United States International Trade Commission to prepare a report on the likely impact of the FTA on the United States economy as a whole and on specific industry sectors and the interests of U.S. consumers.

Meanwhile, AmCham was preparing a promotional campaign for the final stage — approval by Congress. A special edition was published of the AmCham/U.S. Embassy annual commercial guide to Singapore — *Singapore: Gateway to ASEAN* — and 500 additional copies were distributed among Congressional offices.

This was followed by *The Faces of Trade,* a booklet specifically highlighting success stories of small and medium-sized American companies doing business in Singapore. Produced in cooperation with the U.S. Chamber of Commerce, the booklet gave Federal lawmakers 19 examples of companies, ranging in size from two to 1215 employees, whose businesses had gained from trade with Singapore. The companies sold a variety of goods and services, from water purifying systems and medical products to ocean transport services, library software and bar code scanners. More than half of the companies featured had been actively doing business in Singapore for more than ten years, while two had 30 years of involvement. All were vocal supporters of the comprehensive free trade agreement.

The Seattle-based Grand Banks Yachts, an AmCham Singapore member since the early 1970s, had moved its primary building facilities to Singapore in 1968 to take advantage of the regional supply of teakwood and skilled carpenters. According to its Chairman and CEO, Rob Livingston, the FTA would be "a win-win all around".

The President of medical products distributor World Medical Trade Organization, Olivia Ho Cheng, said the company had enjoyed prosperous relations with the city-state for several years. "As a U.S. company, specialising in opening Asian markets for medical-related products, forging a strong network in Asia will only help to further goodwill and promote a better economy," she said.

At the same time, multinational companies expressed their support for the FTA through *The Faces of Trade*. The United Parcel Service (UPS) argued that the FTA will set new standards for open trade. "It will create jobs and improve the economies of both Singapore and the United States. It will bolster business opportunities not only for large corporations, but also for millions of small companies in both markets," the company said.

Kwa Chong Seng, Lead Country Manager, ExxonMobil Companies in Singapore, said the company had been part of the Singapore economy for more than 100 years, growing from a kerosene trading operation to the multibillion dollar manufacturing and marketing business it is today. "We rely on fair and open trade to remain competitive in this region and fully support the passage of the USSFTA," he said.

SHARING THE INSIDERS' VIEWS

One of AmCham's core competencies has always been hosting informative speaker events on a range of topical issues, and the FTA was certainly no exception.

Over a period of two years, the organization held a series of highly publicised events informing members of progress. The first, in August 2001, was a discussion by Director of Trade in the Ministry of Trade and Industry, Ong Ye Kung, of the rules of origin aspects proposed under the agreement.

The Minister of Trade and Industry, George Yeo, addressed members on the FTA at a special luncheon event. The U.S. Ambassador to Singapore, Franklin Lavin, gave a series of briefings, and the Singapore Chief Negotiator, Singapore's Ambassador-at-Large, Tommy Koh, was keynote speaker on the subject of the FTA in U.S.-Singapore relations at the AmCham Annual General Meeting of 2002. The benefits of the FTA were clearly defined at a joint event with the Institute of Policy Studies in February 2003.

By April 2003, AmCham had made a written submission to the International Trade Commission's inquiry. The submission highlighted several areas of the agreement and why AmCham believed it would translate into higher U.S. exports and greater employment opportunities for American workers. The key elements were:

1. Exports — the FTA eliminates Singapore's remaining customs duties on imports from the U.S. and promises improvements in excise tax calculations. Change in rules of origin would create new opportunities for American exporters of fiber, yarn, and fabric. An innovative "Integrated Sourcing Initiative" adapts traditional rules of origin to help U.S. and Singapore companies with greater flexibility for global sourcing.

2. Competition — AmCham welcomed provisions that address potential anti-competitive business practices by state-owned enterprises in Singapore and call for the creation of a competition law in Singapore by 2005.

3. Express Delivery Services — a commitment precludes the cross-subsidization of express delivery operations by Singaporean postal authorities, the first time such a commitment had been made in a trade agreement.

4. Financial Services and Insurance — the agreement levels the playing field for U.S. financial service providers in Singapore's banking and securities sectors.
5. Intellectual Property Rights (IPR) — substantial enhancements in four main areas: trademarks; copyrights; patents and trade secrets.
6. Professional Services — legal, architectural, engineering, and land surveying services see improved market access to Singapore.
7. Telecommunications — provisions ensure greater transparency and non-discriminatory access to the telecom network, leased lines, and related areas.

"We believe a competition law will best serve the interests of both nations and their respective business communities. AmCham believes the Agreement will help to ensure that U.S. companies can compete fairly for the procurement of government contracts, and for the buying and selling of goods and services," the submission said. "We ... wish to congratulate the Singapore and United States governments for negotiating a very comprehensive agreement that will further both nations' trade objectives, while contributing to their respective, future economic growth."

CLEARING THE FINAL HURDLE

On 6 May, President Bush and Prime Minister Goh signed the historic agreement. It was welcomed by AmCham at a special event featuring Minister of State for Foreign Affairs and Trade and Industry, Raymond Lim. A week later, a second briefing, co-hosted by AmCham and the Singapore Academy of Law, looked closely at the details and provided members with insights into the negotiation process.

AmCham had earlier elected a new chairperson, Kristin Paulson, to replace retiring chair Landis Hicks. Paulson, President, South

Asia Pacific, United Technologies (UTC), had been manager of congressional affairs in UTC's Washington office for 11 years. Her experience as a lobbyist was to be of great value over the coming months.

Paulson was optimistic about the chances of the USSFTA passing through Congress with a strong majority. "The prospects are very good," she told the *Business Times* in an interview on her election. She added that while no major objections had been tabled at that stage, the FTA could still trigger a debate. "Trade is always somewhat controversial in the U.S.," she said. "But I think some debate will be good because it'll help highlight to the American public and the American business community what Singapore is all about — and maybe get them to take a closer look at doing business here."

Paulson led Singapore AmCham's delegation to Washington to help support the agreement through its final stages. AmCham, in written evidence, told the House Ways and Means Committee's Trade subcommittee that it offers American companies significant benefits. It increases access for U.S. companies to the Singapore market, provides landmark intellectual property protection and removes restrictions in a number of services. The United States and Singapore had produced a ground-breaking FTA with far-reaching impacts economically and politically.

AmCham's leadership was keen to see the agreement endorsed by a strong vote in both the House and the Senate. So it was with great pleasure that the announcement was heard of the House vote in late July, and then the Senate vote in early August, both firmly in favour of the FTA.

For Paulson, the timing was perfect. "This a great day for both our countries," she told the media. "It is very fitting and very nice that it occurs in-between both of our national days and I think that the business communities in the United States and Singapore have great things to look forward to."

Section IV
Implementing the FTA

19 The Impact of the USSFTA on Our Laws, Regulations and Procedures — The Process and the Substance

Daren TANG[1]

INTRODUCTION

Under Singapore's legal system, all international obligations have to be given domestic effect. This means that the promises we have undertaken in the USSFTA must be "translated" into domestic laws, regulations and administrative procedures. This is no mean task, as the USSFTA is a complex agreement running to almost 1500 pages, written in legal, technical language.

---

[1] Daren Tang started out as a Deputy Public Prosecutor in 1997 with the Attorney-General's Chambers and has been State Counsel with the International Affairs Division of the Attorney-General's Chambers since 2000. In March 2001, he was seconded to the Trade Division of the Ministry of Trade and Industry as Legal Advisor for a period of one year. In the USSFTA, he was one of the lead negotiators for the Cross-Border Trade in Services Chapter, and was lead negotiator for the Temporary Entry Chapter. He also advised the team and drafted provisions relating to the other areas of the USSFTA, including trade in goods, customs, telecommunications, financial services, government procurement, e-commerce, investment, labour and environment. In addition, he was part of the legal team of the USSFTA, which negotiated the dispute settlement and transparency chapters and advised on more general FTA legal issues. Prior to his involvement with the USSFTA, he was one of the legal counsel for negotiations for the Singapore-New Zealand FTA (ANZSCEP) as legal counsel, and was lead counsel for negotiations on the Mexico-Singapore FTA. Daren has a LL.B from the National University of Singapore. The views expressed in this article are those of the author and do not represent the views of the Singapore Government.

THE PROCESS

The USSFTA was signed on 6 May 2003. It was targeted to come into force on 1 January 2004. Therefore, we had slightly more than half a year to ensure that Singapore would have put in place all the necessary laws, regulations and procedures to implement the USSFTA. Given the complexity of the USSFTA and the wide number of issues addressed, an Inter-Ministry Committee (IMC) comprised of representatives from various Ministries and Statutory Boards was set up to oversee this task. A separate Inter-Ministry Committee was set up to oversee the implementation of the Intellectual Property Chapter of the USSFTA, given the different timelines and issues involved.

By and large, where legislative amendments were required, these involved subsidiary legislation rather than primary legislation. This helped to ease the process along as amendments to subsidiary legislation do not need to be tabled in Parliament, unlike amendments to primary legislation. However, given the tight time-frame of six months, it was necessary for the IMC to meet every month to ensure that things were on track for 1 January 2004.

Unlike the U.S., there is no need in Singapore for Parliament to vote on trade agreements which Singapore enters into. Therefore, we were not required to introduce an omnibus USSFTA Bill in Parliament after the signing ceremony of 6 May 2003. While this made the post-negotiation processes in Singapore somewhat less dramatic than that in the U.S., it perhaps helped us to focus on getting the various laws and regulations in place to implement the USSFTA. A list of these laws and regulations are attached as Appendix XIX.

I have roughly described the process by which Singapore put into place whatever laws and regulations were required for the implementation of the USSFTA. But exactly what impact did the USSFTA have on Singapore's laws, regulations and procedures?

THE SUBSTANCE

By and large, the USSFTA does not require us to make sea changes to our laws. Rather, in most of the trade and investment related portions of the USSFTA, for example, the Trade in Goods, Cross-border Trade in Services and Investments Chapters, Singapore basically committed to continuing with the pro-free trade policies it has pursued. Other portions of the USSFTA, for example, Labour and Environment, also do not require us to enact any specific legislation, but oblige us to enforce whatever labour or environment laws are in our statute books. The net effect of these chapters is that very few amendments to our law are required. However, it is important to note that we have now made a commitment that if we amend these laws, they must not be made less trade friendly.

That said, the USSFTA does have an impact on various aspects of our legislative framework. One clear example of this is the obligations relating to transparency which are written in Chapter 19 of the USSFTA. Under the article 19(3) of this chapter, Singapore is obliged, to the extent possible, to publish in advance and allow public consultation of laws and regulations on anything relevant to the USSFTA. Given the breadth of issues addressed in the USSFTA, this means that public consultation should become the norm, rather than the exception, before the promulgation of trade related Bills in Parliament. This obligation echoes Singapore's general movement towards more openness and transparency, and is one example of how the USSFTA complements the policy directions we are taking.

Other more specific examples of how the USSFTA has an impact on our laws and regulations are as follows:

(a) *Customs Duties*

The Customs Duties Order was amended by the Customs (Duties) (Amendment No. 6) Order 2003 to give effect to Singapore's tariff-free obligations under Chapter 2 and Annex 2C of the USSFTA. In addition, the Order provides that only U.S. goods will be allowed to benefit from the preferential treatment given to them under the USSFTA as U.S. goods are deemed to have originated from the U.S. only when they "conform with the Rules of Origin set out in the United States-Singapore Free Trade Agreement". Through this, Chapter 3 of the USSFTA, dealing with Rules of Origin, is made part of our laws.

(b) *Regulation of Imports and Exports*

The Regulation of Import and Exports Act was amended by the Regulation of Imports and Exports (Amendment) Bill 2003 to implement Singapore's obligations under Chapters 4 and 5 of the USSFTA. Chapter 4 of the USSFTA, *inter alia*, obliges Singapore to co-operate with the U.S. in sharing information relating to trade circumvention. Chapter 5 requires Singapore to put in place certain controls on the manufacture and export of textile and apparel goods destined for the United States.

(c) *Import of Chewing Gum with Therapeutic Value*

As part of the USSFTA, Singapore is obliged to allow the import of chewing gum with therapeutic value, subject to laws and regulations relating to health products. In order to implement this obligation, Singapore amended various pieces of subsidiary legislation relating to the sale and supply of chewing gum. Examples of legislation which had to be amended include the Regulation of Import and Export (Amendment) (Chewing Gum) Regulations 2003, the Sale of Food (Prohibition of Chewing Gum) Regulations 2003, the Medicines (Oral Dental Gums) (Specification) Order 2003, the Medicines (Cosmetic Products) (Specification and Prohibition) (Amendment) Order 2003, the Medicines (Prescription Oral Dental Gums) Order 2003, the Medicines (Oral Dental Gums) (Labelling) Regulations 2003, the Medicines (Advertising of Oral Dental

Gums) Regulations 2003, the Medicines (Oral Dental Gums) (Licensing) Regulations 2003 and the Medicines (Registration of Pharmacies) (Amendment) Regulations 2003.

(d) *Services and Investment Related Amendments*

Under the USSFTA, Singapore has committed to opening up certain service sectors to U.S. services providers. For example, Singapore reduced the shareholding requirements for architectural and engineering corporations from 66 percent to 51 percent. Amendments were also made to the Insurance Act (via the Insurance (Amendment) Bill 2003) and the Insurance Regulations to ensure that Singapore complied with its obligations under the Financial Services chapter of the USSFTA.

(e) *Government Procurement*

Under the Government Procurement Chapter (Chapter 13) of the USSFTA, Singapore is obliged to procure a wide variety of goods and services in a manner which does not disadvantage U.S. companies. Violations of the obligations of this chapter may be brought before a domestic tribunal via the bid challenge procedure, which basically allows the tribunal to examine whether a procurement was conducted in conformity with the USSFTA. This obligation will be written into the Government Procurement Act, as part of certain amendments which are being made to the Act to rationalise Singapore's government procurement obligations under various Free Trade Agreements.

(f) *Enactment of a Generic Competition Law*

In May 2002, Minister for Trade and Industry George Yeo announced in Parliament that Singapore will be enacting a generic competition law. This was eventually written into article 12.2 of the

USSFTA, where Singapore committed to enacting a generic competition law by 1 January 2005.

(g) *Intellectual Property Laws*

The Intellectual Property Chapter (Chapter 16) of the USSFTA contains numerous obligations which would require amendments to various pieces of legislation relating to intellectual property, including the Patents Act, Copyright Act and the Trade Marks Act. As of the time of publication, the amendments to these Acts have not been finalized as they are still under consideration by government agencies. However, under the USSFTA, Singapore is obliged to put these amendments into place by 1 July 2004, six months after the USSFTA comes into force. In addition, Singapore is obliged to accede to following the conventions (listed in Article 16.1.2(a) of the USSFTA) within one year of the coming into force of the USSFTA:

(i)   The Convention Relating to the Distribution of Programme-Carrying Signals Transmitted by Satellite (1974);
(ii) The International Convention for the Protection of New Varieties of Plants (1991) (UPOV Convention);
(iii) The WIPO Copyright Treaty (1996);
(iv) The WIPO Performances and Phonograms Treaty (1996); and
(v)   The Patent Cooperation Treaty (1984).

It is evident that acceding to these Conventions may require further legislative amendments to our intellectual property laws and regulations.

It must also be remembered that a fair number of obligations under the USSFTA are implemented administratively. For example, Singapore agreed to relax the requirements relating to the formation of Joint Law Ventures and Formal Law Alliances between U.S. law firms and our local law firms. This is implemented by way of administrative exemptions to the requirements laid down in the Legal Profession Act and Legal Profession (International Services) Regulations. For the sake of comprehensiveness, here is a listing of the various chapters in which our obligations are largely or wholly being implemented administratively:

(a) *Chapter 1: Establishment of a Free Trade Area and Definitions*

This chapter formalizes the legal nature of the free trade area that is created between Singapore and the U.S. and lays down definition of terms which are common throughout the USSFTA. It therefore does not require any amendments to our laws.

(b) *Chapter 6: Technical Barriers to Trade*

This chapter creates the framework for Singapore and the U.S. to co-operate closely on issues relating to technical barriers to trade, including the formation of a Working Group and a Contact Point. These will be implemented administratively.

(c) *Chapter 7: Safeguards*

Singapore generally does not initiate safeguard actions against foreign goods, but in the event that Singapore exercises its rights under this chapter, it will be done so administratively.

(d) *Chapter 9: Telecommunications*

This chapter basically lays down basic principles which should govern how each Party administers the telecommunication services sector. The adoption of these principles do not require legislative amendments for implementation.

(e) *Chapter 11: Temporary Entry*

This chapter commits Singapore to carrying on with its policies of openness to foreign talent, including four defined categories of business visitors, traders, investors and professionals. As such, no legislative amendments are required for its implementation.

(f) *Chapter 12: Anti-competitive Business Conduct, Designated Monopolies, and Government Enterprises*

The obligations of this chapter relate to ensuring that Singapore does not favour its GLCs over other foreign enterprises and will be implemented administratively. We have already dealt with the obligation to enact a generic competition law earlier on in this essay.

(g) *Chapter 14: Electronic Commerce*

Under this chapter, Singapore has committed to not impose any customs duties on the electronic transmission of digital products and, where digital products stored on carrier medium is concerned, to impose duties based on the value of the carrier medium and not the product. In addition, Singapore has committed towards providing non-discriminatory to digital products of foreign origin. Singapore currently already does not impose any customs duties on the electronic transmission of digital products. The obligations relating to non-discriminatory treatment do not require any legislative amendments as our current laws and regulations already meet this standard.

(h) *Chapters 17 and 18: Labour and Environment*

As discussed earlier, the Labour and Environment chapters of the USSFTA require both Parties to effectively enforce their respective domestic labour and environment laws. It therefore does not require any legislative amendments.

(i) *Chapter 19 to 21: Transparency, Administration and Dispute Settlement and Final Provisions*

The obligations of the transparency chapter which are discussed earlier will be implemented administratively. As for the chapters on Administration and Dispute Settlement and Final Provisions, these do not require any legislative amendments as they relate more to the administrative arrangements for the USSFTA and the procedures for dispute settlement before an international tribunal.

CONCLUSION

Although the USSFTA does not result in sea changes to our laws and regulations, the totality of the amendments listed above does have a substantial impact on us. First, the USSFTA "locks in" the pro free-trade policies embodied in our laws and regulations, and commits us to carrying on with these policies. Second, in a number of general areas, such as transparency and intellectual property, the USSFTA will precipitate changes to our practices and laws, and accelerate our movement towards directions which we have already embarked upon. Third, in a number of specific areas, implementing the USSFTA requires legislative amendments. For example, as a result of amendments to the Regulation of Imports and Exports Act, textile manufacturers and exporters targeting the U.S. market will have to comply with more stringent requirements with regard to record-keeping. Nevertheless, these changes will hopefully raise Singapore's competitiveness and help in ensuring that Singapore trade and investment flows with the U.S. continues to increase as the USSFTA kicks into force.

20 The USSFTA: The Impact on Government-Linked Companies and Singapore's Corporate Scene

Vikram KHANNA[1]

An important area of the Singapore economy that will be affected by the USSFTA will be Singapore's government-linked companies (GLCs), in which the single biggest shareholder is, in many cases, Singapore's national investment agency, Temasek Holdings.

The key issues that arise are how the USSFTA will impact GLCs; the implications for Temasek Holdings; and more widely, for the Singapore economy as a whole. This paper will touch on each of these issues.

The total value-added of the so-called Temasek companies is reckoned to account for some 13 percent of Singapore's GDP.[2] These companies span several sectors of the economy, including finance, telecom, media, transport (including air, shipping and rail), logistics, property, infrastructure, engineering and utilities.

---

[1] Vikram Khanna is Associate Editor of *The Business Times*, Singapore, where he has worked since 1993. Prior to this, he served in the External Relations Department of the International Monetary Fund, Washington D.C. (1987–1993). He holds a B.A. (Hons) degree in economics from the University of Bombay, and a B.A., M.A. and M. Phil degrees in economics from the University of Cambridge, UK. In 2002/3, Mr Khanna served on the Entrepreneurship and Internationalisation Subcommittee of the Economic Review Committee, established by the Singapore government. The views expressed in this article are those of the author and do not necessarily represent the views of *The Business Times*.

[2] Speaking points for DPM's round-up speech on "Motion on Temasek Charter and EISC's Recommendations on Government in Business" at Parliament sitting on 28 August 2003. Also see Appendix IX.

The total number of GLCs runs into the thousands if all multi-tiered subsidiaries of all the major companies (including those in which GLCs have minority stakeholdings) are taken into account.[3] There are 22 "first-tier" companies, of which seven are already listed on the Singapore Exchange.[4] The listed entities account for about 20 percent of the market capitalisation of the Singapore Exchange. As at 14 January 2004, the total value of Temasek's stakes in listed companies was just under S$60 billion. However, some major companies remain unlisted. These include PSA, the Media Corporation of Singapore, Singapore Technologies and Singapore Power.

The USSFTA essentially addresses three key issues relating to GLCs: how GLCs will be run, who will run them, and who will own them.

On the issue of how GLCs will be run — in particular, on the degree of influence on government and the commercial orientation of companies, Temasek had already set out its position prior to the signing of the USSFTA in the Temasek Charter,[5] which was released on 3 July 2002. Here, Temasek indicated that it "will exercise its shareholder rights to influence the strategic directions of its companies. But it does not involve itself in their day-to-day commercial decisions".[6] This message was reinforced by the Economic Review Committee (ERC)[7] in its report in February

---

[3] Temasek Holdings is considered to have a deemed interest in a listed company if any of its subsidiaries or associates (as defined in that section) have any voting shares in that listed company.)

[4] The listed companies include DBS Bank, Keppel Corporation, Neptune Orient Lines, SembCorp Industries, Singapore Airlines, SMRT Corporation and Singapore Telecoms.

[5] Temasek Charter. See Appendix IX.

[6] *Ibid.*

[7] Established in December 2001, with a view to comprehensive reviewing of current economic policies. Its members were drawn from both the public and private sectors as well as from academia.

2003, which was accepted by the government. The ERC stated categorically that "all GLCs should be run on strictly commercial principles and be subject to the discipline of the market".[8]

The emphasis on commercialism and market orientation had its origins in both efficiency and equity considerations. On the efficiency side, it was felt, including within government, that facing competition would induce GLCs to make more optimal business decisions as well as better prepare them to go out into the world, while on the equity side, there were concerns — particularly within the small and medium enterprise (SME) sector — that government favouritism towards GLCs results in a "tilted playing field" that works to the disadvantage of the private sector and possibly stifles its growth.

The relevant clause in the USSFTA on the commercial orientation of GLCs reads: "Singapore commits to maintain its existing policy of not interfering with the commercial decisions of Government Linked Companies, ensuring that GLCs are commercially run."

Thus, the USSFTA does not really break new ground on the issue of GLCs being run commercially. Why then is the clause included? One possible explanation is that the explicit commitment on the part of the Singapore government to run GLCs along strictly commercial lines is relatively new, and the clause does have the effect of "locking in" this policy. The inclusion of the clause would also seem to suggest that the commercial orientation (or otherwise) of Singapore's GLCs is of concern, not only to domestic companies, but to U.S. and other foreign companies and investors as well.

On the question of who will run and own GLCs, the USSFTA explicitly addresses two specific issues: transparency and ownership. On transparency, the agreement commits Singapore to, "at least annually, make public a consolidated report that covers, for each

---

[8] Report of the Economic Review Committee, February 2003.

entity, the percentage of shares and percentage of voting rights that Singapore and its government enterprises cumulatively own and the name and government title of any government official serving as an officer or a member of the board of directors."

The concern here seems to be to elicit a clear picture of government interests in GLCs — both in terms of equity stakes and boardroom influence — which has not been comprehensively made public before. It is possible that this requirement of greater transparency in GLC board appointments will provide a change in the nature of these appointments, which some view as being heavily weighted in favour of government-linked personnel, even where the companies concerned are supposed to be operating as purely commercial entities. How these changes will affect corporate governance of GLCs remains, however, to be seen.

DIVESTMENT

On the issue of divestment, the USSFTA states: "Singapore shall continue reducing and substantially eliminating its aggregate ownership and other interests that confer effective influence in entities organised under the laws of Singapore, taking into account the timing of individual divestments and the state of relevant capital markets."

In the telecoms industry, Singapore's commitment to divest was particularly strong. In a side letter to the USSFTA from Singapore's Trade and Industry Minister George Yeo to U.S. Trade Representative Robert Zoellick, Mr Yeo wrote: "The Singapore government is committed to the privatisation of SingTel and ST Telemedia and to the objective of reducing its existing stakes in these companies to zero, subject to the state of capital markets and the interest of other shareholders."

However, there is no formal, explicit mechanism to enforce the divestment provisions and commitments in the USSFTA. Enforcement will likely be done through an informal consultative process for which, indeed, provision has been made in the USSFTA. Given the way the U.S. political process works, it is likely that U.S. business and financial sector interests — and not only the U.S. government — will play a key role in this process.

To be sure, divestment is not new to Temasek. The process has been going on since the 1980s, when stakes in key companies such as Keppel Corporation, NOL and Singapore Airlines were sold to investors. In 1987, a public sector divestment committee headed by one of Singapore's senior corporate figures, Michael Fam, recommended privatising 41 GLCs. Temasek has, in fact, gone further than this, divesting more than 60 of its companies completely or partially since the mid-1980s, including some companies not listed in the 1987 report. However, as some observers have noted, since there is no listing of new GLCs formed since 1987, and some transfer of ownership has taken place from Temasek to GLCs, one cannot accurately gauge the net effective privatisation that has taken place.[9]

Since the Temasek Charter, the divestment process has continued.

During the year from January 2003 to January 2004, Temasek made the following divestments:[10]

* March 2003 — Sale of 100 percent of CPG Corp (formerly, Singapore's Public Works Department) to Downer EDI.
* November 2003 — Sale of 9.5 percent stake in trading firm Intraco (6.4 percent to PSC and 3.1 percent through share placement).
* by December 2003 — Sale of 8.07 percent stake in steelmaker Natsteel to 98 Holdings.

---

[9] Linda Low, "Sustaining the Competitiveness of Singapore Inc.", in *Sustaining Competitiveness in the New Global Economy*, edited by Ramkishen Rajan, Institute of Policy Studies, 2003.

[10] Data from Temasek Holdings.

- 2003/04 — Sale of subsidiaries of 88 percent-owned export-credit and factoring company, ECICS Holdings as follows: 38 percent stake in International Factors reduced to 9 percent; and 88 percent stake in ECICS Credit Insurance and ECICS Guarantee reduced to zero.
- January 2004 — 67.18 percent stake in telecoms company Singtel reduced to 64.98 percent (and up to 61.49 percent if exchangeable notes are converted by 2009).

The clause on privatisation in the USSFTA — which, notably, covers not only so-called GLCs, but "entities organised under the laws of Singapore" (which would include non-corporatised bodies such as Statutory Boards) — will introduce a new transparency into the privatisation process, as well as, possibly, accelerate it.

This prospect — coupled with the expectation of accelerated divestments in the markets — raises some issues for Temasek.

One of them is how it will manage the divestment process. Temasek has divided its companies into three groups. The first group, so-called "Group A" companies, are those which it indicates it has, as yet, no plans to divest. These companies include:

a) companies that control "critical resources." In the Temasek Charter, these are defined as those companies "where ownership of a resource is critical to Singapore's security or economic well-being, or where the business is a natural domestic monopoly for which a market-based regulatory framework has not yet been established. These include water, power and gas grids, airport, and seaport"; and

b) companies where government ownership "enables the government to achieve specific public policy objectives, by providing services or assuring control for the public good". These include gaming, public broadcasting, subsidised services in healthcare, education and housing, and various public amenities like the zoo and bird park.

However, Temasek did not close the door to the eventual privatisation of even some of these companies. It indicated: "The government will continue to hold majority or significant stakes in such Group A companies, **for so long as there is a specific requirement for government ownership or support. Should such businesses become no longer strategic to Singapore, or when viable market alternatives or regulatory frameworks are in place, the government will divest or dilute its shareholdings** (emphasis added)."

A larger number of Temasek companies, however, belong to what is referred to in the Temasek Charter as "Group B" companies, which are "those with the potential to grow beyond the domestic market, into the regional or international markets". For this group, Temasek's willingness to divest appears stronger than in the case of the Group A companies. In its charter, Temasek indicates that it "is prepared to dilute its stake through the issuance of new shares, or mergers or acquisitions in order to support the long-term success of these companies as regional or international players".

For Temasek companies which do not fall into categories A and B — which could well be the majority of Temasek-linked companies — the commitment to divest is strongest. The charter indicates that Temasek "will continue to divest businesses which no longer require government participation, or which have limited potential for regional or international growth".

Overall, Temasek's stated intentions seem to suggest that although it is open to divestment, it is not likely to divest its potential regional or international companies for divestment's sake, but will do so where divestment supports the objective of enabling such companies to internationalise. As the investment agency's Executive Director Ho Ching put it in a major address on the future of Temasek in February 2004: "We are fully open to diluting our stakes in our existing TLCs to minority positions, especially if it creates an opportunity for us to enhance our long-term returns."

However, she added: "We don't intend to raid the larder, nor sell the family jewels. We will jealously guard our interest, and invest, rationalise, consolidate or divest where it makes sense, and where we can achieve clear sustainable value."[11]

Some analysts have argued that "fear of divestment" will pressure GLCs which have not so far gone regional or international to do so.[12]

There have been calls, including some from members of parliament, for Temasek to be more explicit about its divestment plans by providing a timetable as well as details of mechanisms through which divestment would be made. However, the provision of such details — even if these were known in advance, which is itself doubtful — is not a reasonable expectation from any investment agency. As Singapore's Deputy Prime Minister and Finance Minister Lee Hsien Loong responded in parliament: "It would ... be unwise to publish a list of companies that will be divested within a fixed timeframe. The act itself would depress values, alarm customers, demoralise employees and cause viable businesses to run to seed".[13]

Nevertheless, as per the USSFTA and the Temasek Charter, divestment must proceed, even if at a measured pace, over several years. One issue that this raises is "divestment to whom?" As DPM Lee asked during the parliament motion referred to above: "Which private companies or individuals are in a position to take over SingTel, SIA, or PSA? Not just financially, but also in terms of management oversight? Can we really just distribute the shares to

---

[11] Speech at IPS entitled "Temasek Holdings: Building Sustainable Value", 12 February 2004

[12] For example, see: Daniel Lian in Morgan Stanley report dated 8 July 2002, "Temasek Charter Authorises External Economy Mission of GLCs".

[13] Parliament motion on Temasek Charter and EISC's Recommendations on Government in Business, 28 August 2002.

Singaporeans, and expect the companies to naturally prosper?" Temasek will have to grapple with this challenging question.

The investment agency must also anticipate the impact of its divestments on the markets. Market observers suggest that this impact will depend partly on whether the divestments are made to another substantial shareholder (which could result in a new management and a new direction for the divested company) or to fund managers.[14]

Temasek must also manage its divestments such that they do not have a depressive effect (or create expectations thereof) on share prices. This issue was brought into sharp relief in January 2004, when Temasek divested US$1.25 billion dollars worth of its holdings in Singtel.

Market watchers, including a number of broking firms, were quick to link the sale to Singapore's divestment commitments under the USSFTA — adding that there remains an "overhang" in Singtel shares.[15] Typically such an overhang has the effect of depressing share prices.

Temasek denied the divestment was related to the USSFTA, linking it instead to fund-raising for its "active acquisition of regional and international businesses and capital deployment in 2003." The investment agency also indicated that it had no plans to further dilute its shareholdings in Singtel, as its "current target funding needs have been met."[16]

Nevertheless, given the commitment to divest in the USSFTA — particularly in the telecoms sector — it is unlikely that perceptions of the share overhang will go away. Temasek will have to manage these and their price impact. The latter could partly be done through

---

[14] *The Business Times*, 24 January 2004.

[15] "Market Must Cope with Singtel Share Overhang", *The Business Times*, 8 January 2004.

[16] Letter to *The Business Times*, 9 January 2004.

the adoption of mechanisms to divest in ways that do not have a strongly depressive effect on share prices — such as the use of convertible bonds, which allow share sales to be more staggered than they would be through direct placements (and which Temasek has already used). And to manage market perceptions and expectations, the investment agency will have to mount a skilful and pro-active information strategy.

NEW INVESTMENTS

As the divestment process goes ahead as per Singapore's commitments under the USSFTA, another question that arises concerns how Temasek will deploy the proceeds. Although the USSFTA commits Singapore to divest its holdings in existing enterprises, the agreement allows for new government enteprises to be established.[17] Temasek has indicated that it is open to starting new ventures: "Temasek may also, from time to time, invest in new businesses with regional or international potential in order to nurture new industry clusters. These are likely to be in new growth sectors which entail high risk, large investments or long gestation periods, where private enterprise in Singapore is unable or unwilling to assume risks." The investment agency adds, however, that it "will be highly selective in making such new investments".[18]

In the year from January 2003 through January 2004, Temasek made the following investments:[19]

- January 2003: Invested in 4.8 percent stake in local water-treatment company, Hyflux — reduced to 2.9 percent through sales in January 2004.

---

[17] Clause 2a, Chapter 12, page 134: "Nothing in this Agreement shall be construed to prevent a Party from establishing or maintaining a government enterprise."

[18] Temasek Charter. See Appendix IX.

[19] Data provided by Temasek Holdings.

- February 2003: Invested in an 8.5 percent in local equipment supplier to the PCB assembly and semiconductor industries, Autron — reduced to 3.8 percent through share placement in January 2004.
- April 2003: Invested in a 8.0 percent stake in shipbuilding and repair company, Cosco Investments (a subsidiary of China's largest shipping group) — reduced to 5.1 percent in January 2004 through a sale of shares to Sembcorp Marine.
- June 2003: Invested in a 62 percent stake in Indonesian bank, Bank Danamon, through Asia Financial (Indonesia).
- September 2003: Invested in a 16.4 percent stake in U.S.-based company Quintiles, the world's largest provider of clinical trial and commercialisation services.
- November 2003: Invested in an 11 percent stake in planned budget airline, Tiger Airways (other investors: Singapore Airlines and Ryanair).
- December 2003: Invested in a 51 percent stake in Bank Internasional Indonesia through Sorak Financial Holdings.[20]
- December 2003: Invested in 6.7 percent in India's ICICI Bank, by purchasing shares in the secondary market.
- January 2004: Invested in 7.5 percent stake in Olam International, locally-based global supplier of food ingredients.

In January 2004, Temasek also announced that it intended to buy a 14 percent stake in Indian drugmaker, Matrix Laboratories, and that it is looking at investing in LG Card, South Korea's largest credit card company.

---

[20] Sorak consists of Kookmin Bank (25 percent economic, 51 percent voting), Temasek (50 percent economic, 33.33 percent voting), ICB (20 percent economic, 13.33 percent voting), and Barclays (5 percent economic, 3.33 percent voting).

As the list indicates, the majority of new investments made by Temasek during the 12 months to January 2004 were outside Singapore and principally focused on the region — sometimes in partnership with other entities, both local and foreign. Temasek also employed different modes of investment, ranging from secondary market share purchases to establishing special investment vehicles.

In her February 2004 address, Temasek's Executive Director Ho Ching laid out the broad approach Temasek will adopt towards its investments. She indicated that Temasek will focus in particular on: (a) global networks; (b) Asian services; and (c) ASEAN resources. "A common theme that cuts across all boundaries will be our interest in companies and businesses with distinctive IP, competitive strengths and potential to grow regionally or globally," she said. "In short, we will work to transform our portfolio from a proxy for the Singapore GDP, into a balanced GNP portfolio leveraging on the growth and promise of Singapore, ASEAN, Asia and the world."[21]

Singapore's investment agency is thus evolving into a major regional and international investor. This might well have happened in any event. However, its divestment commitments, both under the Temasek Charter as well as the USSFTA, will generate substantial financial resources that the investment agency will have to redeploy productively.

To that extent, the USSFTA could be viewed as a catalyst (though by no means the only one) for the transformation of Temasek from a largely domestic to a regional and international player.

COMPETITION LAW

Under the USSFTA, Singapore also reiterated its earlier commitment to enact a competition law by January 2005. In this

---

[21] Speech at IPS entitled "Temasek Holdings: Building Sustainable Value", 12 February 2004.

context, the USSFTA explicitly required that Singapore "shall not exclude enterprises from that legislation on the basis of their status as government enterprises."[22]

The contours of the competition law envisaged in the USSFTA essentially proscribe anticompetitive business practises and require the maintenance of an authority for the enforcement of the law. It requires Singapore government enterprises to act "solely in accordance with commercial considerations in the purchase or sale of goods or services" and provide nondiscriminatory treatment to U.S. goods and services suppliers. It also prohibits Singapore government enterprises from entering into agreements that restrain competition or from engaging in "exclusionary practices that substantially lessen competition in a market in Singapore to the detriment of consumers".[23]

An important aspect of the competition law provisions in the USSFTA relate to cooperation and consultation.[24] Noting that both parties "recognize the value of transparency of their competition policies", the agreement requires each party to make available to the other:

- public information concerning enforcement of measures proscribing anticompetitive business conduct;
- public information on government enterprises and designated monopolies both public or private; and
- public information concerning exemptions to its measures proscribing anticompetitive business conduct.

When it comes to consultation, Singapore is required under the USSFTA to "inform the United States of the steps it has taken or plans to take to examine the conduct at issue ... apprise the United

---

[22] USSFTA, Chapter 12, page 133.

[23] USSFTA, Chapter 12, Article 12.3.

[24] USSFTA, Articles 12.4 to 12.6.

States when Singapore's responsible authorities decide to initiate or not to initiate enforcement proceedings regarding the conduct, and shall keep the United States regularly apprised of developments in, and the results of, any enforcement proceedings it initiates".

These provisions should ensure stronger enforcement of the competition law and also increase confidence in enhancement, putting paid to doubts about whether this law will have teeth, particularly against GLCs.

To be sure, a competition law — even when highly effective — cannot be sufficient to fully "level the playing field" between SMEs, GLCs and multinational companies, nor will it be sufficient to propel SMEs into the vanguard of the economy or promote innovation. But it will prevent GLCs as well as other large companies from engaging in anticompetitive behaviour and, to that extent, open up more space for SMEs in the economy and possibly lower entry barriers in certain areas.

CONCLUSION

It is arguable that many of the policy commitments included in the USSFTA that will potentially affect the ownership structure, operation and competitive position of Singapore's GLCs would have happened anyway, even without the USSFTA — and there is indeed some evidence to this effect.

However, the USSFTA's inclusion of these important commitments will mean that in addition to the domestic imperatives that are propelling policy changes towards the GLC sector and Singapore's corporate landscape in general, there is also now an "external" discipline. This should have the effect of raising confidence that the policy towards the GLC sector that have been made in, for instance, the Temasek Charter as well as the Economic Review Committee, will be carried out — even if with a margin for flexibility — and will not be reversed in the future.

Appendixes

Appendixes

Joint Statement by President Bill Clinton and Prime Minister Goh Chok Tong on a United States-Singapore Free Trade Agreement, 16 November 2000*

President Bill Clinton of the United States of America (USA) and Prime Minister Goh Chok Tong of Singapore have agreed to start negotiations on a bilateral Free Trade Agreement (FTA).

USA and Singapore are both firm supporters of the Asia-Pacific Economic Co-operation (APEC), and are committed to APEC's Bogor Goals of free and open trade and investment by 2010 for industrialized economies and 2020 for developing economies.

The USA and Singapore reaffirm their strong commitment to the multilateral trading system and the launch of a New Round in 2001.

The FTA will be modeled after the U.S.-Jordan FTA.

We have directed Ambassador Charlene Barshefsky and Minister George Yeo to endeavor to conclude negotiations before the end of the year.

---

* Issued by the Singapore APEC Delegation in Bandar Seri Begawan, Brunei 16 November 2000, 6.00pm.

Singapore Congressional Caucus

1. Representative Solomon Ortiz (D[1]-TX) (Co-chair)
2. Representative Curt Weldon (R[2]-PA) (Co-chair)
3. Representative Eddie Bernice Johnson (D-TX)
4. Representative Joe Knollenberg (R-MI)
5. Representative Joseph Crowley (D-NY)
6. Representative John Larson (D-CT)
7. Representative Alcee Hastings (D-FL)
8. Representative Gene Green (D-TX)
9. Representative Joe Wilson (R-SC)
10. Representative Lloyd Doggett (D-TX)
11. Representative Reuben Hinojosa (D-TX)
12. Representative Bud Cramer (D-AL)
13. Representative Howard Coble (R-NC)
14. Representative Ike Skelton (D-MO)
15. Representative Hilda Solis (D-CA)
16. Representative Martin Frost (D-TX)
17. Representative Grace Napolitano (D-CA)
18. Representative Ciro Rodriguez (D-TX)
19. Representative Richard Burr (R-NC)
20. Representative Silvestre Reyes (D-TX)
21. Representative Joe Baca (D-CA)
22. Representative Charles Gonzalez (D-TX)
23. Representative Anibal Acevedo-Vila (D-PR)
24. Representative Charles Taylor (R-NC)

---

[1] D = Democrat.

[2] R = Republican.

25. Representative Mark Souder (R-IN)
26. Representative Phil English (R-PA)
27. Representative Vic Snyder (D-AR)
28. Representative William Jefferson (D-LA)
29. Representative Ed Pastor (D-AZ)
30. Representative Ellen Tauscher (D-CA)
31. Representative Robert Wexler (D-FL)
32. Representative Marion Berry (D-AR)
33. Representative Jennifer Dunn (R-WA)
34. Representative Tom Lantos (D-CA)
35. Representative Adam Schiff (D-CA)
36. Representative Loretta Sanchez (D-CA)
37. Representative Eliot Engel (D-NY)
38. Representative Norm Dicks (D-WA)
39. Representative Brad Sherman (D-CA)
40. Representative Darrell Issa (R-CA)
41. Representative Ed Royce (R-CA)
42. Representative Mike McNulty (D-NY)
43. Representative Joseph Pitts (R-PA)
44. Representative Albert Wynn (D-MD)
45. Representative Roscoe Bartlett (R-MD)
46. Representative Bill Shuster (R-PA)
47. Representative Paul Gillmor (R-OH)
48. Representative Eni Faleomavaega (D-AS)
49. Representative Elton Gallegly (R-CA)
50. Representative Nancy Johnson (R-CT)
51. Representative Earl Blumenauer (D-OR)
52. Representative Cal Dooley (D-CA)
53. Representative Melissa Hart (R-PA)
54. Representative Jim Davis (D-FL)
55. Representative Jim Kolbe (R-AZ)
56. Representative George Nethercutt (R-WA)

USSFTA Coalition Members

3M Company
ACE INA
Aerospace Ind. Ass'n of Amer.
Affymetrix
AIG
Alexander Strategy Group
Allegheny Valley Chamber of
  Commerce
AmCham Singapore
American International Group,
  Inc.
American Express Company
Americatel
Amway Corporation
Anaheim Chamber of
  Commerce
AOL Time Warner
APL Limited
Arizona Chamber of Commerce
Asia Global Crossing
AT&T
Automotive Trade Policy
  Council
Baker & McKenzie. Wong &
  Leow

Banco Credito Inversiones-
  Miami
Bank of America
Banta Corporation
Barrington Area Chamber of
  Commerce
Beavercreek Chamber of
  Commerce
Bechtel Corporation
Berks County Chamber of
  Commerce
Beverly Hills COC
Black & Veatch International
Boaz Chamber of Commerce
Bootstrap
Bradford Area Chamber of
  Commerce
Bristol-Myers Squibb Co.
Burson Marsteller (Miami)
Cargo Transport Inc.
Cargill
Carlsbad Chamber of
  Commerce
Carroll County Chamber of
  Commerce

Casa Grande Chamber of
Commerce
Caterpillar
Chavilah Corporation
CH2M Hill
Chicago Southland Chamber of
Commerce
Citigroup
Coalition for Open Markets and
Expanded Trade
Coalition of Service Industries,
Inc.
Cochran-Bleckley Chamber of
Commerce
Computer & Communications
Industry Assoc
Columbia-Adair County COC
ConocoPhillips
Council of the Americas
Cyberguard
DaimlerChrysler
Dansutha Printing
Darke County Chamber of
Commerce
Dayton Area Chamber of
Commerce
Decatur and Macon County
COC
Dell
Deringer Intergrated
Transportation
Direct Selling Association

Discovery Networks
International
DOW Corporation
Dublin Chamber of Commerce
Duke Energy International
Eastman Kodak
EDS Corporation
Edison Mission Energy
Emergency Committee for
American Trade
Energy International LLC
ExxonMobil Corporation
Federal Express
Florida FTAA
Fluor Corporation
Enterprise Florida
Fairview Heights Chamber of
Commerce
Fontheim International, LLC
Ford Motor Company
Fort Worth Chamber of
Commerce
Fremont Chamber of Commerce
Gardner International
General Electric Company
General Motors Corporation
Glendale Chamber of
Commerce
Grantha Services
Greater Casa Grande Chamber
of Commerce
Greater Crown Point Chamber
of Commerce

Greater Dallas Chamber of
  Commerce
Greater Houston Partnership
Greater Louisville, Inc.
Green Oaks Chamber of
  Commerce
Greenberg Traurig
Gulf County Chamber of
  Commerce
Healthcare Informatics
  Technology Service
Hewlett-Packard Co.
Holly Real Estate
Hollywood Chamber of
  Commerce
Houghton Lake Chamber of
  Commerce
IBM
Illinois State Chamber
Indiana State Chamber of
  Commerce
Indianapolis Chamber of
  Commerce
Information Technology
  Industry Council
Intel Corporation
InterVestors Capital
International Business –
  Government Counsellors, Inc.
Int'l Trade Alliance, Spokane
  Region
Interport, Ltd.
Joliet Region Chamber of
  Commerce

JP Morgan Chase & Company
Juki Union Special
Kankakee River Valley COC
Kenan Institute of Private
  Enterprise
Kentucky World Trade Center
Knight Manufacturing
  Corporation
Korea-U.S. Exchange Council
Lan Chile
Latin Food Network Corp.
Lawrence County Chamber of
  Commerce
Libertyville Chamber of
  Commerce
Lockheed Martin Corporation
Long Beach Chamber of
  Commerce
Ludington Area Chamber of
  Commerce
Marubeni America Corporation
McGraw-Hill Companies
Merck & Co., Inc.
Mercersburg Area Chamber of
  Commerce
Micro Informatica LLC
Microsoft
Modesto Chamber of
  Commerce
Morgan Stanley
Motion Picture Association of
  America
Motorola

Mundelein Chamber of
Commerce
National Association of
Manufacturers
National Electrical
Manufacturers
National Foreign Trade Council
National Pork Producers
Federation
New Albany Chamber of
Commerce
New Jersey Chamber of
Commerce
New York Life International
Northern Kane County COC
Northern Kentucky Chamber of
Commerce
Northwest and Schaumburg
Assoc. of Commerce and
Industry
Oakland Chamber of
Commerce
Ogilvy PR Worldwide
Orlando Regional Chamber of
Commerce
Over-the-Rhine Chamber of
Commerce
Pacific Architects and
Engineers, Inc.
PA Chamber of Business and
Industry
Pittsburgh Airport Area COC
Pfizer Pharmaceutical Group
PhRMA

Pike County Chamber of
Commerce
Port of Miami
Pratt & Whitney
PricewaterhouseCoopers
Qualcomm
Radcliff-Hardin County COC
Rockwell Automation, Inc.
Rockton Chamber of
Commerce
Riggs International Banking
Corp.
Rushville Area Chamber of
Commerce
Saline Area Chamber of
Commerce
Schering-Plough Corp.
Scottsdale Chamber of
Commerce
Securities Industry Association
Semiconductor Industry
Association
Southern Indiana Chamber of
Commerce
Standard Chartered Bank
Starbucks Coffee Corp.
Sterling Heights Chamber of
Commerce
Sun Microsystems
Superior Multi-Packaging Ltd
Sweet Paper Sales Corp.
Syncad Lift
The Boeing Company
The Business Roundtable

The Direct Impact Company
Toledo Area Chamber of
  Commerce
Tucson Chamber of Commerce
U.S. Ass'n of Importers of
  Textiles
U.S. Chamber of Commerce
U.S. Council for International
  Business
U.S. Wheat Trade Education
United Parcel Service
United Technologies
  Corporation
Unocal Corporation
US - ASEAN Business Council

Verizon Communications
Vernon Hills Chamber of
  Commerce
Vilar, Duty & Montero
VNU
Wachovia Bank
Wal-Mart
The Washington Post
WBC Global
Whirlpool
White & Case
World City Business
York County Chamber of
  Commerce

Joint Statement of the
American Federation of Labor and Congress of
Industrial Organizations (AFL-CIO)
and the Singapore National Trades Union Congress
(SNTUC) on a U.S.-Singapore Free Trade Agreement[1]

The SNTUC and the AFL-CIO welcome our governments' negotiations of a U.S.-Singapore Free Trade Agreement, aimed at fostering deeper economic integration and closer relations between our two countries and peoples. In order to ensure that the benefits of economic integration are broadly shared, the USSFTA must safeguard workers' rights, preserve the environment, and allow for ongoing and meaningful participation by representative civil society organizations, including the SNTUC and the AFL-CIO, in the implementation of the agreement.

We therefore call on our governments to ensure that the USSFTA includes the following:

1. EMPLOYMENT OPPORTUNITIES — We call on both parties to affirm and implement their commitment to creating greater and better employment opportunities, and improving the standard of living and quality of life for all workers.

2. CORE WORKERS' RIGHTS — Both parties must honour obligations and commitments to respect, promote and realise fundamental workers' rights under the ILO Declaration on Fundamental Principles and Rights at Work, as well as their commitment to effectively enforce domestic labor and

---

[1] *Source*: Singapore National Trades Union Congress

environmental laws and all international treaty obligations undertaken in these areas. These provisions must be included in the core of the agreement and covered by effective enforcement mechanisms. These provisions shall not be used as a means for protectionism.

3. TRANSPARENCY AND ACCOUNTABILITY — We call on both parties to agree to consult with their respective publics, including SNTUC and AFL-CIO, at timely intervals, prior to initiating dispute proceedings, to release relevant documents and open dispute panels to the public, and to accept friend-of-the-court submissions from interested parties.

4. GOVERNMENT SCOPE — No trade agreement should undermine the ability of governments to provide public services, to enact and enforce legitimate regulations in the public interest, or to use government procurement policies to achieve legitimate social goals. Investment rules must not create greater rights for foreign investors or take investor disputes with governments out of the public sphere.

The SNTUC and the AFL-CIO believe that freer trade should work in the fundamental interest of workers to create more and better paying jobs, and equitable, democratic, and sustainable development. We call on our governments to assume responsibility for all of the points mentioned here.

November 14, 2002

John de Payva
President
SNTUC

John J Sweeney
President
AFL-CIO

List of Articles and Annexes of the
U.S.-Jordan Free Trade Agreement[1]

Article 1: Establishing Trade and Relationship with Other Agreements

Article 2: Trade in Goods

Article 3: Trade in Services

Article 4: Intellectual Property Rights

Article 5: Environment

Article 6: Labor

Article 7: Electronic Commerce

Article 8: VISA

Article 9: Government Procurement

Article 10: Safeguard

Article 11: Balance of Payments

Article 12: Exceptions

Article 13: Economic Cooperation and Technical Assistance

Article 14: Rules of Origin and Cooperation in Customs Administration

Article 15: Joint Committee

Article 16: Consultation

Article 17: Dispute Settlements

Article 18: Miscellaneous Provisions

Article 19: Entry into Force and Termination

---

[1] For a full text of the FTA, please view http://www.jordanusfta.com/documents/textagr.pdf.

Annex 2.1: Tariff Elimination
Jordan
- Tariff Schedule
- Explanatory Notes to Jordan's Tariff Schedule

United States
- Tariff Schedule
- Explanatory Notes to United States' Tariff Schedule
- Annex to United States' Explanatory Notes

Annex 2.2: Rules of Origin
Annex 2.3: Understanding Concerning Article 2

Annex 3.1: Service Schedules
Jordan
- Schedule of Specific Commitments
- Service Schedules: List of Article II (MFN) Exemptions

United States
- Schedule of Specific Commitments
- Service Schedules: List of Article II (MFN) Exemptions

Annex 3.2: Memorandum of Understanding concerning Certain Reciprocity Requirements
Memorandums and Joint Statements
- Memorandum of Understanding on Issues Relating to Intellectual Property Rights
- Memorandum of Understanding on Transparency in Dispute Settlement
- Joint Statement on Environmental Technical Cooperation
- Joint Statement on World Trade Organization Issues
- Joint Statement on Electronic Commerce

Letters on Marketing Approval of Pharmaceutical Products
- Letter from United States Trade Representative to Jordan's Deputy Prime Minister for Economic Affairs
- Letter from Jordan's Deputy Prime Minister for Economic Affairs to United States Trade Representative

Letters on GATS Commitments
- Letter from United States Trade Representative to Jordan's Deputy Prime Minister for Economic Affairs
- Letter from Jordan's Deputy Prime Minister for Economic Affairs to United States Trade Representative

Letters on FTA's Entry into Force
- Letter from Ambassador Muasher to Asst. USTR Novelli
- Letter from Asst. USTR Novelli to Ambassador Muasher

Members of the Singapore Negotiating Team[1]

Chief Negotiator
Tommy **Koh** Thong Bee

Deputy Chief Negotiator
Ong Ye Kung

Internal Coordinators
Fang Min
Neo Gim Huay
Quah Ley Hoon
Tay Chng Yeow

Special Assistant to Chief Negotiator
Iris **Chen** I Zu (10th Round to completion)
Jophie **Tang** (1st to 9th Round)

Chapter 1: Establishment of a Free Trade Area and Definitions
Sivakant **Tiwari** (Lead Negotiator)
Deena Abdul Aziz Bajrai
Daren **Tang** Heng Shim

Chapter 2: National Treatment and Market Access for Goods
Rossman Ithnain (Lead Negotiator)
Deena Abdul Aziz Bajrai
Jeraldine **Ong**
Tan Juan Fook

---

[1] The members have been listed according to the chapters they negotiated for. The list was compiled from various government sources. We regret if any names were omitted inadvertently.

Chapter 3: Rules of Origin
Rossman Ithnain (Lead Negotiator)
Deena Abdul Aziz Bajrai
Lai Jiunn Ning
Wong Chian Voen

Chapter 4: Customs Administration
Tay Chng Yeow (Lead Negotiator until December 2001)
Ng How Yue (Lead Negotiator from January 2002)
Deena Abdul Aziz Bajrai
Lim Teck Leong

Chapter 5: Textiles and Apparel
Ng Kim Neo (Lead Negotiator)
Deena Abdul Aziz Bajrai
Peter **Low**
Minn Naing Oo
Aireen **Phang**
Tan Juan Fook
Tan Li Lin
Wong Hwee Ngo
Yeo Sew Meng

Chapter 6: Technical Barriers to Trade
Ng Kim Neo (Lead Negotiator)
Deena Abdul Aziz Bajrai

Chapter 7: Safeguards
Rossman Ithnain (Lead Negotiator)
Deena Abdul Aziz Bajrai
Aireen **Phang**

Chapter 8: Cross-Border Trade in Services
Daren **Tang** Heng Shim (Lead Negotiator)
Minn Naing Oo
Sheila **Saw**
Audrey **Tan**

Chapter 9: Telecommunications
Valerie **D'Costa** (Lead Negotiator)
David **Alfred**
Muhammad Hanafiah Bin Abdul Rashid
Gerald **Wee**

Chapter 10: Financial Services
Ravi **Menon** (Lead Negotiator)
Adrian **Chua** Tsen Leong

Chapter 11: Temporary Entry of Business Persons
Daren **Tang** Heng Shim (Lead Negotiator)

Chapter 12: Anticompetitive Business Conduct, Designated
Monopolies, and Government Enterprises
Yeo Kia Thye (Lead Negotiator)
Minn Naing Oo
Daren **Tang** Heng Shim

Chapter 13: Government Procurement
Lee How Sheng (Lead Negotiator until August 2001)
Chew Hock Yong (Co-Lead Negotiator from August 2001)
Tan Eng Beng (Co-Lead Negotiator from September 2002)
Tay Chng Yeow

Chapter 14: Electronic Commerce
Valerie **D'Costa** (Lead Negotiator)
David **Alfred**
Muhammad Hanafiah Bin Abdul Rashid
Gerald **Wee**

Chapter 15: Investment
Teoh Yong Sea (Lead Negotiator)
Deena Abdul Aziz Bajrai
Christopher **Lim** Hang-Kwang
Joyce **Low** Wai Ching

Minn Naing Oo
Kawitha **Vardeva**

Chapter 16: Intellectual Property Rights
Sivakant **Tiwari** (Lead Negotiator)
Lee Li Choon
Liew Woon Yin
Neo Gim Huay

Chapter 17: Labour
Ong Yen Her (Lead Negotiator)
Deena Abdul Aziz Bajrai
Low Pei Ching

Chapter 18: Environment
Loh Ah Tuan (Lead Negotiator)
Chua Yew Peng
Deena Abdul Aziz Bajrai
Khoo Seow Poh
Fion **Tan**

Chapter 19: Transparency
Sivakant **Tiwari** (Lead Negotiator)
Deena Abdul Aziz Bajrai
Daren **Tang** Heng Shim

Chapter 20: Administration and Dispute Settlement
Sivakant **Tiwari** (Lead Negotiator)
Deena Abdul Aziz Bajrai
Daren **Tang** Heng Shim

Chapter 21: General and Final Provisions
Sivakant **Tiwari** (Lead Negotiator)
Deena Abdul Aziz Bajrai
Daren **Tang** Heng Shim

Members of the Singapore Negotiating Team
(by alphabetical order)[2]

David **Alfred**
Legal Counsel, Infocomm Development Authority of Singapore

Iris **Chen** I Zu
Country Officer, Directorate II, Ministry of Foreign Affairs

Chew Hock Yong
Director, Central Services, Ministry of Finance (August 2001 to August 2002)
Director (Budget) Ministry of Finance (From September 2002)

Adrian **Chua** Tsen Leong
Assistant Director, Monetary Authority of Singapore

Chua Yew Peng
Deputy Director, International Relations, Ministry of the Environment

Valerie **D'Costa**
Director, International, Infocomm Development Authority

Deena Abdul Aziz Bajrai
State Counsel, Attorney-General's Chambers

Fang Min
Assistant Director, Trade, Ministry of Trade and Industry

---

[2] The designations listed are the positions that the members held during the negotiations. Some have since moved to other organisations or have left the civil service. The members are listed in alphabetical order of their family names which are in bold.

Linda Esther **Foo**
Assistant Director, Market & Business Conduct Department,
Monetary Authority of Singapore

Tommy **Koh** Thong Bee
Ambassador-At-Large, Ministry of Foreign Affairs

Lai Jiunn Ning
Assistant Director, Trade, Ministry of Trade and Industry

Lee How Sheng
Director, Central Services, Ministry of Finance (until August 2001)

Lee Li Choon
Principal Assistant Registrar, Intellectual Property Office of Singapore

Liew Woon Yin
Registrar and Director-General, Intellectual Property Office of
Singapore

Christopher **Lim** Hang-Kwang
Head, International Economics, Economic Development Board

Lim Teck Leong
Research and International Officer, Customs and Excise Department

Loh Ah Tuan
Director, Environmental Policy, Ministry of the Environment

Low Pei Ching
Senior International Labour and Policy Officer, Ministry of Manpower

Joyce **Low** Wai Ching
Assistant Head, International Agreements, Economic Development
Board

Khoo Seow Poh
Director, Corporate Communications & International Relations Division, Ministry of the Environment

Peter **Low**
Assistant Manager, Trade Enforcement Unit, International Enterprise Singapore

Ravi Menon
Assistant Managing Director (Complex Institutions), Monetary Authority of Singapore

Minn Naing Oo
Legal Officer, Ministry of Trade and Industry

Muhammad Hanafiah Bin Abdul Rashid
Assistant Director, International, Infocomm Development Authority

Neo Gim Huay
Deputy Director, Trade, Ministry of Trade and Industry

Ng How Yue
Deputy Director-General (Policy), Customs and Excise Department

Ng Kim Neo
Consultant, Trade, Ministry of Trade and Industry

Jeraldine **Ong**
Assistant Director, Trade, Ministry of Trade and Industry

Ong Ye Kung
Director, Trade, Ministry of Trade and Industry

Ong Yen Her
Director, Labour Relations Department, Ministry of Manpower

Aireen **Phang**
Assistant Director, Trade, Ministry of Trade and Industry

Quah Ley Hoon
Assistant Director, Trade, Ministry of Trade and Industry

Rossman Ithnain
Deputy Director, Trade, Ministry of Trade and Industry

Sheila **Saw**
Assistant Director, Trade, Ministry of Trade and Industry

Audrey **Tan**
Assistant Director, Trade, Ministry of Trade and Industry

Tan Eng Beng
Director, Corporate Development Division, Ministry of National Development

Fion **Tan**
Assistant Director, International Policy, Ministry of the Environment

Tan Juan Fook
Officer, Export Certification Unit, International Enterprise Singapore

Tan Li Lin
Deputy Director, Trade, International Enterprise Singapore

Tan York Chor
Senior Deputy Director/Directorate II, Ministry of Foreign Affairs

Daren **Tang** Heng Shim
State Counsel, Attorney-General's Chambers

Jophie **Tang**
Assistant Director, Directorate II, Ministry of Foreign Affairs

Tay Chng Yeow
Free Trade Agreement Coordinator, Ministry of Finance

Teh Thiam Siong
Research and International Officer, Customs and Excise Department

Teoh Yong Sea
Senior Director, International Business Development Division, Ministry of Trade and Industry

Sivakant **Tiwari**
Principal Senior State Counsel, Attorney-General's Chambers

Kawitha **Vardeva**
Senior Officer, International Agreements, Economic Development Board

Gerald **Wee** Jin Ann
Manager, International, Infocomm Development Authority

Wong Chian Voen
Assistant Director, Trade, Ministry of Trade and Industry

Wong Hwee Ngo
Manager, Lifestyle Division, International Enterprise Singapore

Yeo Kia Thye
Assistant Director, Investment Project, Ministry of Finance

Yeo Sew Meng
Head, Trade Control Branch, International Enterprise Singapore

Elaine **Ying**
Head, Intellectual Property Branch, Ministry of Home Affairs

The Singapore and U.S. Missions

The Singapore Mission to the United States in Washington D.C.[1]

Ambassador Chan Heng Chee
Mr. Stanley Loh, Deputy Chief of Mission
Mr. Balagopal Nair, Counsellor (Economics)
Ms. Neo Gim Huay, First Secretary
Mr. Jaime Ho, First Secretary
Mr. Syed Noureddin, First Secretary
Ms. Ariel Tan, First Secretary
Mr. Tan Soon Kim, First Secretary (Economics)
Mr. Lim Yuin Chien, First Secretary (Information)

The United States Mission to Singapore[2]

H.E. Ambassador Franklin L. Lavin
Mr. John Medeiros, Deputy Chief of Mission
Mr. Laurent Charbonnet, Counselor for Economic-Political Affairs (2002–present)
Mr. Douglas Spelman, Counselor for Economic-Political Affairs (1999–2002)
Mr. Paul A. Brown, First Secretary

---

[1] Members of the lobbying team in the Singapore Mission in Washington D.C.

[2] Members of the lobbying team in the United States Mission in Singapore.

Remarks by U.S. President George Bush at the Signing of the U.S.-Singapore Free Trade Agreement at the White House, Tuesday, 6 May 2003, Washington D.C.[1]

Thank you, good afternoon, and welcome to the White House. I'm honoured to host Prime Minister Goh as we sign an historic free trade agreement between the United States and Singapore.

Our two countries have a proud history of friendship and cooperation. We're working together to meet the threats of a new era, and we share a belief in the power of free enterprise and free trade to improve lives. The U.S.-Singapore Free Trade Agreement marks a crucial step forward for both our countries. And with the approval of the Congress, this agreement will help generate well-paying jobs and opportunities for people in Singapore and in the United States.

The Prime Minister is a man with whom I enjoy good conversations. He's got good advice, and I'm proud to call him "friend".

I appreciate so very much our — members of my Cabinet who are here: the Secretary of State; Secretary of Commerce; Trade Minister Robert Zoellick, Ambassador Zoellick. I want to thank very much the Singaporean delegation for coming. Madame Ambassador, it's good to see you again. I appreciate our Ambassador, Frank Lavin, for being here, and I appreciate his service to our country.

I'm so grateful for the members of Congress for being here. Thank you all for coming; strong free traders, people who believe in the possibility of trade, in the hope of trade. I want to thank members

---

[1] *Source*: Office of the U.S. White House Press Secretary.

of our business community who are here. Mr. Prime Minister, you've drawn quite a crowd.

America supports free trade because it creates new opportunities for millions of people, new wealth for entire nations, and benefits that are widely shared. NAFTA, in the Uruguay Round, for example, show us what free trade can accomplish. They've created more choices and lower prices for consumers, raising living standards for a typical American family of four by at least $2,000 a year. Free trade has a direct benefit for our citizens.

In NAFTA's first six years, more than half of Mexico's new manufacturing jobs were connected to trade. Trade helps people in our neighbourhood. It helps people find work. A prosperous neighbourhood is in the interest of the United States of America. Trade helps people emerge from poverty. Trade helps people realise their hopes and ambitions. Trade is an important part of improving the lives of people around the globe.

And that's why this administration strongly stands for free trade. From the first days of this administration, we have been working to extend the benefits of trade to every region of the world. We're a leader in the negotiations of the WTO. We've advanced bold proposals to open up global markets. We seek to build on the success of NAFTA with the Free Trade Area of the Americas.

We're also encouraging the free flow of trade and investment in the Pacific, among our partners in APEC and ASEAN. America has implemented a free trade agreement with Jordan, our first ever with an Arab nation. And we're finalising our pact with Chile. Similar negotiations are underway with Australia, Morocco, and five nations in the Central American region. And soon we'll be beginning negotiations with the Southern African Customs Union to bring new opportunities to a part of the world where the need is great.

The agreement that the Prime Minister and I sign today is the first of its kind between the United States and an Asian Pacific country. The four million people of Singapore have built a strong and vibrant economy. Singapore has long set an example for its neighbours in the world of the transforming power of economic freedom and open markets. Singapore is already America's 12th largest trading partner, and buys a full range of American products, everything from machine parts and computers to agricultural products.

This free trade agreement will increase access to Singapore's dynamic markets for American exporters, service providers and investors. The agreement contains state of the art protections for Internet commerce and intellectual property that will help drive growth and innovation in our dynamic technology sectors.

The agreement also safeguards the right of workers and protections for our environment. It's a modern agreement. And it's a good agreement for both countries. By granting free trade — by granting trade promotion authority last year, Congress showed support for an agenda of free and open trade. And I want to thank them for that. I hope the Congress will act in this same spirit and quickly give final approval to this agreement — and I'm sure they will. Singapore is a nation that is small in size, but large in influence. With this agreement, Singapore becomes an even more valued economic partner of the United States.

Mr. Prime Minister, your nation has also been a vital and steadfast friend in the fight against global terror. Singapore has made determined and successful efforts to break up terror plots before they can take innocent lives.

As a member of the U.N. Security Council, Singapore worked hard to secure the passage of Resolution 1441, requiring Iraq to live up to its international obligations. And now with Iraq's liberation, Singapore will send police and health care workers to help with Iraq's reconstruction.

Mr. Prime Minister, I appreciate your nation's contribution as we overcome great dangers and defend the peace. I'm grateful, as well, for your commitment to a world that trades in freedom and for all the hard work on both sides that have made this agreement possible. We take great pride in the strong relationship between our countries.

Remarks by Singapore Prime Minister Goh Chok Tong at the Signing of the U.S.-Singapore Free Trade Agreement at the White House, Tuesday, 6 May 2003, Washington D.C.[2]

I am delighted to join President Bush to sign the U.S.-Singapore Free Trade Agreement.

We launched negotiations during the APEC Economic Leaders' Meeting in Brunei two years ago. The reasons were both economic and strategic. The FTA would enhance our close economic relations. It would also signal the U.S.'s long term commitment to engage Southeast Asia and contribute to its development.

These reasons are even more valid today. In particular, defeating terrorism in Southeast Asia requires American leadership. President Bush's resolute stand on this issue has given courage and heart to our people, especially the victims and intended victims of terrorism. The world must not be intimidated by the terrorists. We must not allow them to derail our development. Southeast Asia supports the U.S. in the fight against terrorism.

Indeed, since the Second World War, no country has played as important a role in Southeast Asia as America. You shed blood defending freedom in Korea and Vietnam. Your sacrifice bought the non-communist countries of Southeast Asia precious time and protective cover to consolidate our new nations. In the last three decades, the U.S. has continued to work closely with ASEAN on security issues. You have also generously opened your markets, shared technology and invested capital in our economies at crucial times in our development. America's presence has helped to shape contemporary Southeast Asia. Without the U.S., ASEAN would not have prospered as quickly as we did.

---

[2] *Source*: Singapore Government Media Release, Media Division, Ministry of Information and the Arts.

Over the years, exchanges of goods, services, investments, people, ideas and technology between Singapore and America have strengthened. The U.S.-Singapore FTA builds upon this solid foundation of growing economic links.

Today, we have one of the closest trans-Pacific relationships. Our relationship is multidimensional: in defence as well as economics, with a shared strategic vision. We are a small country, with about the same population as Rhode Island — four million. But Singapore is your 12th largest trading partner and the second largest investor from Asia. And the U.S. has consistently been Singapore's most important trading and investment partner.

The U.S.-Singapore FTA is an ambitious and comprehensive agreement. It removes barriers in the goods and services trade and in investments. It breaks new ground in emerging areas like e-commerce. It also establishes high standards in intellectual property, transparency and customs.

The FTA will expand opportunities for American businesses in Singapore. More importantly, the U.S.-Singapore FTA can be a model for other FTAs under President Bush's Enterprise for ASEAN Initiative (EAI). I hope the EAI will quickly result in more FTAs between the U.S. and Southeast Asia.

In short, Singapore appreciates your friendship. Our strong relations are based on shared interests in many areas. We now fight terrorism together. We have good defence links. We both strongly advocate open trade and investment and the multilateral trading system.

There are many people to thank for this historic agreement, the first between a country in Asia and the U.S.: the Chief Negotiators, Ralph Ives and Tommy Koh, and their teams; USTR Bob Zoellick and Minister George Yeo; and the business community, especially the U.S.-Singapore Business Coalition led by Boeing, Exxon Mobil and United Parcel Services, the U.S.-ASEAN Business Council, and the U.S. Chamber of Commerce and its local chapter in Singapore.

I thank also the Singapore Congressional Caucus led by Congressman Solomon Ortiz, Congressman Curt Weldon, the Ways and Means Committee and the Senate Finance Committee. Some of them are here today.

Finally, let me thank you, President Bush, most warmly for your friendship to Singapore and to me, and for your vision and your leadership. Without President Bush, our FTA would not have come to such an expeditious and successful conclusion.

I look forward to even closer relations between our countries under the FTA.

Thank you.

Temasek Charter[1]

Temasek Holdings holds and manages the Singapore Government's investments in companies, for the long term benefit of Singapore.

By nurturing successful and vibrant international businesses from its stable of companies, Temasek will help to broaden and deepen Singapore's economic base.

Temasek will work with its companies to:

Values
Promote and maintain a strong culture of integrity, meritocracy, excellence and innovation;

Focus
Foster a strong focus on core competence, value creation, customer fulfilment and shareholder returns; and divest non-core businesses, so as to maximise long-term shareholder benefit;

Human Capital
Nurture and cultivate a strong and internationally competitive cadre of board and management leadership, as well as outstanding employees to build successful businesses;

Sustainable Growth
Support and institutionalise high standards of business leadership, financial discipline, operational excellence and corporate governance to achieve scaleable and sustainable growth; and

---

[1] Issued by Temasek Holdings on 3 July 2002.

Strategic Development

Shape strategic developments, including consolidations, mergers, acquisitions, rationalisation or collaborations as appropriate; to build significant international or regional businesses.

Temasek will divest businesses which are no longer relevant or have no international growth potential.

Temasek may also, from time to time, invest in new businesses, in order to nurture new industry clusters in Singapore.

Elaboration

Background

1 Temasek Holdings was formed in 1974 as a focal point to hold and manage the Singapore government's investments in companies for the long-term benefit of Singapore.

2 Many of its businesses have their roots in the history of Singapore's economic development. For instance, Singapore Airlines was formed through the de-merger of Malaysia-Singapore Airlines after Singapore's separation from Malaysia, and SembCorp Marine evolved from the commercialisation of the naval dockyard facilities when British military forces withdrew from the Far East. In each case, the goals were to develop economically viable businesses, retain and create jobs, and contribute to Singapore's economic survival, progress and prosperity.

Relationship with Temasek Companies

3 In the next phase of Singapore's economic development, Temasek aims to build and nurture internationally competitive businesses. These can leverage on Singapore's competitive strengths and, in turn, enhance Singapore's economic resilience.

4 Temasek expects all its companies to continually innovate, explore new technologies or markets, operate on sound

commercial principles, and deliver commercial returns in a globally competitive environment.

5   Temasek will exercise its shareholder rights to influence the strategic directions of its companies. But it does not involve itself in their day-to-day commercial decisions.

6   Temasek will continually review its stable of companies, and rationalise or consolidate them where it makes commercial and strategic business sense, so as to enhance long-term shareholder returns.

Group A Businesses — Government Ownership and Control
7   Government needs to own and control companies for various reasons. These include:

(a) *Critical resources* — where ownership of a resource is critical to Singapore's security or economic well-being, or where the business is a natural domestic monopoly for which a market-based regulatory framework has not yet been established. These include water, power and gas grids, airport, and seaport; or

(b) *Public policy objectives* — where ownership enables the government to achieve specific public policy objectives, by providing services or assuring control for the public good. These include gaming, public broadcasting, subsidised services in health care, education and housing, and various public amenities like the zoo and bird park.

8   The government will continue to hold majority or significant stakes in such Group A companies, for so long as there is specific requirement for government ownership or support. Should such businesses become no longer strategic to Singapore, or when viable market alternatives or regulatory frameworks are in place, the government will divest or dilute its shareholdings.

9 Where Temasek has stewardship of Group A companies on behalf of the government, Temasek will ensure their financial discipline and sound management, with a clear focus on customer orientation, strategic and operational effectiveness and economic viability in order to fulfil their respective missions.

Group B Businesses — International / Regional Potential

10 Regardless of ownership, Singapore companies cannot depend solely on the domestic market for their long-term growth, particularly in view of the trends in technology, liberalisation and deregulation.

11 Group B businesses within the Temasek stable are those with the potential to grow beyond the domestic market, into the regional or international markets. Companies such as PSA Corporation have internationalised to leverage onto the global network, while others, such as DBS Bank, have expanded beyond their domestic market base to take advantage of regional opportunities.

12 Temasek is open to Group B companies partnering other companies or shareholders to regionalise or internationalise where it makes strategic or commercial sense. Temasek is prepared to dilute its stake through the issuance of new shares, or mergers or acquisitions in order to support the long-term success of these companies as regional or international players.

13 Temasek may also, from time to time, invest in new businesses with regional or international potential in order to nurture new industry clusters. These are likely to be in new growth sectors which entail high risk, large investments or long gestation periods, where private enterprise in Singapore is unable or unwilling to assume risks. Temasek will be highly selective in making such new investments.

Rationalisation and Divestments

14 Since its inception, Temasek has progressively divested its stake in companies which are no longer strategic to Singapore or relevant to Temasek's mission. It has also publicly listed major companies which have evolved from statutory boards, such as Keppel Corporation and Singapore Telecommunications, to broaden their share ownership base and support their growth. Temasek companies have in turn divested their non-core assets and listed some of their major shareholdings over the years.

15 Temasek will continue to rationalise and consolidate its shareholdings, where there are opportunities to improve shareholder returns. It will continue to divest businesses which no longer require government participation, or which have limited potential for regional or international growth. This will enable Temasek to focus its financial and management resources in areas where it can make a distinct contribution to developing the Singapore economy through successful international and regional enterprise.

The USSFTA Article 2.12: Tariff Treatment of Non-originating Cotton and Man-made Fiber Apparel Goods (Tariff Preference Levels)

1. Subject to paragraphs 3 and 4, the United States shall apply the applicable rate of duty under paragraph 2 to imports of cotton or man-made fiber apparel goods provided for in Chapters 61 and 62 of the Harmonized System and covered by the U.S. categories listed in Annex 2B that are both cut (or knit to shape) and sewn or otherwise assembled in Singapore from fabric or yarn produced or obtained outside the territory of a Party, and that meet the applicable conditions for preferential tariff treatment under this Agreement, other than the condition that they be originating goods.

2. The rate of duty applicable to goods described in paragraph 1 is the United States most favoured-nation rate of duty reduced in five equal annual increments, beginning on the date this Article enters into force, such that the rate of duty shall be zero beginning on the first day of the fifth year after that date .

3. Paragraph 1 shall not apply to imports of goods described in that paragraph in quantities greater than:

  (a) 25,000,000 square meter equivalents ("SME") in the first year following entry into force of this Article;
  (b) 21,875,000 SME in the second year following entry into force of this Article;
  (c) 18,750,000 SME in the third year following entry into force of this Article;
  (d) 15,625,000 SME in the fourth year following entry into force of this Article;

(e) 12,500,000 SME in the fifth year following entry into force of this Article;

(f) 9,375,000 SME in the sixth year following entry into force of this Article;

(g) 6,250,000 SME in the seventh year following entry into force of this Article; and

(h) 3,125,000 SME in the eighth year following entry into force of this Article.

For purposes of this paragraph, quantities of textile and apparel goods shall be converted into SME according to the conversion factors set forth in Annex 2D.

4. This Article shall cease to apply beginning on the date that is nine years after entry into force of this Article.

Annex 2D: Conversion Factors

The following conversion factors shall be used to calculate quantities in SME for purposes of Article 2.12.

U.S. Category	Conversion Factor	Description	Primary Unit of Measure[1]
237	19.20	Playsuits, sunsuits, etc	Dz
239	6.30	Babies' garments & clothing access	Kg
330	1.40	Cotton handkerchiefs	Dz
331	2.90	Cotton gloves and mittens	Dpr
332	3.80	Cotton hosiery	Dpr
333	30.30	M&B suittype coats, cotton	Dz
334	34.50	Other M&B coats, cotton	Dz
335	34.50	W&G cotton coats	Dz
336	37.90	Cotton dresses	Dz
338	6.00	M&B cotton knit shirts	Dz
339	6.00	W&G cotton knit shirts/blouses	Dz
340	20.10	M&B cotton shirts, not knit	Dz
341	12.10	W&G cotton shirts/blouses, not knit	Dz
342	14.90	Cotton skirts	Dz

continued

U.S. Category	Conversion Factor	Description	Primary Unit of Measure[1]
345	30.80	Cotton sweaters	Dz
347	14.90	M&B cotton trousers/breeches/shorts	Dz
348	14.90	W&G cotton trousers/breeches/shorts	Dz
349	4.00	Brassieres, other body support garments	Dz
350	42.60	Cotton dressing gowns, robes etc	Dz
351	43.50	Cotton nightwear/pajamas	Dz
352	9.20	Cotton underwear	Dz
353	34.50	M&B cotton downfilled coats	Dz
354	34.50	W&G cotton downfilled coats	Dz
359	8.50	Other cotton apparel	Kg
630	1.40	MMF handkerchiefs	Dz
631	2.90	MMF gloves and mittens	Dpr
632	3.80	MMF hosiery	Dpr
633	30.30	M&B mmf suittype coats	Dz
634	34.50	Other M&B mmf coats	Dz
635	34.50	W&G MMF coats	Dz
636	37.90	MMF dresses	Dz
638	15.00	M&B mmf knit shirts	Dz
639	12.50	W&G mmf knit shirts & blouses	Dz
640	20.10	M&B not-knit mmf shirts	Dz
641	12.10	W&G not-knit mmf shirts & blouses	Dz
642	14.90	MMF skirts	Dz
643	3.76	M&B MMF suits	No
644	3.76	W&G MMF suits	No
645	30.80	M&B MMF sweaters	Dz
646	30.80	W&G MMF sweaters	Dz
647	14.90	M&B MMF trousers/breeches/shorts	Dz
648	14.90	W&G MMF trousers/breeches/shorts	Dz
649	4.00	MMF bras & other body support garments	Dz
650	42.60	MMF robes, dressing gowns, etc	Dz
651	43.50	MMF nightwear & pajamas	Dz
652	13.40	MMF underwear	Dz
653	34.50	M&B MMF downfilled coats	Dz
654	34.50	W&G MMF downfilled coats	Dz
659	14.40	Other MMF apparel	Kg

1 Dz = dozen; Dpr = dozen pairs; Kg = kilograms.

Negotiators of the Goods/Rules of Origin/Safeguard Chapters

Mr. Rossman Ithnian (Lead Negotiator)
Deputy Director, Trade Division-Directorate B,
Ministry of Trade & Industry
(Full bio is available on page 61, footnote 1.)

Ms. Wong Chian Voen (Rules of Origin)
Assistant Manager, Trade Policy Division, IE Singapore and
Assistant Director, Trade Division-B, Ministry of Trade and
Industry from 1 April 2002
She left the Ministry in August 2002 to join the private sector.

Ms. Lai Jiunn Ning (Rules of Origin)
Senior Trade Officer, Trade Policy Department, IE Singapore and
Assistant Director, Trade Division-B, Ministry of Trade and
Industry from 1 April 2002
Her FTA experience includes negotiations with the U.S., Australia
and EFTA. She is currently involved in negotiating the FTA with
Jordan and India.

Mr. Tan Juan Fook (Market Access)
Higher Superintendent, Classification and Statistics Audit Branch,
Singapore Customs
His job focuses on interpreting the rules of origin and Certificates of
Origin documentary procedures for products exported from Singapore.
He joined the trade service in 1986 and converted to the customs
service when the Trade Facilitation Division of IE Singapore

merged with Customs and Excise Department to form Singapore Customs in April 2003.

Ms. Aireen Phang (Safeguards and Safeguards in the Textiles Chapter)
Senior Trade Officer, Trade Policy Deparment, IE Singapore and Assistant Director, Trade Division-B, Ministry of Trade and Industry from 1 April 2002
Her FTA experience includes negotiating with Japan and EFTA. She left the Ministry in July 2003.

Ms. Jeraldine Ong (Goods)
Senior Trade Officer, Trade Policy Deparment, IE Singapore and Assistant Director, Trade Division-B, Ministry of Trade and Industry from 1 April 2002
Her FTA experience includes negotiating with Japan and the U.S.

Ms. Deena Abdul Aziz Bajrai
State Counsel, International Affairs Division, Attorney-General's Chambers
Deena has been with the Altorney-General's Chambers since 1993. Prior to joining the International Affairs Division, Deena was a deputy public prosecutor with the Crime Division of the AGC. In the International Affairs Division, Deena has advised the government on various matters relating to international law like aviation, human rights, and international trade, and represented the Singapore government in various international negotiations and conferences in various international law forums.

Negotiators of the Customs Administration Chapter

Mr. Tay Chng Yeow (Lead Negotiator until end 2001)
Coordinator (Free Trade Agreement), Ministry of Finance
Chng Yeow joined the customs service as a senior officer in 1969 and was the Deputy Director-General of the Customs Department since 1995 before he was seconded to the Ministry of Finance as Coordinator (FTA) in January 2002. As the Deputy-Director General of Customs, he managed the department's manpower and resources to meet the corporate goals and objectives as well as formulate organisational and revenue policies. His present work in the Ministry of Finance (MOF) involves formulating policies and development of a holistic approach to FTA issues in MOF as well as representing Singapore in FTA negotiations in the areas concerning MOF.

Mr. Ng How Yue (Lead Negotiator)
Director-General of Customs
How Yue joined the USSFTA negotiating team for the Customs chapter in January 2002. He was then the Deputy Director-General (Policy), overseeing customs policy matters.

Mr. Lim Teck Leong
Head Intelligence, Singapore Customs
(Full bio is available on page 75, footnote 1.)

Negotiators of the Textiles and Apparel Chapter

Ms. Ng Kim Neo (Lead Negotiator)
Consultant, Trade Division A, Ministry of Trade and Industry
(Full bio is available on page 83, footnote 1.)

Mrs. Tan Li Lin (Market Access)
Deputy Director, Lifestyle Division, Corporate Group,
International Enterprise Singapore (IE Singapore)
She has been involved in the textiles and apparel trade and bilateral negotiations under the WTO-ATC. She oversees industries such as textiles & garment, food & beverages, food services, furniture & furnishing, wellness, retail and travel. The Division helps Singapore-based companies to internationalise. This includes the managing of the textile quota allocation. Tan has been with IE Singapore since 1978.

Ms. Wong Hwee Ngo (Market Access)
Senior Account Manager of the Lifestyle Division, Corporate
Group in International Enterprise Singapore (IE Singapore)
She is in charge of the textiles and garment industry sector. She administers the Textile Quota System. She is also tasked to help Singapore-based textile and garment companies to internationalise successfully. She joined IE Singapore since 1979.

Mr. Tan Juan Fook (Market Access)
Higher Superintendent, Classification and Statistics Audit Branch, Singapore Customs
(Full bio is available on page 266, Appendix XI.)

Mr. Yeo Sew Meng (Customs Cooperation)
Head, Trade Control Branch, Singapore Customs
He oversees matters relating to strategic goods controls and enforcement of rules of origin under the various Free Trade Agreements signed by Singapore. Prior to Singapore Customs, he served as an Assistant Director in International Enterprise Singapore and as a senior officer in the Singapore Police Force.

Mr. Peter Low (Customs Cooperation)
Higher Superintendent, Trade Control Branch,
Singapore Customs
He was among the officers transferred from the Trade Facilitation Division in the Trade Development Board, now known as IE Singapore, to Singapore Customs in April 2003.

Negotiators of the Telecommunications and Electronic Commerce Chapter

Ms. Valerie D'Costa (Team Leader)
Director, International Division, Info-Communication
Development Authority of Singapore (IDA)
(Full bio is available on page 95, footnote 1.)

Mr. Muhammad Hanafiah Bin Abdul Rashid
Assistant Director, Infocomm Development Authority
of Singapore (IDA)
Since joining the IDA in 2000, Muhammad Hanafiah has worked in the International Division of IDA. He oversees a team of officers who represent IDA on ICT issues at the free trade negotiations and at international fora like APEC, ASEAN, the WTO and the ITU. Before joining the IDA, Hanafiah held positions at the Ministry of Information Communications and the Arts and the Public Works Department.

Mr. Gerald Wee Jin Ann
Senior Manager, Infocomm Development Authority
of Singapore (IDA)
Wee joined the IDA's International Division in 2000. His areas of work have included assisting in the negotiation of the ICT aspects of the Singapore-Japan free trade agreement, the agreement between the EFTA states and Singapore and the USSFTA. He also serves by representing the IDA at International fora like the OECD, the ASEAN Telecommunications Regulators Council and UPU. Before

joining IDA, Wee worked as an international relations executive in Singapore Airlines.

Mr. David Alfred
Legal Counsel, Infocomm Development Authority of Singapore (IDA)

As IDA's legal counsel for the USSFTA, Alfred represented IDA and advised the USSFTA negotiating team on legal aspects of ICT issues arising from the negotiations on Intellectual Property Rights. He is currently pursuing further studies and is on no-pay leave from the IDA.

Singapore and U.S. Reach Agreement on the Issue of Free Transfer of Capital, 16 January 2003[1]

The Singapore and U.S. Governments have reached an agreement on the issue of free transfer of capital, which was the only outstanding matter in the U.S.-Singapore Free Trade Agreement. The agreement provides for the free transfer of capital in both countries and enhances the protection and rights of U.S. investors, while maintaining Singapore's freedom of action to take appropriate measures in the event of an economic crisis.

Singapore and the U.S. share a strong commitment to the free and unfettered flow of capital. Both countries have therefore taken on an obligation in the FTA to guarantee investors free transfers into and out of their countries. The protection and rights afforded to investors under this agreement are substantially higher than under the WTO Agreements.

An open capital account has been and remains a critical factor underpinning Singapore's economic growth and development as a financial centre. Singapore fully intends to maintain its reputation as an international financial centre, and does not envisage having to impose restrictions on capital flows.

However, in an extreme balance of payments crisis that threatens to severely destabilise the economy, Singapore needs the flexibility to take all appropriate measures, including, where absolutely unavoidable, restrictions on capital flows. The agreement therefore contains special provisions under which Singapore would not be

---

[1] Press statement issued by the Monetary Authority of Singapore (MAS), 16 January 2003.

liable for claims for damages by investors if it imposes restrictions on capital account transactions, provided the restrictions last for less than one year and do not substantially impede transfers.[2]

These special provisions apply only to short term capital account transactions, such as portfolio investments and inter-bank loans and placements. They do not apply to current payments and transfers such as debt servicing, profit repatriation, and dividend payments as well as proceeds from the sale of foreign direct investments. Thus even in a crisis, while Singapore retains the flexibility to place temporary restrictions on potential short-term flows, current payments and direct investments will be fully protected by the free transfers provision.

---

[2] The agreement clarifies that a restriction is presumed to not substantially impede transfers if it meets certain conditions such as being non-confiscatory, non-discriminatory, price-based (e.g. in the form of a tax or levy), and not interfering with the investor's ability to earn a market rate of return in Singapore. The agreement also clarifies the scope of compensation that investors affected by measures that are deemed to substantially impede transfers may seek.

Negotiators of the Financial Services Chapter

Mr. Ravi Menon (Lead Negotiator)
Deputy Secretary, Ministry of Finance
(Full bio is available on page 105, footnote 1.)

Mr. Adrian Chua Tsen Leong
Assistant Director, Monetary Authority of Singapore
Since joining the Monetary Authority of Singapore (MAS) in 2000, Adrian has worked in the areas of banking liberalisation policy, strategic planning, and regulation of exchanges. He also served in the Secretariat to the Economic Review Committee's Financial Services Working Group, and as a member of the USSFTA negotiating team for financial services.

Negotiators of the Intellectual Property Rights Chapter

Mr. Sivakant Tiwari (Lead Negotiator)
Principal Senior State Counsel of the International Affairs
Division in the Attorney-General's Chambers, Singapore
(Full bio is available on page 151, footnote 1.)

Ms. Liew Woon Yin
Director-General of the Intellectual Property Office of Singapore
(IPOS)
(Full bio is available on page 123, footnote 1.)

Ms. Lee Li Choon
Director of Trade Marks and Legal Counsel, Intellectual Property
Office of Singapore
Since joining the Intellectual Office of Singapore (IPOS) in 1996, Li Choon has been actively involved in the implementation work to give effect to the World Trade Organisation Agreement on Trade-Related Aspects of Intellectual Property Rights (TRIPS Agreement) through her role as a member of an Inter-Ministerial Committee chaired by Mr. S. Tiwari. She has looked into areas of copyright policy and policy review which culminated in amendments to the copyright legislation in 1999. She has also been representing Singapore in the World Intellectual Property Office (WIPO) Standing Committee on Copyright and Related Rights. In addition, she handles trademark opposition cases and trademark applications. In her legal counsel portfolio, she specialises in copyright policy and legislative work.

Ms. Neo Gim Huay
Deputy Director (Government and Investment),
Ministry of Finance
(Full bio is available on page 177, footnote 1.)

Negotiators of the Labour Chapter

Mr. Ong Yen Her (Lead Negotiator)
Divisional Director, Labour Relations & Welfare Division,
Ministry of Manpower
(Full bio is available on page 135, footnote 1.)

Ms. Low Pei Ching
International Labour and Policy Section, Labour Relations
Department, Ministry of Manpower
Ms. Low is the Senior Labour Desk Officer of the International
Labour and Policy Section. She handles various issues relating to
international labour, including matters concerning ILO's activities
as well as regional labour issues within ASEAN's cooperative
framework on labour. She also helps in the review and formulation
of policies relating to international and regional labour affairs.
Ms. Low is currently on secondment at the Singapore National
Trades Union Congress for greater exposure to trade union and
workers' issues.

List of Singapore Laws and Regulations Relating to the USSFTA (As of 11 March 2004)

1. Customs (Duties) (Amendment No. 6) Order 2003
2. Regulation of Import and Export (Amendment) (Chewing Gum) Regulations 2003
3. Sale of Food (Prohibition of Chewing Gum) Regulations 2003
4. Medicines (Oral Dental Gums)(Specification) Order 2003
5. Medicines (Cosmetic Products) (Specification and Prohibition) (Amendment) Order 2003
6. Medicines (Prescription Oral Dental Gums) Order 2003
7. Medicines (Oral Dental Gums) (Labelling) Regulations 2003
8. Medicines (Advertising of Oral Dental Gums) Regulations 2003
9. Medicines (Oral Dental Gums) (Licensing) Regulations 2003
10. Medicines (Registration of Pharmacies) (Amendment) Regulations 2003
11. Regulation of Imports and Exports (Amendment) Bill 2003
12. Regulation of Imports and Exports (Amendment No. 4) Regulations 2003
13. Insurance (Amendment) Bill 2003
14. Insurance Regulations 2003

Joint Declaration on the Proposed U.S.-Singapore Free Trade Agreement, 17 January 2001[1]

On November 16, 2000, President Clinton and Prime Minister Goh Chok Tong agreed to launch negotiations for a free trade agreement (FTA) between the United States and Singapore.

The United States and Singapore conducted two rounds of negotiations for the U.S.-Singapore Free Trade Agreement (FTA), the first from December 4-21 and the second from January 10-January 18,2001, in Washington D.C. During the week of January 8, 2001, U.S. experts visited Singapore for fact-finding missions.

As a result of these efforts, substantial progress has been achieved, and we have a document of consolidated texts reflecting our countries' respective proposals as of January 17, 2001. Much work remains to be done to result in a final Agreement.

The United States and Singapore remain committed to achieving a comprehensive FTA that will increase the flow of trade and investment. We share the vision of a closer commercial relationship that reinforces our already strong political ties. We recognize that the U.S.-Singapore FTA is an important initiative that will enhance our mutual interest in a strong ASEAN and East Asia and will further strengthen the partnership across the Pacific.

The U.S.-Singapore FTA will contribute to regional and global trade liberalization and strengthen the multilateral trading system. We commit to an FTA that covers substantially all trade and is consistent with our World Trade Organization obligations. The FTA

---

[1] *Source*: Singapore Government Media Release, Media Division, Ministry of Information and the Arts.

will be fully in line with APEC goals and principles, particularly the Bogor Declaration and the Osaka Action Agenda.

We agreed to hold a new round of negotiations in Singapore as soon as possible and, in the meantime, that our experts should continue discussions of technical issues.

Charlene Barshefsky
United States Trade Representative
For the Government of The United
States of America

George Yeo
Minister for Trade and Industry
For the Government of
Singapore

Listing of U.S. Trade Advisory Committees

1 Advisory Committee for Trade Policy and Negotiations (ACTPN)
2 Trade and Environment Policy Advisory Committee (TEPAC)
3 Intergovernmental Policy Advisory Committee (IGPAC)
4 Labour Advisory Committee (LAC)
5 Agricultural Policy Advisory Committee (APAC)

Agricultural Technical Advisory Committee for Trade (ATAC)[1]
6 Animal and Animal Product ATAC
7 Fruits and Vegetables ATAC
8 Tobacco, Cotton and Peanuts ATAC
9 Sweeteners ATAC
10 Grains, Feed and Oilseeds ATAC

Industry Functional Advisory Committee (IFAC)[2]
11 IFAC 1 — Customs Matters
12 IFAC 2 — Standards
13 IFAC 3 — Intellectual Property Rights
14 IFAC 4 — Electronic Commerce

Industry Sector Advisory Committee (ISAC)[3]
15 ISAC 1 — Aerospace Equipment
16 ISAC 2 — Capital Goods
17 ISAC 3 — Chemicals and Allied Products
18 ISAC 4 — Consumer Goods

[1,2] These committees are sub-divided into smaller committees.

[3] ISAC committees have subsequently been reorganised in November 2003.

A Chronology of the USSFTA

Launching the USSFTA

United States President William J. Clinton and Singapore Prime Minister Goh Chok Tong announced their agreement to launch the United States-Singapore Free Trade Agreement (USSFTA) on 16 November 2000 in Brunei Darusalam.

Clinton Administration's Request for Public Feedback

On 29 November 2000, the Office of the United States Trade Representative (USTR) requested for public comments on the proposed USSFTA. The public had 60 days to respond.

Negotiating the USSFTA

A total of 11 formal rounds of negotiations took place in Washington D.C., Singapore and London. Many intersessional meetings were held in between the formal rounds. London was selected as the third location as it was easily accessed by the two delegations by non-stop flights. Intersessional meetings (IM) are italicised below.

Round	Dates	Meeting	Location
	2000		
1	**4–21 December**	**Formal Round**	**Washington, D. C.**
	2001		
	9–11 January	Fact finding mission to Singapore led by Martin Walsh, Department of Commerce	
2	**10–18 January**	**Formal Round**	**Washington, D. C.**
3	**21–25 May**	**Formal Round**	**Singapore**
	23 May	IM: Video-conference: Financial Services	

continued

Round	Dates	Meeting	Location
4	**16–21 July**	**Formal Round**	**London**
	2 August	IM: Video-conference: Financial Services	
	7 August	IM: Video-conference: ICT/ E-commerce	
	17 August	IM: Video-conference: Trade in Goods	
	19 September	IM: Video-conference: Financial Services	
	26–28 September	IM: Video-conference: ICT/ E-commerce	
	9–10 October	IM: Financial Services	Geneva
5	**22–26 October**	**Formal Round**	**London**
	22 October	IM: Teleconference: ICT/ E-commerce	
	31 Oct – 1 Nov	IM: ICT/E-commerce	London
	18 December	IM: Video-conference: Financial Services	
	2002		
6	**28 Jan – 1 Feb**	**Formal Round**	**London**
	11 January	IM: Video-conference: Services	
	17 January	IM: Video-conference: Services	
	4–8 February	IM: Textiles and Apparel	London
	22 February	IM: Video-conference: ICT/ E-commerce	
	4–8 March	IM: Trade in Goods	Washington, D.C.
	11–15 March	IM: Textiles and Apparel	London
	18–20 March	IM: Financial Services	Washington, D.C.
7	**11–14 March**	**Formal Round**	**London**
8	**15–26 April**	**Formal Round**	**London**
	15–19 April	IM: Trade in Goods	Washington, D.C.
	16–25 April	IM: Textiles and Apparel	Washington, D.C.

continued

Round	Dates	Meeting	Location
	17 April	Visit to Singapore by William Lash, U.S. Asst. Secretary of Commerce	Singapore
		IM: Video-conference: Services	
	22–24 April	IM: Safeguards	Washington, D.C.
	2 May	IM: Video-conference: Intellectual Property Rights	
	10 May	IM: Video-conference: Government Procurement	
		IM: Video-conference: Financial Services	
	3–8 June	IM: Trade in Goods	Washington, D.C.
	7 June	IM: Video-conference: Financial Services	
9	**20 June–4 July**	**Formal Round**	**London**
	1–2 July	IM: Textiles and Apparel U.S. Textile Team led by David Spooner on fact-finding mission to Singapore	Singapore
	2–3 July	Financial Services	London
	5–6 August	IM: ICT/E-commerce Issues	Washington, D.C.
	18 August	IM: Video-conference: Financial Services	
	28 August	IM: Video-conference: Government Procurement	
	6 September	IM: Video-conference: Competition	
	8–13 September	IM: Rules of Origin and Trade in Goods	Washington, D.C.
	25 September	IM: Video-conference: Temporary Entry	
10	**30 Sept–5 Oct**	**Formal Round**	**London**
	21 October	IM: Video-conference: Services and Investment	

continued

Round	Dates	Meeting	Location
	22 October	IM: Teleconference: Services and Investment	
		IM: Video-conference: Temporary Entry	
	23 October	IM: Video-conference: Financial Services	
	21–24 October	IM: Trade in Goods/ICT/E-commerce	Washington, D.C.
	21–24 October	IM: ICT/E-commerce	Washington, D.C.
	25 October	IM: Video-conference: Services	
	30 October	IM: Video-conference: Services	
	7 November	IM: Video-conference: Government Procurement	
	11–18 November	IM: Textiles and Apparel	Singapore
	13 November	IM: Video-conference: Government Procurement	
	25 November	IM: Video-conference: Financial Services group	
11	**11–19 November**	**Formal Round**	**Singapore**
	16–19 December	IM: Rules of Origin	Washington, D.C.
	20 December	IM: Video-conference: Financial Services group	
	2003		
	16 January	Resolution of the Capital Control Issue after the last formal round of negotiations	
	4 March	Teleconference call: Textiles and Apparel	
	7 March	Teleconference call: Textiles and Apparel	
	17 April	Teleconference call: Textiles and Apparel	
	22–24 April	Teleconference call: Textiles and Apparel	

continued

Round	Dates	Meeting	Location
	18 September	Teleconference call: Textiles and Apparel	
	1 October	Teleconference call: Textiles and Apparel	
	22 December	Teleconference call: Textiles and Apparel	

Formation of the USSFTA Business Coalition[1]

In March 2002, the U.S.-ASEAN Business Council and the U.S. Chamber of Commerce announced the formation of the USSFTA Business Coalition. Chaired by Boeing, ExxonMobil and United Parcel Services (UPS), the Coalition's purpose is to support the FTA. At the conclusion of the USSFTA, the coalition had attracted 114 members comprising leading U.S. companies and trade associations that support the conclusion and passage of the USSFTA.

Passage of the Trade Promotion Authority (TPA)[2] Legislation

On 27 July 2002, the House of Representatives passed the TPA legislation. This legislation was passed by the Senate on 1 August 2002.

---

[1] Refer to Appendix III.

[2] U.S. Trade Promotion Authority (TPA) is the trade negotiating authority the Congress has granted to each of the previous five presidents. It has been an integral part of U.S. trade policy since it was first granted in 1974. Under this authority, the Executive branch is required to consult regularly with the Congress, and solicit advice from advisory committees and the public, as trade agreements are being negotiated. In return, the Congress agrees not to amend legislation implementing trade agreements, voting up or down on these agreements. The cooperative relationship at the heart of Trade Promotion Authority helps ensure that U.S. trade negotiators will strike agreements that have the support of the Congress and the American people. See http:/www.tpa.gov.

Formation of the Singapore Caucus[3]

On 8 October 2002, the Congressional Caucus for Singapore was officially launched. The Caucus is co-chaired by Democrat Congressman Solomon P. Ortiz and Republican Congressman Curt Weldon. As this Caucus is not a trade-specific but a country-specific group, it continues to exist and as of January 2004, has 56 congressional members.

Creation of the USSFTA Task Force in the U.S. House of Representatives

In early April 2003, Congressmen Solomon P. Ortiz and Pete Sessions, selected by their respective Democratic and Republican leaderships, informally formed a Task Force to champion the USSFTA in the House of Representatives.

Legal Scrubbing

The scrubbing of the agreement by the lawyers of the two delegations began on 16 January 2003 and was completed on 5 May 2003.

Notifying Congress

United States President George W. Bush notified the U.S. Congress on 30 January 2003 of his intention to sign the USSFTA. The period of notice was 90 days and expired on 30 April 2003.

Feedback from the Trade Advisory Committees[4]

The trade advisory system provides the private sector and civil society the opportunity to advise the Administration on trade issues and is an important part of the Administration's outreach efforts.

---

[3] Refer to Appendix II.

[4] Refer to Appendix XXI.

The system was established by Congress in the Trade Act of 1974. Today more than 700 advisors participate on committees jointly administered by USTR, the Departments of Commerce, Labor and Agriculture, and the Environmental Protection Agency. On 28 February 2003, the advisory committees released their reports. Out of the 31 committees, only the Labour Committee did not endorse the USSFTA.

Draft Text released
On 7 March 2003, the United States Trade Representative's Office released the draft text of the USSFTA for public and congressional review.

U.S. International Trade Commission (USITC)[5] Calls For Public Hearing
On 24 April 2003, USITC held a hearing in persuance of its investigation on "U.S.-Singapore Free Trade Agreement: Potential Economywide and Selected Sectoral Effects". Singapore Ambassador to the United States, Professor Chan Heng Chee testified at this hearing. The ITC is required by the Trade Promotion Authority to release its report on the impact of an FTA on the U.S. economy within 90 days of the signing of the FTA. The Congressional process kicks in after the ITC report is released.

Signing the Agreement
On 6 May 2003 President Bush and Prime Minister Goh signed the USSFTA at the White House in Washington, D. C.

---

[5] USITC is an independent, nonpartisan, quasi-judicial federal agency that provides trade expertise to both the legislative and executive branches of the U.S. government, determines the impact of imports on U.S. industries, and directs actions against certain unfair trade practices, such as patent, trademark, and copyright infringement.

Hearings

On 25 June 2003, the Asia and the Pacific Subcommittee of the House Intenational Relations Committee held a hearing on the "U.S. Trade and Commercial Policy in Southeast Asia and Oceania." Details on this and the other hearings can be found on the US Congress committee homepage and http://www.ussfta.gov.sg.

Congressional Hearings
House of Representatives

On 1 April 2003, the House Committee on Financial Services, Subcommittee on Domestic and International Trade Policy, Trade, and Technology held a hearing on "Opening Trade in Financial Services — The Chile and Singapore Examples".

On 8 May 2003, the House Committee on Energy and Commerce, Subcommittee on Commerce, Trade, and Consumer Protection held a hearing on "Trade in Services and E-Commerce: The Significance of the Singapore and Chile Free Trade Agreements".

On 10 June 2003, the House Committee on Ways and Means, Subcommittee on Trade held a hearing on "Implementation of U.S. Bilateral Free Trade Agreements with Chile and Singapore".

Senate

On 17 June 2003, the Senate Finance Committee held a hearing on "The Implementation of U.S. Bilateral Free Trade Agreements with Singapore and Chile".

On 14 July 2003, the Senate Judiciary Committee held a hearing on the "Proposed United States-Chile and United States-Singapore Free Trade Agreements with Chile and Singapore".

U.S. International Trade Commission Results

In June 2003, USITC released the results of its investigation into the probable economic effects of a U.S.-Singapore FTA. The Commission's findings concluded that the economy-wide effects on

U.S. trade, production, and economic welfare of the FTA tariff reductions were likely to be negligible to very small.[6]

U.S. Legislative Process

Following the signing of the Agreement, the U.S. Administration was expected, within the period of 60 days, to submit to the U.S. Congress a report on the necessary changes which would have to be made to U.S. laws. The U.S. House of Representatives Ways and Means Committee Trade Subcommittee conducted a hearing on the implementation of U.S. Bilateral Free Trade Agreements with Chile and Singapore on 10 June 2003.

In the meantime the U.S. Congress began to draft legislation for the Administration to submit to Congress. This was called a "mock" legislative process because the real process would only begin only when the Congress receives from the Administration its proposed implementing legislation. Taking into account the suggestions of the Congress, arising from the mock legislative process, the Administration submitted draft implementing legislation to the Congress for its action.

On 10 July 2003, the House Ways and Means and Senate Finance Committees and House Judiciary Committee held mock markups of the draft implementing legislation for the USSFTA. On 14 July 2003, the Senate Judiciary Committee held a mock markup of the legislation.

On 15 July 2003, House Majority Leader Congressman Tom DeLay introduced the USSFTA Implementation Act in the House of Representatives and Senator Charles Grassley introduced the USSFTA Implementation Act in the Senate.

On 17 July 2003, the House Ways and Means Committee and Senate Finance Committee approved the USSFTA Implementation Act by a vote of 32 to 5. Both the Senate Finance Committee and Senate Judiciary Committees also approved the Act.

---

[6] For a full report see http://www.usitc.gov/wais/reports/arc/w3603.htm.

U.S. Congress Passes Implementing Legislation

The Congress must act within 90 days of the submission by the Administration of the draft implementing legislation. Under the Trade Promotion Authority Act, the Congress could either accept or reject the USSFTA. It cannot amend it. On 24 July 2003, the House of Representatives passed the USSFTA with 272–155 votes. The U.S. Senate voted on 31 July 2003 with 66–31 votes.

Regulation of Imports and Exports (Amendment) Bill

On 11 November 2003, Singapore Parliament approved the changes to the Regulation of Imports and Exports Bill. The amendments include measures to ensure that the preferential tariff concessions apply strictly to Singapore goods. It would, *inter alia*, criminalise the changing of labels on products not of Singapore origin to state falsely that they are made in Singapore.

USSFTA Comes into Force

On 1 January 2004, the USSFTA came into force.

Implementing Legislation to be passed by Singapore Parliament

It is anticipated that implementing legislation for the intellectual property rights section of the USSFTA in relation to patents, pharmaceutical and agricultural chemical products will be passed in the first half of 2004. The key obligations in the intellectual property rights chapter will come into force on 1 July 2004.